"From the Gene Autry epigraph that opens it, this entire book is a revelation—a lively and comprehensive look at a subculture, but one that spills its bounds to become a sweeping panorama of American life. Depression-era foreclosures, the Tomb of the Unknown Soldier, crashing the Oscars, John Wayne's Dollar and Roy Rogers's Trigger, plus cameos from Willie Nelson, Medgar Evers, Aretha Franklin's ex-husband, and Muhammad Ali (on horseback!)—hold on for the ride, because *Black Cowboys of Rodeo* will buck off every one of your preconceptions."
—Alexander Wolff, best-selling author of *The Audacity of Hoop: Basketball and the Age of Obama*

"*Black Cowboys of Rodeo* is a much-needed look at the lives of modern Black cowboys. For too long this story has been overlooked. But that omission stops with this book. Keith Ryan Cartwright takes readers on a journey from farm life in Oklahoma, to the Jim Crow South, the bright lights of Hollywood, and the streets of Harlem. Filled with stories of famous men like the legendary Bill Pickett and many other unheralded Black men who scraped their way to make a living in rodeo, Cartwright has produced a beautifully written manuscript about Black manhood."
—Louis Moore, best-selling author of *We Will Win the Day: The Civil Rights Movement*

"With the vivid, detailed portraits in *Black Cowboys of Rodeo*, Keith Ryan Cartwright not only chronicles a series of brave and pioneering lives; he also fills in a missing and vital piece of America's cultural history."
—Alan Light, SiriusXM host, best-selling author, and former editor-in-chief of *Vibe* and *Spin* magazines

"There is nothing quite so tantalizing as hidden history. Remember what it felt like to be a young person, when it seemed like grownups were conspiring to hide the truth? In this case, they were. In reading a book like *Black Cowboys of Rodeo*, young people searching for identity find their heroes."
—Erin Alvarado, high school librarian and co-founder of the Southeastern Young Adult Book Festival

BLACK COWBOYS OF RODEO

BLACK COWBOYS
OF RODEO

UNSUNG HEROES FROM HARLEM TO HOLLYWOOD AND THE AMERICAN WEST

KEITH RYAN CARTWRIGHT
FOREWORD BY DANNY L. GLOVER

UNIVERSITY OF NEBRASKA PRESS   LINCOLN

An earlier version of chapter 25 previously
appeared in *The Undefeated*, February 3,
2020. Reprinted courtesy of ESPN.

Publication of this volume was assisted by a grant from
the Friends of the University of Nebraska Press.

Library of Congress Cataloging-in-Publication Data
Names: Cartwright, Keith Ryan, author.
Title: Black cowboys of rodeo: unsung heroes from
Harlem to Hollywood and the American West / Keith
Ryan Cartwright; foreword by Danny L. Glover.
Description: Lincoln: University of Nebraska Press,
2021. | Includes bibliographical references.
Identifiers: LCCN 2021006509
ISBN 9781496226105 (hardback)
ISBN 9781496229489 (epub)
ISBN 9781496229496 (pdf)
Subjects: LCSH: African American rodeo performers—
Biography. | Rodeos—Social aspects—United
States. | Rodeos—United States—History.
Classification: LCC GV1833.5 .C37 2021 |
DDC 791.8/4089607300922 [B]—dc23
LC record available at https://lccn.loc.gov/2021006509

Set in Lyon by Mikala R. Kolander.
Designed by N. Putens.

Former *Washington Post* president and publisher Philip L. Graham
once lamented that news serves as "the first rough draft of history."
Unfortunately, when it comes to more than 150 years of Black
cowboys, a vast majority of those drafts were wrong, and the few
that had it right were either ignored, lost, or, at best, forgotten.
The profiles chronicled in *Black Cowboys of Rodeo*, and the
thousands of other Black cowboys those stories represent,
are my small part in a much larger and ongoing effort to write
a second draft and, in the process, correct history.
This is for those who never had their story told.

Much love,
KRC

He must not advocate or possess racially or religiously intolerant ideas.

—FROM GENE AUTRY'S COWBOY CODE

Contents

Foreword

DANNY L. GLOVER

In many ways, the story of the cowboy is a story of how America's cultural identity came to be. The rugged bravado, heroism, triumph over the wilderness, individualism, and iconoclasm that animate America's mythology are partially rooted in the cowboy mythos and have been universalized in the United States as emblematic of a quintessentially American national character. But as much as these ideals can be taken as a definitive piece of Americana, the story of the American cowboy is also implicitly about race. As a result, we must ask who and what constitutes an American and then interrogate the basis upon which one would make that determination.

For most people in the twentieth and twenty-first centuries, the cumulative impact of Buffalo Bill's Wild West Show, the "Western" memorabilia industry, and, of course, the Western movie genre has been a portrait of the American cowboy as invariably white and prototypically male. But is that popular perception accurate? How did African Americans factor into the history of the American cowboy? Cowboys, first and foremost, were agricultural workers in the latter half of the nineteenth century. In centering the Black cowboy, it seems almost pedantic yet counterintuitive to note that newly freed African American slaves and sharecroppers—who almost by definition were highly skilled agricultural workers—were a critical component of the cowboy labor force—nearly 25 percent. Why then is there such a paucity of representation for them?

Slavery fundamentally impacted the relationship of people of African descent to land and animals in the Western hemisphere. Yet in the antebellum South, armed men on horseback—who were equipped with ropes—comprised fugitive slave patrols. A generation later, some of the descendants of the very people that slave patrolmen terrorized became cultural heroes through their mastery of tools previously used to oppress them. For African Americans, who themselves were likened to animals with everything from vile caricatures to government policies, to achieve notoriety by dominating formidable animal opponents was a direct confrontation of the primal core of American racism. Thus, Black cowboys faced down both angry steers and the even angrier beast of white supremacy simultaneously. As a result, the concept of a cowboy as the victor in a battle between humans and beasts carries a special connotation for African Americans that unmoors much of our understanding of who cowboys were and why they are important in the story of American identity.

The rodeo itself, as a competitive exhibition of athletic skill, was and is a venue in which Black cowboys could vie for legitimacy not only as exemplars of the American spirit but also as leaders within their industries. Black cowboys who competed in rodeos were among the first Black professional athletes. The political connotations of Black athletic excellence and the ways in which Black athletes have historically used their popularity and influence to fight against racism are part and parcel of the story of Black cowboys. At its core, *Black Cowboys of Rodeo* seeks to capture the stories of Black cowboys as they endured and resisted racism, violence, and discrimination as the United States grappled with its congenital contradictions about race throughout the twentieth century. It sets the record straight through a priceless series of vignettes, often straight from the horse's (and cowboy's) mouth. Although cowboys, Westerns, and rodeos declined in popularity toward the end of the twentieth century, this collection of stories speaks to the urgency of not only remembering Black cowboys as key originators of American identity but also to the need to memorialize Black cowboys in the pantheon of great Black athletes in other sports.

Yet the legacy of Black cowboys is not only a relic of the past. Black cowboys have continued to excel in rodeo events and have competed at the sport's highest levels into the twenty-first century. Black cowboys indeed have an incredible and consistent legacy of excellence that is worthy of sustained admiration and support. People of all ages, but especially young people, should know that Black cowboys still exist, that they matter, and that their inspirational achievements are fundamentally and inextricably linked to the development of what constitutes an American.

Lifting the veil of obscurity—if not invisibility—from Black cowboys is not merely an academic exercise. As members of marginalized groups take to the streets to demand justice in the face of fascist tyranny only to be met, in some instances, by mounted police officers, what can the symbolism and real-life accomplishments of Black cowboys do to inspire heroism? The untold stories of Black cowboys, situated within the timeline of more widely known chapters of Black history, show that Black cowboys represent a commitment to resisting oppression and to mastering their craft. Black cowboys like Roy LeBlanc founded professional associations in response to the indignities they faced in competitive spaces and even founded their own rodeos in which they could compete, preside, and prosper. In doing so, Black cowboys commanded respect for their athletic abilities and asserted themselves as businessmen. Although they did not get as much limelight as they deserved, Black cowboys like Herbert Jeffries, the "Bronze Buckaroo," triumphed on the silver screen as well. Black cowboys passed their knowledge down within their families and sought additional ways of contributing to their communities, like Glynn Turman, who founded Camp Gid-D Up to serve inner-city youth in the aftermath of the 1992 uprising in response to the Rodney King verdict. The image of the Black cowboy is thus one of a grassroots freedom fighter that refuses to be denied his rightful place in history.

Whether as rodeo title winners, movie stars, community members, or even folk heroes, Black cowboys have inspired the world, including other luminaries in the Black sporting tradition like Muhammad Ali. *Black Cowboys of Rodeo* is a profound correction to the popular conception of the cowboy. It calls on us to rethink what it means to be an African American and to contemplate what the forgotten legacy of the Black cowboy says about American identity. In an era in which African Americans own less than 1 percent of the rural land in the United States, the continued appeal and inspirational potency of the Black cowboy points to the necessity of healing our collective relationship to land, nature, and nation.

Abbreviations

ABBI American Bucking Bull Inc.
ACRA American Cowboy Rodeo Association
ARA American Rodeo Association
BPIR Bill Pickett Invitational Rodeo
CNFR College National Finals Rodeo
CRRA Cowboys Regional Rodeo Association
IFR International Finals Rodeo
IPRA International Professional Rodeo Association
IRA Interstate Rodeo Association (later International and then IPRA)
NFR National Finals Rodeo
PBR Professional Bull Riders
PRCA Professional Rodeo Cowboys Association
RCA Rodeo Cowboys Association (later PRCA)
SNCA Southwestern National Cowboys Association
USTRC United States Team Roping Championships

Chronology

* Black cowboy events are in bold

1619   First African slaves are brought to North America, on an English privateer ship, arriving at Point Comfort, in the colony of Virginia

1863   Emancipation Proclamation issued by President Abraham Lincoln

1865   Thirteenth Amendment abolishing slavery is passed

1868   Fourteenth Amendment guaranteeing African Americans full citizenship is passed

1870   Fifteenth Amendment guaranteeing right to vote for all citizens regardless of race is passed

       Bill Pickett is born on December 5 in Williamson County, Texas

1883   **Jesse Stahl is born**

1890s   Jim Crow laws segregating Blacks from whites become common in Southern states

1896   Supreme Court rules in favor of "separate but equal"

1902   **William "Frank" Haygood—Negro League player, co-founder Okmulgee Colored Round-Up—is born**

1904   George Poage finishes third in the 200-meter and 400-meter hurdles to become first African American to win an Olympic medal

1909   NAACP founded by W. E. B. DuBois and Ida B. Wells

1912   **Jesse Stahl performs at Salinas Rodeo, famously remembered for riding a bareback horse backward**

1913   Rosa Parks is born

1914   **By most accounts Herb Jeffries was born, but he once claimed to have been born in 1911**

1918   **Floyd Frank is born**

1919   Jackie Robinson is born

1921   Tulsa Race Riots

1924   **Marvel Rogers is born**

1925   Medgar Evers is born

       Malcolm Little, later known as Malcolm X, is born

1928   **Roy LeBlanc is born**

       Rev. James Lawson is born

1929   **At fifty-nine, Bill Pickett retires from performing with the 101 Ranch and Wild West Show**

       Martin Luther King Jr. is born

1930   **Willie Thomas Sr., Charles Evans are born**

1932   **Thyrl Latting and Bailey Prairie Kid (birth name Taylor Hall Jr.) are born**

       Bill Pickett dies on April 2

1935   **Myrtis Dightman Sr., Freddie Gordon, Calvin Greely Jr., and Nathaniel "Rex" Purefoy are born**

1936   Cowboys' Turtle Association is created

1937   **Bud Bramwell is born**

1938   **Jesse Stahl dies**

1939   **Cleo Hearn and Sidney Reagor are born**

1940   **Nelson Jackson Jr. is born**

       John Lewis is born

       Tuskegee Airmen break color barrier in becoming first African American military aviators

1941   Emmett Till is born

1942   Cassius Clay is born; later changes his name to Muhammad Ali

1943   **Jesse "Charlie Reno" Hall is born**

1945   Cowboys' Turtle Association changes name to Rodeo Cowboys Association (RCA)

1946   **Sherman Richardson wins first Southwestern National Cowboys Association all-around title**

1947   Jackie Robinson becomes first African American to play
Major League Baseball, for the Brooklyn Dodgers

Eugene "Cowtown Gene" Walker and Glynn Turman are born

1948   President Harry S. Truman ends segregation of the armed forces

**Willie Thomas competes in rodeo at
Diamond L Ranch for the first time**

Harold Cash and Tex Williams are born

1949   National Intercollegiate Rodeo Association forms and
then holds first College National Finals Rodeo

1940s   Second migration of African Americans from the South
to the North takes place and continues to 1970s

1950   **Jimmy Lee Walker and Barry Moore are born**

Malcolm Little becomes known as Malcolm X

1951   **Clarence LeBlanc, Larry Callies, and Obba
Babatundé (aka Donald Cohen) are born**

1952   Zack Miller passes away

**Mike Latting and James Pickens Jr. are born; Kenneth
LeBlanc is born ten months after his older brother Clarence**

Lonnie Bunch III is born

1953   **Willie Ed Walker is born**

1954   In *Brown v. Board of Education*, Supreme Court rules
segregating schools is unconstitutional

Sedgwick Haynes is born

1955   **Donald and Ronald Stephens are born**

Rosa Parks is arrested for not giving up her seat
on a bus in Montgomery, Alabama

Emmett Till, fourteen, lynched in Mississippi after being
accused, yet not guilty, of offending a white woman

1956   **Steve Robinson is born**

Cleatus Stephens, father of Donald and Ronald Stephens,
is one of first six African Americans hired by the Tulsa
Fire Department, they became known as "The Six"

Interstate Rodeo Association founded (later renamed International Rodeo Association)

Charles and Roy LeBlanc and twenty others co-found the Okmulgee (Oklahoma) Colored Round-Up Club

Okmulgee Round-Up produces first all-Black rodeo; still continues second weekend every August

1957   **Charlie Sampson is born**

The Little Rock (Arkansas) Nine become first African Americans to attend a previously all-white school

Civil Rights Act serves as first major legislation since Reconstruction, allowed prosecution of anyone who prevented anyone else from voting

1958   **Marcous Friday is born**

Okmulgee Colored Round-Up Club purchases forty acres; builds own arena for annual Black rodeo

Rodeo Cowboys Association (later named the Professional Rodeo Cowboys Association, PRCA) establishes the National Finals Rodeo (NFR)

1959   First National Finals Rodeo (NFR) in Dallas; later held in Los Angeles and Oklahoma City before moving to Las Vegas in 1985

Cleo Hearn becomes first African American cowboy to turn pro as a calf roper in the Rodeo Cowboys Association

1960   Four college students take stand against segregation in Greensboro, North Carolina, at Woolworth's lunch counter

1961   The Freedom Riders; seven Black and six white students board bus in Washington DC on tour of South

President John F. Kennedy names draftee Cleo Hearn to the Presidential Honor Guard

Dwayne Hargo Sr. is born

Thyrl Latting starts Latting Rodeo School south of Chicago, Illinois, in nearby Robbins

1963   **At fourteen, Tex Williams wins the saddle bronc riding title at the Southwestern National Cowboys Association**

John F. Kennedy, Medgar Evers are assassinated

Martin Luther King Jr. writes "Letter from Birmingham Jail" and later delivers his "I Have a Dream" speech

1964   Civil Rights Act of 1964 is signed by President Lyndon B. Johnson

Cassius Clay officially changes his name to Muhammad Ali

Thyrl Latting starts Latting Rodeo Company; first rodeo is fundraiser for Robbins (Illinois) Fire Department

Interstate Rodeo Association rebranded International Rodeo Association

Ervin Williams Jr. and Donald Ray Goodman are born

Myrtis Dightman becomes first Black cowboy to "compete" at the National Finals Rodeo as an alternate for injured bull rider

1965   **Gus Trent (aka Harlan Tyrone Ware) is born**

Voting Rights Act of 1965 is signed by President Lyndon B. Johnson

Malcolm X is assassinated

Watts Race Riots

Black Panther Party is founded in Oakland, California

1966   **Myrtis Dightman becomes the first Black cowboy to "qualify" for the National Finals Rodeo**

Barbara Jordan, a Democrat from Houston, is the first African American born after Reconstruction to be elected to the Texas State Senate

1967   **"Cowtown Gene" Walker becomes first Black cowboy to qualify for the College National Finals Rodeo**

Thurgood Marshall becomes first African American Supreme Court Justice

Black Stuntmen's Association is founded

Citing opposition to Vietnam War, Muhammad Ali refuses draft; barred from boxing, stripped of title

Tex Williams is first African American to win Texas state high school rodeo title (bareback) as a junior

Fred Whitfield is born

1968   Martin Luther King Jr., Robert F. Kennedy are assassinated

Tex Williams wins two more state titles as a high school senior (bareback and bull riding)

Dennis Davis is born in Runge, Texas

Otis Young becomes first African American to co-star in a Western television series, *The Outcasts*

1969   **Black Rodeo Association founded in New York; Bud Bramwell wins coin flip and named president; Cleo Hearn named vice president**

Willie Thomas retires from rodeo

1970   **Cleo Hearn becomes first Black cowboy to win calf roping at a major PRCA rodeo (Denver)**

Myrtis Dightman receives the Guy Weadick Award given to the Calgary Stampede competitor who best embodies what the cowboy stands for

1971   **Bill Pickett becomes first African American inducted into National Cowboy Hall of Fame**

First all-Black rodeo in Harlem takes place September 4; Muhammad Ali attends pre-event parade

1972   **Rarely seen, much-talked-about documentary film *Black Rodeo* is released; directed by Jeff Kanew**

Jackie Robinson passes away

Barbara Jordan served one day, June 10, as acting governor of Texas; to date, she is the only African American woman to serve as governor of a state; same year she was elected to Congress

1973   **American Black Cowboy Association hosts its final Black rodeo in June**

1974   **Lee Akin is born**

Cleo Hearn forms what becomes the Cowboys of Color rodeo series

1975   **Dihigi Gladney is born**

Rodeo Cowboys Association becomes known as the Professional Rodeo Cowboys Association

Arthur Ashe becomes the first African American to win Wimbledon

1976   The first Black History Month is officially celebrated

1979   Jesse Stahl inducted into National Rodeo Cowboy
        Hall of Fame in Oklahoma City, Oklahoma

        PRCA headquarters established in Colorado Springs;
        home of Pro Rodeo Hall of Fame and Museum

1982   Charlie Sampson becomes first Black cowboy
        to win a PRCA world title (bull riding)

1983   International Rodeo Association rebranded
        International Pro Rodeo Association

        Dwayne Hargo Jr., Steve Reagor are born

        William "Frank" Haygood dies

        Charlie Sampson among those who compete at the Presidential
        Command Performance Rodeo in Washington DC; nearly killed
        when a bull, Kiss Me, breaks nearly every bone in his face

        Ervin Williams becomes first Black cowboy to win an
        Oklahoma state high school rodeo title; he took home
        three buckles—bull riding, bareback, and all-around

1984   Bill Pickett Invitational Rodeo (BPIR), an all-
        Black rodeo series, is founded by Lu Vason

        Glynn Turman and Danny Glover serve as grand
        marshals for the BPIR's event in Los Angeles

        Clarence LeBlanc wins the International Professional
        Rodeo Association (IPRA) steer wrestling championship

        Ervin Williams Jr. named IPRA Bull Riding Rookie of the Year

        Black rodeo cowboys return to New York with Black
        World Championship Rodeo series; produced by Dr.
        George Blair, the events continue through 1997

1985   Dwayne Hargo Sr. wins freestyle bullfighting at
        Cheyenne Frontier Days Rodeo, facing Crooked Nose

        Clarence and Kenneth LeBlanc make history
        as first brothers to qualify for the International
        Finals Rodeo (IFR) in the same event

1986   Aaron Hargo is born

1989   Dwayne Hargo Sr. becomes first Black cowboy to win Wrangler
        Freestyle Bullfighting Tour at the National Finals Rodeo (NFR)

1990   **Fred Whitfield is named the PRCA Rookie
of the Year (tie-down roping)**

Russell Williams wins Oscar for Best Achievement in Sound (*Glory*)

1991   Russell Williams is first African American to win two
Oscars (*Dances with Wolves*, Best Sound Mixer)

**Glynn Turman, Reginald T. Dorsey win
team penning championship**

1991   **Fred Whitfield wins the first of eight PRCA
world titles (tie-down roping)**

1992   Twenty of the top-ranked bull riders in the PRCA meet in
Scottsdale, Arizona, and create the Professional Bull Riders (PBR)

Los Angeles riots following the beating of Rodney King

**Reginald T. Dorsey is cast in *Return to Lonesome
Dove* alongside Louis Gossett Jr.**

**Glynn Turman and wife, Jo-Ann, form IX Winds
Ranch Foundation, host first Camp Gid-D Up**

1994   PBR begins its first season of competition

Byron De La Beckwith was tried and convicted
for the murder of Medgar Evers

1995   **Fred Whitfield wins the second of eight
PRCA world titles (tie-down roping)**

**Freddie Gordon inducted into Black Go Texan
Gala at Houston Livestock and Rodeo**

1996   **James Pickens Jr. portrays Medgar Evers
in the biopic *Ghosts of Mississippi***

**Charlie Sampson inducted into the Pro Rodeo
Hall of Fame in Colorado Springs, Colorado**

**Fred Whitfield wins the third of eight PRCA
world titles (tie-down roping)**

1997   **Myrtis Dightman inducted into National Cowboy
Hall of Fame in Oklahoma City, Oklahoma**

**Mayor Rudy Giuliani proclaims May 17 "Black World
Championship Rodeo Day in New York City"; Black World
Championship Rodeo promotes its final Black rodeo**

Clara Brown (1800–1885) becomes first African American inducted into National Cowgirl Hall of Fame

1999 Fred Whitfield wins the fourth and fifth of eight PRCA world titles (tie-down roping and all-around)

Angel Floyd launches her C91 Ranch and Livestock Rodeo Productions

2000 Fred Whitfield inducted into National Cowboy Hall of Fame in Oklahoma City, Oklahoma

Fred Whitfield wins the sixth of eight PRCA world titles (tie-down roping)

2001 Mollie Taylor Stevenson Sr. and Jr. are inducted into National Cowgirl Hall of Fame

Colin Powell becomes first African American confirmed as secretary of state

Myrtis Dightman, Bailey's Prairie Kid (aka Taylor Hall Jr.) inducted into Texas Rodeo Cowboy Hall of Fame

College National Finals Rodeo relocates to Casper, Wyoming

2002 Fred Whitfield wins the seventh of eight PRCA world titles (tie-down roping)

Vonetta Flowers becomes the first African American to win a gold medal at the Winter Olympics

2003 Steve Reagor becomes first African American to win College National Rodeo Finals

Myrtis Dightman, Bill Pickett, Charlie Sampson, and Herb Jeffries inducted into National Multicultural Western Heritage Hall of Fame

Myrtis Dightman becomes first African American inducted into PBR Ring of Honor

2004 Fred Whitfield inducted into Pro Rodeo Hall of Fame in Colorado Springs, Colorado

Charles Sampson inducted into PBR Ring of Honor in Las Vegas, Nevada

Willie Thomas, Leon Coffee inducted into Texas Rodeo Cowboy Hall of Fame

2005   Leon Coffee inducted into National Multicultural
        Western Heritage Hall of Fame

        Fred Whitfield wins his eighth and final
        PRCA world title (tie-down roping)

        Rosa Parks passes away

2007   Nathaniel "Rex" Purefoy and Rufus Green Sr. inducted into
        National Multicultural Western Heritage Hall of Fame

2008   Barack Obama becomes first African American
        elected president of the United States

        James Pickens Jr. Foundation is founded

        Willie Thomas, Art T. Burton inducted into National
        Multicultural Western Heritage Hall of Fame

2009   Calvin Greely Jr. passes away

        Roy LeBlanc passes away

        Calvin Greely Jr., Mayisha Akbar inducted into National
        Multicultural Western Heritage Hall of Fame

        Tony Dungy becomes first African American
        coach in the NFL to win a Super Bowl

2010   James Pickens Jr. Foundation hosts first of its
        annual charity team-roping events

        Okmulgee Colored Rodeo renamed Roy
        LeBlanc Invitational Rodeo

        Harold Cash, Abe Morris inducted into National
        Multicultural Western Heritage Hall of Fame

2011   Freddie Gordon, Glynn Turman inducted into National
        Multicultural Western Heritage Hall of Fame

        Myrtis Dightman inducted into Texas Cowboy Hall of Fame

        Fred Whitfield, Woody Strode inducted into National
        Multicultural Western Heritage Hall of Fame

2014   "Cowtown Gene" Walker dies of cancer

        California Chrome wins the Kentucky Derby

2015   Dihigi Gladney hired as exercise trainer for California
        Chrome year after winning the Kentucky Derby

        Patricia E. Kelly inducted into the National Cowgirl Hall of Fame

Leon Coffee inducted into Texas Cowboy Hall of Fame

Danell Tipton inducted into National Multicultural Western Heritage Hall of Fame

2016 Myrtis Dightman inducted into Pro Rodeo Hall of Fame; Bull Riding Hall of Fame

Floyd Frank inducted into National Multicultural Western Heritage Hall of Fame

Calvin Greely Jr. inducted into Texas Rodeo Cowboy Hall of Fame

Muhammad Ali passes away

Colin Kaepernick sat during National Anthem of 49ers' third preseason game; began kneeling next week

2017 Ezekiel Mitchell becomes first African American to win the PBR Touring Pro Division title

2018 Bill Terrell, Charles Evans, Sedgwick Haynes pass away

Leon Coffee inducted into the Pro Rodeo Hall of Fame in Colorado Springs, Colorado

Gene Smith inducted into National Multicultural Western Heritage Hall of Fame

2019 Compton, California, native Mayisha Akbar is inducted into the National Cowgirl Hall of Fame

James Pickens Jr., Bailey's Prairie Kid (aka Taylor Hall Jr.), Lu Vason inducted into National Multicultural Western Heritage Hall of Fame

Freddie Gordon, Bailey's Prairie Kid, Willie Thomas, and Clinton Wyche inducted into South Central Texas Rodeo Ring of Honor

Charlie Sampson, Leon Coffee inducted into the Bull Riding Hall of Fame

Barry Moore dies of cancer

Dennis Davis qualifies for American Bucking Bull Inc. (ABBI) Finals in Las Vegas, with bull owned by UFC president Dana White

Bud Bramwell receives Forgotten Trailblazer Award at annual Legacy of West Gala in Las Vegas

2020   Cleatus Stephens and "The Six" are inducted into the Tulsa Fire Department Hall of Fame

In midst of worldwide pandemic, vast majority of rodeos—including the Bill Pickett Invitational Rodeo and Cowboys of Color—are canceled

George Floyd killed at the hands of four Minneapolis police officers, sparking several weeks of racial unrest

Tre Hosley wins the California Circuit title in bareback riding

Shad Mayfield wins the PRCA tie-down title by a mere $230.66

Willie Thomas dies of cancer

John Lewis, C. T. Vivian pass away

2021   Obba Babatundé, Lynn Hart, Aldrich Everett, Thomas Everett Sr., Clarence Gonzales inducted into National Multicultural Western Heritage Hall of Fame

PBR co-produces its first Bill Pickett Invitational Rodeo at MGM Grand Arena in Las Vegas; a week later, on Juneteenth, an hour-long special is broadcast on CBS; PBR plans to continue collaborating with BPIR to feature Black rodeos on network television in 2022

Willie Thomas posthumously inducted into the Bull Riders Hall of Fame

Floyd Frank passes away three months shy of turning 103 years old

Juneteenth becomes only the twelfth federal holiday and the first since 1983

Note from the Author

Some of the unsavory characterizations used in this book—all of which appear in quotation marks—tend to evoke strong emotions in readers, but to change this language would mitigate or outright fail to chronicle the impact of the racial tension faced by those who are recalling the trials and tribulations of their unsung, yet no less heroic journeys as *Black Cowboys of Rodeo*.

BLACK COWBOYS OF RODEO

Introduction

Wherever you go in the history of America, there have been Black people making contributions, but their contributions have been obscured, lost, buried.
—DR. HENRY LOUIS GATES JR.

MURFREESBORO, TENNESSEE

They ride horses and bulls, rope calves, buck broncs, fight bulls, and even wrestle steers. They are cowboys. But because of the color of their skin, the legacies of their pursuits intersected with America's struggle for racial equality, human rights, and social justice.

Beginning at the dawn of the twentieth century, *Black Cowboys of Rodeo* is a collection of more than one hundred years' worth of cowboy stories set against the backdrop of Reconstruction, Jim Crow, segregation, the civil rights movement, and, eventually, the integration of a racially divided country. Every chapter reveals a revolutionary Black pioneer whose accomplishments and rightful place in history have largely gone unrecognized.

They no longer will be among the nameless in American history.

Their individual and collective stories are compiled from firsthand conversations with the cowboys themselves—all of whom share their unique and deeply personal narratives—and those who witnessed history. In keeping with the likes of Jack Johnson, Jesse Owens, Jackie Robinson, Muhammad Ali, Tommie Smith and John Carlos, Bill Russell, Kareem Abdul-Jabbar, and, more recently, Colin Kaepernick, the stories of Black rodeo cowboys also have had social and political implications.

Cleo Hearn was more than the first Black rodeo cowboy to rope professionally in the Rodeo Cowboy Association. After being drafted by the U.S.

Army, in 1960, he was named to the Presidential Honor Guard a year later and became the first African American to carry a casket in Arlington National Cemetery. Like integrating the Secret Service, the Honor Guard was an act of equality that then-president John F. Kennedy and others in the administration felt would be easier to carry out than pushing the Civil Rights Act for a vote early in his presidency.

Following Kennedy's assassination, Lyndon B. Johnson carried out civil rights legislation, but even after it passed in 1964, there was not always accountability or enforcement. Laws merely govern, and in Wharton County, Texas, those laws were not enforced until local officials were made to do so in the early 1970s.

It should come as little surprise that a young Black cowboy from El Campo, Texas, was not allowed to compete at high school rodeos with his white classmates in the mid-1960s. Instead, from the time he was fourteen, Tex Williams was made to compete at semipro events with grown men. Finally, as a junior and senior, the mental toughness he developed led to him becoming the first Black cowboy to win a high school state title in Texas.

"I wasn't trying to break a racial barrier," Williams said. "That never crossed my mind. The only thing I wanted to do is to ride with the white kids, ride with kids my age. That's all I wanted to do. To me, it wasn't a Black or white deal. It was just let me compete with their kid. I think I can beat him, and it finally came to turn."

Williams, who has never been listed among his hometown's noteworthy residents, won three state titles in his final two years at El Campo High School—1967 and '68—yet in a state where amateur rodeo is perceived to be more important than anywhere else in the country, Williams is often overlooked among the all-time rodeo greats.

There were examples of this all across the South, especially in athletics.

"It meant that America lost out on talents of amazing people," said Lonnie Bunch, founding director of the National Museum of African American History and Culture. "We will never know how much they could have reshaped the field. We'll never know, in many ways, how much they inspired other generations, and to me, the greatest challenge with segregation and discrimination is you yourself, as Americans, by limiting the best talents you can choose from."

Today's generation of Black cowboys—Shad Mayfield and Ezekiel Mitchell, both of whom were born nearly twenty years after Charlie Sampson became the first African American to win a gold buckle at the 1982 National Finals Rodeo—are benefactors of Williams, Hearn, and others who graciously endured and overcame civil and social injustice.

In November 2019 Mitchell and Dalton Kasel became only the fourth and fifth African American cowboys to qualify for the Professional Bull Riders (PBR) World Finals and the first in fourteen years. Kasel was the first African American in the history of the PBR to be named Rookie of the Year. Together, they were the first to *qualify* for the finals since Lee Akin in 2005. Gary Richard last qualified in 2002 and Nick Buckley qualified in 1999, while Neil Holmes competed at PBR Finals in 2015 and again in 2016 but was a lower-level qualifier and an alternate in back-to-back seasons before his retirement. In just two seasons with the PBR, Mitchell became one of the most marketable cowboys in Western sports. Young, friendly, and unafraid to address his own less-than-storybook upbringing, he has largely avoided controversy, which makes Mitchell appealing to Hollywood movie producers, a powerful entertainment agency—William Morris Endeavor—and a corporate sponsor like Ariat. Unlike the headlines torn from the pages of GQ, *Garden and Gun*, *Good Morning America*, FOX *and Friends*, and the BBC, Mitchell, who starred in the Snapchat docuseries *Life by the Horns*, simply sees himself as "a bull rider who happens to be Black."

Mayfield, the 2018 National High School Rodeo Association Champion tie-down roper, finished his 2019 rookie season twelfth in the Professional Rodeo Cowboys Association (PRCA) world standings. Eight months later, he had a nearly $100,000 lead atop the tie-down standings, making the nineteen-year-old from Clovis, New Mexico, the favorite to win his first world title in only his second season in the PRCA. By the end of the National Finals Rodeo (NFR), in December 2020, Mayfield became only the third Black cowboy to win a PRCA world title when he claimed the gold buckle in the tie-down roping by a mere $230.66.

Seen as the immediate future of Black rodeo cowboys, Kasel, Mitchell, and Mayfield have been able to carve out their own paths thanks to the Black pioneers and trailblazers—Bill Pickett, Cleo Hearn, Myrtis Dightman and Steve Reagor, among them—who came before them.

Historians often suggest that the greatest victories of Black Americans were somehow accomplished by the stroke of a presidential pen, but Dr. Yohuru Williams, founding director of the Racial Injustice Initiative at the University of St. Thomas, noted *Black Cowboys of Rodeo* challenges that outdated narrative and reveals Black cowboys as having stood up in the face of adversity.

Bunch agreed.

"I think your notion of the skills it takes, the horsemanship . . . you're countering the notion that enslaved people had no skills and, see, that's an important part of the story," said Bunch, who is now the first Black secretary of the Smithsonian Institution.

Like Jackie Robinson, Dr. Martin Luther King Jr., Rosa Parks, Thurgood Marshall, and the Little Rock Nine, these pioneering Black cowboys endured hardships and collectively broke through racial barriers and glass ceilings from Harlem to Hollywood and the American West.

"In the fifties and sixties, there was a drive among Black folks . . . to excel and overcome all sorts of barriers in order to achieve what they wanted to achieve," said civil rights activist Rev. James Lawson. "I'm not surprised at all that a sizable number of Black cowboys, who've been misrepresented and not represented in our history books and films, were among those who did that."

Each of the cowboys profiled in this collection pushed against the boundaries imposed by segregation and transcended the racial animus they faced to create an opportunity to showcase their respective cowboy skills.

For many readers, the pages that follow are origin stories featuring first- and second-generation cowboys—some even third- and fourth-generation—who served in the military or worked as firemen, cow punchers, cattle ranchers, actors, and educators. It would be unreasonable to think that nearly four hundred pages of stories would be a definitive look at more than a century of accomplishments—after all, Jesse Stahl, Moses Fields, Will Dawson, Marvel Rogers Sr., Calvin Greely Jr., or Tony Brubaker could have just as easily been included in this collection as well—yet *Black Cowboys of Rodeo* serves as a vibrant, unvarnished, and comprehensive look at a seldom-documented segment of the African American experience.

1

Bill Pickett and the 101 Ranch

After climbing a great hill, one only finds that there are many more hills to climb.
—NELSON MANDELA

PONCA CITY, OKLAHOMA

The years had stacked up on an aging Bill Pickett.

At sixty-one, the world's most famous Black cowboy was confident he could singlehandedly separate two hundred horses from the almost two thousand that would otherwise be auctioned off at an estate sale.

Pickett had worked as a ranch hand at the famous Miller Brothers 101 Ranch, in Ponca City, Oklahoma, for nearly three decades.

It was March 1932 and the 101 had fallen on hard times.

The Great Depression coupled with the onset of the dust bowl hit the 101 hard. It was no longer the largest ranching operation in the country or the center of Oklahoma's oil boom. On the brink of bankruptcy, the ranch was forced into a conservatorship.

The government and creditors had laid claim to much of the property. Once spanning 110,000 acres, the 101 Ranch was nearly equal to the combined acreage of New York City boroughs Manhattan, Queens, and the Bronx. Auctioneers were going to sell off whatever was left, including farming equipment and livestock, to the highest bidders. Zack Miller, the lone survivor of three brothers who had inherited the ranch from their father, was bedridden and gravely ill when a local judge granted him one day to separate his personal horses from those owned by the ranch.

All but one longtime ranch hand—Bill Pickett—had packed up and headed west.

Pickett was a loyalist.

He and Miller, whose family's history traces back to Kentucky prior to the Civil War, thought of one another as kin.

Pickett did not look like half the cowboy he was. He was a lanky fellow, who never weighed more than 145 pounds, but what he lacked in stature he more than made up for with experience and knowhow. He was a South Texas brush-popper with big, strong hands. He was an expert horseman and handy as any man—regardless of their ethnicity—with a rope. And even though Miller could no longer cover his weekly earnings, Pickett remained.

That loyalty got him killed.

Miller tasked Pickett with the impossible chore of getting his personal horses separated ahead of the auction. Once he was healthy, Miller planned for the two of them to use the money from the sale of the horses to travel overseas in search of a fresh start in South Africa.

That winter had been uncommonly dry and windy.

The horses' coats were long, but Pickett—familiar with the livestock—could still make out the brands on their upper thighs. He rode into the corral by himself and began separating a few of the horses. It was a job for ten men, but the inexperienced and unskilled ranch hands the conservator had hired as replacements, for subpar wages, stood by and watched a legend at work.

There was a four-year-old chestnut-colored colt with an unmistakable reddish tone that stood out from the others. He was big. He was ornery and unsettled and thrashed back and forth from one side of the corral to the other.

In his biography, *Fabulous Empire*, author Fred Gipson—who, in 1956, wrote the classic young adult novel *Old Yeller*—said Miller remembered the colt as "boogery and skittish," but no one ever described him as mean.

Pickett had not ironed him out a year earlier when the colt ran off into the pasture, so Pickett had never finished the job of breaking him. On this day—March 22, 1932—he got down off his horse and looped his rope around its head and then began slowly walking hand-over-hand up the rope until he reached the horse. The colt went into a frenzy and reared up on his hind legs.

By this point, everyone nearby had stopped what they were doing and joined the other ranch hands to watch the famous Black cowboy as he struggled to calm the wild colt.

The horse was confused and swiped one of his forefeet at Pickett. It tore the front brim of his hat and before the aging cowboy could back off, the other hoof hit him on the side of the head and knocked him to the ground.

Pickett was hurt.

But not mortally—not yet anyway.

As they all watched and heard Pickett groaning, the horse stomped and kicked the old man squarely in the side of the head as he turned to run off. The gash was bleeding but had even one of the onlookers come to his aid, he *might* have survived. Be it a lack of experience or lack of courage, not a single one of them went in among all those wild horses to help.

Motionless, Pickett lay within arms' reach of his cowboy hat—the brim torn from its crown—as the dust from the Oklahoma rain bristled in the wind across the sundried landscape.

His head was busted open and Pickett's skull was cracked. Fluids and part of his brain pooled like spoiled cottage cheese beneath his head. Help finally arrived. They were too late. "The bulldogger was slated for death; all he needed was time to die," Gipson wrote.

In spite of the everyday risks of being a ranch hand and the vulnerabilities of being a Black man in a racially segregated Oklahoma—between 1907 and 1930 lynching took the lives of dozens of Blacks—Pickett lived twenty years longer than the average life expectancy for someone born just five years after the end of the Civil War.

Pickett took his last breath on April 2, 1932, eleven days after being kicked in the head.

It is generally believed that Willie M. Pickett was born December 5, 1870, in the Jenks-Branch community of Williamson County, Texas. However, the Travis County (Texas) census of 1880 listed his age as eight, not ten.

He was the second of thirteen children—five boys and eight girls—born to Thomas Jefferson Pickett, a former slave from South Carolina and Louisiana, and Mary Virginia Elizabeth Gilbert, who is said to be of Choctaw Indian descent. There are a few accounts of Mary being a combination of Black, white, Mexican, and Cherokee. Like a lot of kids his age, Willie was still a boy when he went to work to help his growing family. It's not known where he went to school through the fifth grade, but Willie learned to read and write and was considered lucky. Sometime before his eighteenth birthday, the family moved to nearby Taylor, Texas. In 1890 he met and married Maggie Turner, a former slave, whose father was a white plantation owner. They had nine children, including seven daughters who lived into adulthood.

At this point, he was using the name Bill and had earned a reputation as a salty ranch hand—not just for his unyielding work ethic, but also his undeniable cowboy skills. For several years, he worked for various ranchers around Taylor, Georgetown, Round Rock, and Rockdale.

At sixteen, he was bulldogging cattle and laid claim to having pioneered the art of jumping from a horse and biting the upper lip of a steer to subdue it, so the cowboy could twist its horns and force the steer onto its side. Unlike today's steers, which average four hundred to five hundred pounds, back then they were eight hundred pounds, on the small side, and as big as a thousand pounds. "Pickett discovered this act while watching herding dogs subdue cattle in this manner," according to the Williamson County Historical Commission.

There is no way of validating Pickett's claim, but no one—then or now—ever denied or even questioned him.

Bill Pickett is noted in legend and lore as the father of modern-day steer wrestling.

His first performance of the feat in front an audience is believed to have taken place at the turn of the twentieth century during the Confederate Soldiers Reunion in Nashville, Tennessee. The crowd stood amazed as they looked on. Bill and his brothers then formed the Pickett Brothers Bronco Busters and Rough Riders Association. They mostly performed in small Texas towns and surrounding southern states. As an African American he could not perform with white cowboys, so because of his lighter complexion—a physical characteristic he likely inherited from his mother's side of the family—they billed him as a Native American named the Dusky Demon.

The deception worked, and his "steer rasslin'" performance became a wildly popular phenomenon. Performing as the Dusky Demon, he became revered as the most daring cowboy alive.

By the time Pickett arrived at the Fort Worth Stockyards in 1905, Zack Miller and his older brothers, George and Joseph, had heard stories about him. Zack rode down from Oklahoma to Texas to look for him in the stockyards.

A few days later, the pair headed north to Ponca City and Pickett went to work for the Miller brothers, where he spent the better part of the next three decades establishing himself as "the greatest sweat and dirt cowboy that ever lived—bar none."

Pickett, who shed his Dusky Demon moniker, was known for his colorful and dynamic personality upon joining the 101 Wild West Show alongside Tom Mix, Buffalo Bill, Geronimo, and Will Rogers. Over the next quarter of a century, he became an international sensation—performing throughout the United States, Canada, Mexico, South America, and Europe.

If promoters had any misgivings about having a Black man perform in their arenas, they never spoke of it. Not to mention, race was less of an issue in the Midwest, throughout the Rust Belt, Northeast, and out West. The Miller brothers also had too much money and too much power to care one way or the other about how anyone felt about the ethnicity of their famous cowboy. From Oklahoma and Texas to California back east to Ohio, Pennsylvania, Massachusetts, and New York, Pickett became the main attraction. He brought crowds to their feet at the Chicago Coliseum and the world's most famous arena, the original Madison Square Garden.

One year after another, Pickett and Zack Miller, who oversaw the production of the 101 Wild West Shows, enjoyed the greatest adventures of their lives.

One not-so-great adventure took place in Mexico City when Zack bet a man 5,000 pesos that Pickett could bulldog a purebred Mexican fighting bull. Not just any fighting bull. This one was a bull named Chiquito Frijole, or "Little Bean."

Pickett had only one request; if he was killed, he asked Miller to make sure he was buried at the 101 Ranch. He did not want to be left behind in Mexico.

Pickett's prized horse, Spradley, was gored and Pickett's ribs were busted up. Finally, some thirty-eight minutes after entering the arena—well past the five-minute bet—Pickett staggered to the front of the bucking chutes.

Gipson wrote that the unruly crowd yelled, "Kill the Black man. Kill all the American dogs." Before he made it to the gate, Pickett was hit in the head with a thick, longneck beer bottle thrown from the stands.

Dazed, he was still able to make it out of the arena, and more importantly, he and Miller both made it back to the States alive.

They stayed on the road performing at iconic rodeos like the Calgary Stampede and Cheyenne Frontier Days until Pickett retired in 1929.

The Millers did not merely value Pickett as an employee; they loved him dearly, especially Zack and his family.

Zack's granddaughter Jimmie Munroe said her mom, Tassie Blevins Miller, learned how to ride a horse from Pickett. She got a pony and he made sure to spend time working with her every day. Much of what Pickett taught Tassie, she passed down to Jimmie, who developed into one of the greatest world champion barrel racers of all time and has been inducted into the National Cowgirl Hall of Fame, Pro Rodeo Hall of Fame, and Rodeo Hall of Fame at the National Cowboy and Western Heritage Museum.

While Pickett lay dying, Tassie, who was having her tonsils removed, insisted on being taken to see Pickett, who was kept in another section of the same hospital.

He was so popular, well-liked, and beloved by the Miller family that Pickett was only the second man to be eulogized on the steps in front of the Miller's stately white house, overlooking the ranch. The massive funeral was presided over by the Reverend Sylvester Fairley, and it's been estimated that as many as a thousand people—including Blacks, whites, and Native Americans—attended.

Doctors told Miller if he got out of his bed, he might not have the strength to get back to it alive. He did not listen.

Back in 1932, white men, especially those who were once as rich and powerful as Zack Miller, rarely attended funerals for any ranch hands, let alone a Black one. Not to mention, Ponca City is merely ninety miles northwest of Tulsa, where one of the most deadly incidents of racial violence in U.S. history had taken place eleven years earlier. But as Gipson wrote, "When the Negro preacher had finished, Zack had a few words to say."

We're telling Bill good-bye. He's dead now, and this is one time when a Negro and a white man are all the same. If there ever was a white Negro, it was Bill. His hide was Black, but his heart was white. If all white men had been as honest and loyal as this Negro, the world wouldn't be in the shape it's in today.

Miller's words only illustrated just how complex race and racism was and still is in America.

Heard through modern ears, his words are abhorrent; but Miller's granddaughter insists it is important to see them through the prism of race relations in the first decades of the twentieth century. In 1930s Oklahoma, proclaiming that if whites were as loyal as a Black man—even a popular Black man like Pickett—could have very well gotten Miller killed on the steps of his own home, especially at a time when he was no longer as rich and powerful as he once was, she said.

Miller, who had already lost both bothers and his family's fortune, tried as best he could to express the sense of love, loss, and grief he felt about now losing his one remaining friend. Miller returned to his bedroom and eventually recovered.

They laid Pickett to rest nine miles south of what locals still refer to as the "white house" at the base of White Eagle Monument. He had buried Spradley there four years earlier and made it well-known that he wanted to be buried alongside his horse and not his wife, at another site several miles away. His grave was extra deep, and the pinewood box was covered with soapstone rocks to keep the coyotes from clawing at his bones. The gravesite is inaccessible; and yet almost ninety years later, souvenir seekers and vandals have chipped away Pickett's headstone marker.

Will Rogers memorialized Pickett on his nationally broadcast radio program and wrote an obituary for the *New York Times*. It took until 1971 before Pickett became the first African American to be inducted into the Rodeo Hall of Fame, in Oklahoma City. Only three other Black rodeo cowboys—Myrtis Dightman (1997), Fred Whitfield (2000), and Charlie Sampson (2008)—have been inducted into the most prestigious of the Western halls of fame.

Looking back, Miller's granddaughter, Jimmie, said few people knew that, at the point of Pickett's untimely death, Miller was planning to move with him to South Africa. Her grandfather hoped each of the two hundred horses Pickett was separating from the rest of the herd would fetch $200, and he planned to use the $40,000 to fund one last great adventure.

They never made it to South Africa.

Pickett was dead.

Miller regained his health but lost everything and eventually wound up living in Waco, Texas, with his daughter, Tassie, and her husband. The couple was expecting Miller's first granddaughter, Jimmie, at the time of his death in January 1952.

Over the last twenty years of his life, Zack Miller remained haunted by Bill Pickett's death.

2

Robert "Money" Jackson

I don't want a Black History Month. Black history is American history.

—MORGAN FREEMAN

ANGLETON, TEXAS

Robert "Money" Jackson is a well-liked man who is equal parts working cowboy, rodeo cowboy, and businessman. He owned his own arena, produced rodeos, hauled livestock to rodeo events throughout Texas, Oklahoma, and Louisiana, owned and operated a gas station, worked as a ranch foreman, and was a consummate family man who employed his siblings—sixteen in all—and raised his own children to carry on the Jackson tradition of hard work *and* rodeo.

The history of Black rodeos in the Gulf Coast region of Texas is nothing without his inclusion.

His life story is legendary yet pales in comparison to his early kinfolk and their stories of wealth, plantations, slaves, mistresses, interracial children, a family divided by the Civil War, bankruptcy, and murder.

Robert is the great-great-grandson of Major Abner Jackson, an owner of three plantations—Retrieve, Lake Jackson, and Darrington—spread across 6,400 acres along the gulf coastline. A census taken in 1860 listed Abner as owning 285 slaves, making him the second-largest slave owner in Texas, according to various sources, including texasbeyondhistory.net.

By most accounts, Abner was born in 1810, in Virginia, before moving to South Carolina, twenty years later. He fathered four sons with Margaret Strobel, who may or may not have been his first wife. Two of those sons—Andrew and Abner Jr.—were killed in the Civil War. A third son, George, also served in the Confederacy, while their eldest son, John, helped their father manage the plantations.

John is believed to have fathered an illegitimate son, Frank, with a slave named Rosa, who is of African and Native American ancestry. However, Abner also is said to have fathered an illegitimate son with Rosa, leading some family members—Robert's son Ramone, among them—to wonder if John merely covered for his father to save him from the embarrassment. In either case, John raised Frank as his own son. John later was murdered by his brother George, who was jealous of the power and prestige he perceived his brother having. Unfortunately, John had mismanaged what little remained of the family fortune and George died of tuberculosis a couple years later.

Frank, who was half white and half a mix of African and Native American descent, married a woman who also was a mix of African and Native American ancestry. They had fifteen kids who survived to adulthood, including John, who was named after his "father." John, who made a living as a rancher, identified as Black and Native American. He and his wife had seventeen kids together, including Robert "Money" Jackson.

Robert Jackson—his nickname was Money, but he's known to his family and closest friends as Bobby—was born September 29, 1933.

He was working alongside his father by the time he was ten so that he could help his parents provide for his sixteen siblings. He has been a working cowboy for so damn long, he only got an eighth-grade education.

But, Jackson said, "I had fun, too."

At ten he was not only riding ranch horses, but his dad, John Jackson, also had started to show him how to break wild horses and rope calves. For a short time, Bobby even took an interest in horseracing and started to learn what it would take for him to be a jockey. However, his dad barred him from pursuing it any further when a local Black jockey was found murdered after a couple of wins. Years later, Bobby learned his dad was concerned that he, too, would be lynched. Instead, he went to rodeos, including during the earliest days of the Southwestern National Cowboys Association (SNCA).

The Jacksons had a place in the country. It was across the street from where Bobby would eventually build his home and his own rodeo arena. He purchased the land in 1953—when he was twenty years old—the same year he produced his first rodeo at the William Dudley Arena in Angleton.

In 1955 he married his wife, Catherine (pronounced Cath-reen).

While other Black cowboys from the Gulf Coast region would leave home to compete in Chicago and New York and other far-off and seemingly exotic metropolises, Bobby would compete locally on the weekends at events sanctioned by the SNCA. He started to produce jackpot rodeos a couple times a month at his own RV Ranch Arena. The first of those was held Mother's Day weekend in 1953, and the family has produced that event every year since.

"I had a good turnout," recalled Bobby, who added, "I knew a lot of people and a lot of people knew me, and they come to see [the rodeo]."

"He did some things that people of color weren't doing," said Bobby's youngest son, Ramone. As a matter of fact, Ramone noted that his dad was the first African American to secure a permit to have a trail ride in Brazoria County.

As much as he was a cowboy, he was also a businessman and respected as such.

He had a hay business with all his own equipment. He would cut and bail hay and then haul and sell it all over Texas and Louisiana. In the 1960s Bobby owned his own Conoco gas station adjacent to his arena. Whether they were arriving at or leaving his biweekly rodeos—many of which were sanctioned by the SNCA—it seemed like all the competitors and spectators bought gas from Bobby, which Ramone said was "unheard of for a Black man."

Today the pumps are gone, but the building remains.

"My dad, I would say, had an influence and an impact on his whole, entire family," Ramone said. "He kept the family with jobs and things to do because he was in a position to do so."

In addition to everything he had of his own doing, Bobby was a foreman for a land surveyor who hired him to oversee all four of his ranches. Bobby was his righthand man, with full authority to buy and sell cattle, but he wasn't always welcomed. At one point in the sixties, Bobby was at a nearby sale barn when he ran into trouble. He had never been to that particular barn but was certain they knew Mr. Thompson and that Bobby worked for him. They didn't like having a Black man at their auction and took exception to a Black man thinking he could write a check for as much money as he had done.

They called the local sheriff, who detained Bobby.

Bobby called Mr. Thompson who tried to clear things up over the phone, but he was met with resistance, so he and the sheriff from Angleton made the short flight over by helicopter.

They got there and "they were all gunned-up," said Ramone. They asked that Bobby be let free. Mr. Thompson and the sheriff stood by as Bobby loaded up the cattle and got the hell out of town.

Though he's hauled livestock to Black rodeos, his own events were always open to cowboys of any ethnicity. That includes the SNCA events he produced for years. In the sixties, Bobby served as the group's treasurer and then, in the seventies, he was elected president of the SNCA for several terms. Though it was a year-round series centralized in the Gulf Coast region—events were held from McBeth and Angleton to Pendleton, Hamilton, Dickinson, Brazoria, Jones Creek, West Columbia, and Houston—there were white promoters jealous of the SNCA's local success. They would replace the word "National" with "Negro" or substitute "Colored" in place of "Cowboys," even though the events were open to all ethnicities and over the years attracted PRCA world champions—the likes of which included Joe Beaver and Fred Whitfield.

"I don't think it was just 'Negro,'" Bobby said.

Ramone asked, "Are you talking about the n— word?"

"Yes," Bobby replied.

Bobby doesn't like hearing the word, much less saying it. His kids and their kids and now their kids have all been raised to walk away from people for saying it. In fact, Ramone said, his father would crack him and his brothers across the ass if he heard them say it.

"They wouldn't say 'Negro.' They would say 'nigger,'" said Bobby, who felt bad saying it but wanted to make sure there's a record of just what was being said back in the days of the Southwestern *National* Cowboys Association and that in no uncertain terms was it ever known as the Southwestern Negro Cowboys Association or the Southwestern National Colored Association.

"The best thing was to walk away," continued Bobby, who never wanted to give those who were racist or prejudiced the satisfaction of seeing him get emotional. "I don't hold no grudge. I let them overcome that. . . . I wouldn't be here now if I hadn't learned to turn the other cheek."

He knew it was not him they disliked; it was the color of his skin.

He made sure his kids were never denied because they were Black.

"Some of them didn't want to see me do the things I've done because I was Black. They didn't think a Black man could do that," said Bobby.

Ramone added, "Keep in mind, this is coming from a man with only an eighth-grade education."

More importantly, Bobby never let how he was treated by a select few affect how he treated anyone else—whether they were cowboys or not, and whether they were white or Black, Hispanic or Native American. He treated everyone as if they were special.

Bobby and Catherine were always there to lend a hand to those in need or just passing through.

For a cowboy, there is no greater prized possession than his horse and Bobby was open to letting even the most inexperienced rider in the arena use his roping horse if it meant the difference between that cowboy competing or turning out of the draw.

"My dad has no enemies," Ramone said. "If you want to come to the house [and practice], he'll turn the lights on for you if it's dark. If you need to drop your trailer and leave your horse for a day or two, fine. Ain't no problem. If you're from out of town and you're coming through and you need a place to stay, something to eat, you got it. Stop by the house."

Darrell Petry, one of approximately twenty Black cowboys ever to qualify for the National Finals Rodeo, stopped by unannounced one year on Thanksgiving.

He knew the door would be open to him and that Bobby and Catherine, a schoolteacher by trade who during segregation was a dietitian at the Black school in McBeth, would just add another plate to the dinner table.

The open-door policy is a way of life for rodeo cowboys.

Bobby, an accomplished bulldogger, won his last steer-wrestling championship with the SNCA in 1981. He was forty-eight. Over the next seventeen years, the old man was still climbing on his horse and dogging steers with his boys. His son Tommy beat him for a title in the early eighties, and then Rodney beat his brother Tommy a year later to win the same title. In 1985 Rodney beat them both again to win the all-around in what turned out to be one of the last couple years of the now-defunct SNCA.

Like his brothers, Ramone grew up going to junior rodeos, but his father made him quit prior to his senior year of high school. Rodney had lost out on a Division I football scholarship because the NCAA considered him a "professional athlete." Even junior rodeos pay out prize money, and Bobby did not want another of his sons to lose out on having an athletic scholarship pay for his college education.

"I considered myself a pretty good bull rider," Ramone said, "but I never got a chance to prove myself. My dad made me quit, and he was going to see to it I went to school."

After graduating in 1986, Ramone went to junior college in Ranger, Texas, where he played football and ran track, before transferring to Sam Houston State University for his junior and senior years. There, he ran the 100 meters.

While he was away at school, Rodney helped his father produce rodeos at the RV Ranch Arena. Ramone graduated in 1990 and returned home. He dabbled in rodeo, took an interest in his family's history and that's when he realized his family's unique story and his father's place in rodeo history, especially in the Gulf Coast region. "I already knew things were special for the rodeo itself—the longevity—because when I left and came back home, a lot of the arenas we used to go to as kids had died off."

He and his dad were determined to keep the Jackson legacy from becoming a story of the past.

For years, Bobby bought and sold young calves and then used stock contractors like Smokey Davis, a contractor with the International Professional Rodeo Association (IPRA), and Sloan Williams, who once owned the famous hall-of-fame bucking bull, known only as V-61, in the 1960s and '70s. Those two would always bring top stock to the Jacksons' rodeos along with T Diamond Ranch. In the eighties and nineties, Ramone said, some of the other "white contractors weren't bringing their good stuff to the Black rodeos. They were bringing their sorry stuff."

Instead of using bulls and horses that needed to be chute-broke, Ramone and his father started buying their own cattle and developing a livestock program. By 1999 Ramone was a fulltime stock contractor, and in addition to the three rodeos he and his dad still produce at the RV Ranch Arena, he was and still is on the road hauling bulls within a day's drive of Angleton.

Today, the Jackson legacy is in the hands of Bobby's grandsons—Glenn, a rodeo cowboy who became a Hollywood stuntman, and Little Rodney, who was a high school state qualifier in the tie-down roping for the Texas finals as a sophomore in 2020.

"Proud of Glenn and glad somebody is out there doing what I did and trying to do more," said Bobby, who paused and then made a point of recognizing his whole family, "I'm happy for all of them."

3

Charles, Roy, Clarence, and Kenneth LeBlanc

Sometimes history takes things into its own hands.
—THURGOOD MARSHALL

OKMULGEE, OKLAHOMA

Roy LeBlanc was a welder by trade.

He was also a damn good amateur calf roper. He rode broncs and did some steer wrestling, too.

His parents, Charles and Eyola, owned farmland going back to the early 1900s and it was there that Roy, born March 29, 1928, learned how to ride and rope and began to hone his skills as an amateur rodeo cowboy.

Roy started competing in the late 1940s and his career continued into the '50s. It was rare for him to compete during the rodeo. He was either relegated to the slack competition earlier that day or made to wait until the crowds left the arena.

The *New York Times* chronicled a rodeo in Checotah, Oklahoma, when Roy won the steer-wrestling event, but the first-place prize money was awarded to the second-place finisher—a white cowboy.

The producer of the rodeo offered to return Roy's entry fee.

He declined.

When Roy, then twenty-seven, entered the calf roping at his hometown Pow Wow Rodeo in Okmulgee, Oklahoma, there was an expectation that he would be treated fairly. It was 1955 and, as a Black contestant, not only was Roy made to compete after the predominantly white crowd had left the arena, but when his father made his way into the grandstand to watch his son compete, the elder LeBlanc was upset to discover a "Colored Only" section that had been roped off from the rest of the bystanders.

When he asked why he had to sit there, Charles was told, "We just want you to be more comfortable with your own people."

He replied, "I'm comfortable wherever I'm at."

Charles was not a stranger in town. In the 1950s, Okmulgee's population peaked at more than eighteen thousand people, and not only was Charles friendly with everyone, they respected him as an honest, hardworking businessman.

In the wake of that year's Pow Wow, Charles used his entrepreneurial spirit to form the Okmulgee Colored Round-Up Club. The group's sole purpose was to produce its own "All-Colored Rodeo."

There were twenty-two co-founders. The club was led by Charles and Roy along with local farmers, schoolteachers, and William "Frank" Haygood, a former professional baseball player, who played in the Negro League. Haygood, born in 1902, played shortstop for several teams in Texas and Oklahoma from the 1920s to the 1940s, including the Merchants in Okmulgee, which he called home until he died in November 1983.

As the driving force of the Round-Up Club, Charles took on the role of president. Roy was secretary.

They held their first rodeo less than two miles outside of town on Wood Drive on August 25 and 26, 1956. Coincidentally, it was held at the same arena used by the Pow Wow Rodeo, which the owners rented to the Round-Up Club for a $50 facility fee.

That year, there was $600 in prize money, and it featured four of seven traditional events: calf roping, steer wrestling, bareback riding, and bull riding. Admission was only one dollar for adults and fifty cents for children.

After seeing how big of a crowd the Black rodeo drew—stories passed down over the years recall it outdrawing the white rodeo—jealous and resentful Pow Wow organizers surprised the club by charging them $250 the following year.

By the time they held their third rodeo, in August 1958, the Okmulgee Colored Round-Up Club had purchased forty acres on Thirty-Sixth Street for a mere $4,000 and built their own outdoor arena.

They called the arena home until 1991, even though it was only used once a year and getting more difficult to maintain. Charles passed away in 1981, and several other founders were getting older—Larnell Williams is the last of the original Round-Up members still alive—so they decided to sell it for $40,000.

The annual rodeo has been held at the outdoor Bob Arrington Rodeo Arena, which is owned by the Creek Nation Casino Muscogee, ever since.

Roy had long taken over the role his father played. He eventually enlisted his second-born son, Kenneth, to produce the rodeo with him.

Roy would handle the public relations and marketing, while Kenneth would do everything related to the rodeo—hire the stock contractors and judges and invite the cowboys. Roy died in November 2009 and the event was rebranded the Roy LeBlanc Invitational Rodeo.

Roy LeBlanc's two oldest boys—Clarence and Kenneth, born just ten months apart—were five and four years old when their father and grandfather produced the first all-Black rodeo in Okmulgee.

Both boys and the siblings who followed grew up and came of age attending Black rodeos in Oklahoma.

They went to Boley in May, Seminole in June, Langston in July, and Drumright the first weekend in August. Okmulgee was always the second weekend. Only Boley and Okmulgee continue today. Boley quit for a few years, making Okmulgee the longest continuously running Black rodeo in the country—they produced their sixty-fifth and sixty-sixth in a row in August 2020 and '21 in spite of the COVID-19 pandemic.

Roy was tough and he made his sons into the men they are today. There was never a question of whether or not they were going to be cowboys. They were born cowboys.

Kenneth was seven and Clarence was eight when they started riding calves. Their mother, Teresa, was upset with their father when Kenneth busted his lip open falling off his first calf, but she remained supportive. By the time they were eight and nine, Roy put the boys to work, even if it was just passing out programs.

Clarence roped calves, while Kenneth transitioned from riding calves to bulls.

J. B. "Cigarette" Gibson gave Kenneth his first bull rope.

Gibson did it all. He roped calves, bulldogged, rode bulls, and competed in just about every other event. For several years, he would stay with the LeBlancs for the first half of August. They would go to Drumright together and then he would compete in Okmulgee. Kenneth cannot recall a single time he ever saw Gibson without a cigarette dangling from his lower lip.

Kenneth was about twelve when he recalled standing on the back of the bucking chutes in Drumright. Gibson was riding his bull dead easy into his hand when he abruptly fell off just before the eight-second whistle.

"J.B., what happened?" asked Kenneth. "I thought you had him rode."

Gibson shrugged, "It just happens like that sometimes."

Kenneth could not believe what he saw. He brought it up several times on the way home before Roy finally told him the truth. Mr. Grey had spotted Gibson $5 for his entry fee, so did Mr. Hampton and six others. Each had quietly agreed to pay his entry fee in exchange for half his winnings.

"He really couldn't ride him," Roy tried explaining, "because there wasn't nearly enough halves to go around and he's already made $40."

It was common for some white cowboys and rodeo insiders to front poor Black cowboys their entry fees in exchange for half their winnings. Gibson turned the practice against unsuspecting lenders by quietly collecting fees from multiple people without anyone knowing and then "bucking off" just shy of the whistle. Then, he would use their money to enter himself in higher-paying rodeos and keep all the winnings to himself. Unlike other Black rodeo cowboys who would often forgo half their winnings, Gibson outsmarted everyone.

"I just shook my head, because I couldn't believe he would do that," Kenneth said. "If he had his own money up, he'd always ride."

Clarence was a non-scholarship walk-on at Oklahoma State University. In college, he would win the calf roping, but they only gave away trophy saddles to the all-around winners, so he needed a second discipline.

As a junior, he started steer wrestling. Clarence wound up being better at bulldogging than he was at roping, and he was a damn fine roper.

An agile athlete with good reflexes, Clarence played both tight end and defensive end on his high school football team and was a forward on the basketball team. With that kind of size and strength, steer wrestling came naturally to him, but that was mostly because he was better than most kids his age when it came to handling horses.

"There's a lot of guys who have the ability to steer wrestle," Clarence said, "but they don't ride a horse well enough to where they can win."

Kenneth was always at the practice pen with his brother, and both were expert horsemen, so, like Clarence, shortly after trying steer wrestling for the first time, Kenneth focused on being a bulldogger.

But that is where the parallels between the two ended. Or so they claim.

"I don't think we're anything alike," Kenneth said. "When we was kids, we used to fight all the time, but nobody could fight us. If somebody fought Clarence, they had to fight me, and if they fought me, they would have to fight Clarence. But we fought each other all the time."

Kenneth stayed close to home when it came to entering rodeos, while Clarence envisioned a career in rodeo and was much more adventurous. In September 1971 Clarence had just started his sophomore year at OSU when he traveled to New York to compete in the first all-Black rodeo ever held in Harlem. Muhammad Ali was there, and so too were all the Black cowboy legends—Bud Bramwell, Cleo Hearn, Marvel Rogers Sr., Nelson Jackson, Bailey's Prairie Kid, and Willie Thomas.

After graduating with a degree in animal science, Clarence moved to Wichita, Kansas. For less than a year, he worked in a cooler with no windows at Kansas Beef, Inc. When he inquired about taking a meat inspector test, his supervisor laughed.

"Son, you gotta have a college degree," the man said.

Clarence replied, "I got one."

"You mean you're back here hauling guts and you got a college degree?" he said. "Why didn't you let us know earlier?"

Clarence shrugged and said, "I didn't plan on being here that long."

In the spring of 1975, a friend asked if he wanted to compete at a rodeo in St. Louis. Clarence said he did. When the friend asked how long he could be gone, Clarence joked, "From now on."

When Clarence told his boss he was quitting, he was told to take a leave of absence and Kansas Beef would hold his position for him whether he was gone two weeks, two months or two years.

He never did return to his job as a meat inspector.

Clarence was a few months shy of his twenty-fourth birthday when he joined the IPRA. According to the *New York Times*, Clarence was one of only six African Americans among the three thousand members.

"He'd leave home with entry fees for one rodeo and he'd figure out a way to get to the next one," Kenneth said of his brother. "That's all he wanted to do was rodeo. That was his passion."

Clarence said, "If they was having one somewhere, I wanted to be there. I didn't care where it was. If I could drive there overnight, I would be there."

It was nothing for Clarence to go from Michigan to Texas, home to Oklahoma, and back to Illinois inside of a week. He loved competing, but he loved winning more. He credits his travel partner, Calvin Greely Jr., with his success.

"If I was out there by myself, I probably wouldn't have lasted," admitted Clarence, who said he benefitted from Greely's universal popularity. Both men grew to be well-liked by everyone—competitors, promoters, and fans—regardless of color and ethnicity.

After nearly qualifying for the International Finals Rodeo his first year, Clarence went on to qualify sixteen times, including a stretch of thirteen consecutive years—a streak that only ended when he took a year off to build a house for himself and his family. There had been successful Black rodeo cowboys before him—Myrtis Dightman, Bud Bramwell, and Cleo Hearn all competed as members of the RCA—but his sustained success in the IPRA provided a gateway for Charlie Sampson and later Fred Whitfield to have success at the elite level of rodeo—Professional Rodeo Cowboys Association (formerly known as the Rodeo Cowboys Association)—and Black cowboys could in fact be a force of nature in the arena.

Clarence was on the rodeo trail with the IPRA for eighteen years, and looking back, he said, only once did he feel he was the victim of racism.

His first year as a pro, he was down in Tallahassee, Florida. Clarence ran a steer and, to his recollection, caught him "really fast." Skip Akers, a Florida native who won the IPRA steer-wrestling title in 1973 and again in '74, ran his steer two-seconds further than Clarence, but when they announced Akers's time it "was one-tenth [of a second] faster than me."

A couple of fellow cowboys hollered up to the timekeeper and said, "That ain't right."

Clarence didn't say a word. He quietly led his horse back to his trailer and was getting ready for the trip home to Oklahoma when Akers walked up. He held out his hand and offered to switch his first-place check with the second-place one Clarence had been given.

"I don't know those people up there," Akers explained. "I ain't got nothing to do with that."

"Skip tried to give me the money," Clarence said. "I wouldn't take it. I said, 'Nah. That's fine.'"

A decade later, he told Stone Love of the *Tulsa Tribune*, "In the places I thought they might be against me—the South—they have applauded me more than anywhere else."

Clarence was runner-up for the IPRA steer-wrestling title in 1977 and won the average at the International Finals Rodeo a year later, in 1978. But his best years almost never happened when his career nearly came to an abrupt end in April 1980.

Clarence was one of four men traveling in a pickup truck when a car directly in front of them had a blowout. After narrowly avoiding a wreck, they stopped to offer help and Clarence was standing between the two vehicles when a third car slammed into the backend of the truck. His left leg was crushed, and doctors feared they would have to amputate.

Miraculously, they were able to save his leg, and a month later, Clarence was released from the hospital. Three months later, he was cycling up to fifty miles a day.

In January 1981 he returned to competition. Later that year, he was back in New York for the first time in a decade. This time he was entered in the Stetson World's Toughest Rodeo at Madison Square Garden.

Clarence won his first steer-wrestling world title in 1983. He was the first African American to win a title in the IPRA. A year later, there was a change to the IFR format, and instead of winning back-to-back world titles, he won the 1984 National Championship and was runner-up in '85.

In 1985 Clarence and Kenneth made history by becoming the first brothers—regardless of color or ethnicity—to ever qualify for the IFR in the same event.

The brothers were rarely able to travel with one another on a regular basis because Kenneth still had a fulltime nine-to-five job as a case manager for a job placement company in Okmulgee. But much like when they were younger, the two would haze for one another whenever they were competing at the same rodeo. They coached each other to be their best and pushed each other to succeed. They certainly made one another better, but Kenneth once found himself in Lufkin, Texas, without his older brother there for support.

He did not make a particularly good run. James Neighbors, a fellow steer wrestler, who later became a stock contractor, was not one to mince words.

Neighbors walked up to Kenneth and said, "Son, you bulldog like a man with a job."

Kenneth knew what Neighbors meant; he needed to be serious every opportunity he had. That year, he was the runner-up for steer-wrestling title in the IPRA and won the Bill Pickett Invitational Rodeo (BPIR) title.

Once they were too old to compete, Clarence focused on building a successful concrete business, while Kenneth continued to work as a case manager for a job placement company, spending eleven months out of the year preparing for the annual Okmulgee rodeo.

Before his death, the late Sedgwick Haynes, arena director in Okmulgee and a cowboy who spent thirty years managing the BPIR, referred to Roy LeBlanc's annual rodeo as "the Cheyenne [Frontier Days] of Black rodeo."

Unfortunately, community leaders have not always treated it as such.

Over the years, the rodeo has brought large groups of people to town, but until recently, any unruly behavior that weekend was blamed on the rodeo. If there was a fight, authorities blamed the rodeo.

For a number of years, Kenneth said, if you came to Okmulgee the second weekend of August and you were Black, "You might as well get ready to get stopped by the city police."

Once they went so far as to set up a checkpoint outside of the exit from Creek Nation Casino.

"They checked every Black person," Kenneth recalled, "and let every white person go through. That was the reality and that was as recent as the seventies and eighties. My wife even got stopped on her way home from the rodeo one night."

She had left her purse in his truck.

It was a bad situation that could have been worse.

"They did that constantly," Kenneth continued, "and I think the purpose was to try and kill the rodeo."

That all changed in 2010 when Chris Asbell was elected to the Okmulgee City Council. Prior to Asbell's election, the council saw the rodeo as an annual nuisance. Despite the tax dollars generated, the council had never allocated any tourism funds for the LeBlancs to market their event. Yet, they allegedly gave $15,000 to the organizers of a car show.

"The car show didn't bring anybody to town," said Kenneth. After Asbell was elected, the new councilman told him, "With all the people your rodeo brings to Okmulgee, the city should be behind you."

In recent years, the council has contributed $5,000 from a tourism fund for the rodeo. Clarence knows it has not been easy for Kenneth. He is proud of what his brother has managed to do in working to keep the rodeo relevant.

"People that leave here plan their vacations to come back on that weekend," Clarence said. "When they grow up, they come back and bring their kids."

But Okmulgee is more than a tradition. It's an event with historical significance that often goes unrecognized. For more than sixty-five years, three generations of one of the most influential families in the history of all-Black rodeos—Charles, Roy, Clarence, and Kenneth LeBlanc—have managed to keep their dream alive and offer a showcase for Black cowboys.

4

Nathaniel "Rex" Purefoy with Herb Jeffries

The greatest gift you can give someone is the gift of inspiration.
—CORNEL WEST

DURHAM, NORTH CAROLINA, AND HOLLYWOOD, CALIFORNIA

Nathaniel "Rex" Purefoy knew all the television and movie cowboys by name. He knew the crooks and the outlaws, too.

On Friday and Saturday nights in Durham, North Carolina, where he was born in 1935, the local theater screened popular Westerns. There was Roy Rogers and Gene Autry, along with Tex Ritter, Monte Hale, Sunset Carson, Bill Elliott, Lash Larue, Eddie Dean, Tom Mix, and then came John Wayne.

Purefoy never left without watching the end credits. He knew all the stuntmen by name and the stunt coordinators, too.

He never saw himself on the screen, though.

Purefoy, who was Black, was twelve by the time he saw Herb Jeffries on the big screen in *Harlem on the Prairie*. Jeffries was one of the original singing cowboys in the early days of Hollywood Westerns, but what made him unique was that he was Black.

Directed by Sam Newfield, *Harlem on the Prairie*, which had been released a decade earlier in 1937, was billed on movie posters as the first all-colored

Western musical, and it encouraged Purefoy's dream. Prior to then, the easily influenced sixth-grader had only seen white cowboys on the silver screen.

Yet for some reason, Purefoy "still wanted to be a *cowboy*."

By all accounts, Jeffries was born in 1914 and raised in a Detroit ghetto. However, on occasion, he would claim to have been born in 1911. His mother was Irish and the father he said he never knew was Sicilian.

In 2004 Jeffries told the *Oklahoman* newspaper, "One of my great-grandparents was Ethiopian. . . . I'm an Italian-looking mongrel with a percentage of Ethiopian blood, which enabled me to get work with Black orchestras."

He began playing with those bands after moving to Chicago in 1933.

Born with a luscious tenor voice, it was Duke Ellington who would eventually convince Jeffries to lower himself to the baritone that made him famous. In Chicago he landed a gig as a vocalist for jazz bandleader Erskine Tate. He experienced discrimination and racism for the first time during a tour down South, where he discovered segregated movie theaters for Black audiences. Westerns were so popular, in fact, that along with Autry and Rogers, Black audiences were enamored by Ritter, Mix, and Hale.

It was said that Jeffries "vowed to correct this inequity via race films," according to a story that was published in the *LA Times Magazine*. He left Chicago and played his way to Hollywood.

It remains unclear how Jeffries befriended and began working with B-movie producer Jed Buell. Jeffries claims to have seen *Terror in Tiny Town*, a Western featuring a cast of all little people, and thought he and Buell could accomplish the same with an all-Black cast. However, *Tiny Town* was released in 1938, a year after Jeffries made his debut in *Harlem on the Prairie* and the same year he returned to the silver screen in *Harlem Rides the Range* and *Two-Gun Man from Harlem*.

Ultimately, all three movies and a fourth release, *The Bronze Buckaroo*, released in 1939, were filmed in less than a week at N. B. Murray's dude ranch outside Victorville, California, with a paltry budget of less than $25,000 each.

Decades later, however, Reginald T. Dorsey, one of a few Black cowboys who found success in Hollywood as an actor, met Jefferies during an event celebrating Black cowboys at the Gene Autry Museum of the American West. Dorsey recalled Jeffries, who starred in the films but was not credited for his role as a producer, telling him Jeffries was inspired to make an all-Black Western after meeting a young African American boy who was crying because his friends would not let him play "cowboys and Indians" with them because there was no such thing as Black cowboys.

Whatever the inspiration, at the time, *Harlem on the Prairie* was reportedly the highest grossing all-Black film.

Jeffries was not Buell's first choice for the lead role, but the two men had a hard time finding an African American who could ride a horse, sing, and act, which led Jeffries to suggest himself. He told the *Los Angeles Times* that Buell initially told him "no way" and went so far as to claim, "They'll never buy you; you're not Black enough."

Not only could Jeffries sing, but as a young boy, he also learned to ride horses on his maternal grandparents' dairy farm in northern Michigan. With no alternatives, Buell relented, but according to several firsthand accounts, he insisted the light-skinned Jeffries wear makeup to darken his skin.

"It looked like I had a good suntan," Jeffries was quoted in the *Times*.

The same article also noted that Jeffries never removed his Stetson hat in an effort to hide his brownish-red hair from movie audiences. Jeffries stood six feet three and is, perhaps, best remembered for his Clark Gable–like mustache. New York University film professor and noted historian Donald Bogle described Jeffries as a sex symbol and said, "He might have been a different kind of star had America been a different kind of place."

While *Harlem on the Prairie* touted its "all-Negro" cast, the others featured Black and white actors and were dubbed "horse operas" by trade magazines, the *Times* article recalled.

Aside from Jeffries's low-budget turn as a cowboy crooner, Black cowboys in the Old West—and their importance—were mostly written out of Hollywood scripts. In 1947 Louis Jordan made *Look-Out Sister* about a bandleader who finds himself at a dude ranch. The film also featured Bobby Scott, a Black cowboy, in an uncredited role. It was not until 1971, when Sidney Poitier and Harry Belafonte took top billing in *Buck and the Preacher*, that Hollywood produced a realistic all-Black Western.

A decade later and more than 2,500 miles due east of Hollywood, in Durham, an impressionable Purefoy saw Jeffries's singing cowboy films, and more importantly, he saw himself as a singing cowboy.

Nathaniel Purefoy was born November 11, 1935, and grew up on Mathews Street in downtown Durham, North Carolina. He was the middle child of five siblings and does not remember if his mother, Beulah Purefoy, ever told him who his father was.

Over the years, someone told him his father was white. Someone else told him he was Native American. Every time the conversation came up, it seemed to be something different, but Purefoy said he always identified as being African American.

He was in junior high school when he first taught himself how to trick rope on the street in front of his childhood home. By thirteen he was emulating the tricks he saw performed by singing cowboys on television shows in the 1940s and '50s. He idolized anyone with a lasso, especially Jeffries in *Harlem Rides the Range* and *Two-Gun Man from Harlem*.

In 1984 Purefoy told *Ebony* magazine, "I figured that one day, since there weren't that many Black cowboys, I would take that cowboy's place."

In the late forties, he would perform during the local junior high and high school basketball games. He didn't know a lot of tricks, but he still wowed the crowd from the stage during timeouts and halftime. Dressed in fancy cowboy attire, Purefoy started roping at a tavern in Durham called City News Stand. He would twirl his rope while jumping in and out of the loop and then take his hat around and collect money from the beer drinkers. Like his heroes, he never drank or smoked.

"I couldn't do that many tricks then," Purefoy said, "but I did enough."

There were tricks called the butterfly, reverse butterfly, and upside-down butterfly. There was the ocean wave, wedding ring, and flying star. He named one trick zigzag, and another was called drunk and preach. It took three to five months to learn new tricks, and another year or two for Purefoy to perfect the artistry of trick roping.

He was dedicated to his craft. From day one, an hour of practice turned into two. Two days became a whole week and then a month. It was that kind of time and commitment that kept others from pursuing it. Trick roping, Purefoy would say, "is one of the hardest arts for a cowboy to learn."

After graduating from Hillside High School, Purefoy enlisted in the U.S. Air Force and spent four years stateside working as a military police officer. It was the first time he experienced racism. Durham was different from the surrounding towns, according to Purefoy, who said, "More Negros owned their homes than any other place in the world."

After being honorably discharged, Purefoy changed his name from Nathaniel to Rex because "it had more of an Old West ring to it."

Purefoy trained both of his horses—Ringo and Smoky—to perform what eventually became his one-man, Hollywood-style cowboy show. He dazzled onlookers by twirling as many as seven lariats, cracking whips, and spinning his replica six-shooters. He performed fancy Charro tricks and jumped his horses through his rope while standing atop their silver saddles.

Purefoy became a professional roper in 1969, but he did not start touring on his own until 1970. In 1971 former New Jersey congressman George Richardson offered him $50 a performance to entertain audiences at a trio of all-Black rodeos on the East Coast, including the first of its kind in Harlem.

By 1972 he was back in Durham where he found work at a local amusement park, the Daniel Boone Railroad, fifteen miles out of town in nearby Hillsborough. He performed rope tricks for tourists and park visitors every Saturday and Sunday for the entire season. He also found work in Longview, Texas; Shreveport, Louisiana; and Washington DC, performing at rodeos and carnivals as well as shopping malls and civic gatherings. However, it was never a steady source of income, so he became a professional photographer by trade and eventually moved to New Jersey.

He worked as a photojournalist for the *Star Ledger* in Newark and freelanced for twenty years as a stringer for both *Jet* and *Ebony* magazines, which profiled Purefoy in an article titled "That Fancy Roping Man."

"I was a good photographer," proclaimed Purefoy, who said they still owe him a check for his last assignment and joked about today's technology, "but now these telephones done took over making pictures."

At one point, like the cowboys who inspired him, Purefoy ventured out to Hollywood. He arrived in an Oldsmobile with Ringo behind him in a one-horse trailer. He did not know anyone when he got there and randomly pulled off the 101 freeway in Chinatown, where he befriended a stranger who had just been released from the Los Angeles County jail for petty larceny.

The man pointed Purefoy in the direction of El Segundo Boulevard and Figueroa Street, where he told him he would find a horse stable at the intersection. It took some time to find the entrance in an alley, but that's where he met the stable's owner Tommy Cloud, a Hollywood stunt coordinator, who often helped African Americans find work in films.

He introduced Purefoy to a friend named Cactus. Like Purefoy, Cactus was a light-skinned Black trick roper. Upon meeting, the two immediately traded off doing tricks. They became fast friends and briefly lived together. Nearly fifty years later, there's an excitement when Purefoy talks about Cactus, who got his name from a character he played in one of Jeffries's films.

Cactus and his live-in girlfriend invited Purefoy to stay with them and her nephew, Don Mitchell, an actor best known for his role alongside Raymond Burr in the television series *Ironside*. Or, at least, that is how Purefoy recalls the memory. He said Cactus, whose real name, he claims, is Thomas Hoard, was in his eighties when they met, but film credits list him as John Thomas. He was only sixty-seven years old when he passed away in 1981.

Purefoy's time in Hollywood was short-lived. He performed regularly on *The Flip Wilson Show*—combining his roping routine and singing talent—but a career in movies and television never materialized.

Other than Mitchell, Cactus failed to introduce Purefoy to anyone of any significance who could help launch a career. Mitchell offered to help him find work as his stunt double, but once *Ironside* wrapped following the 1974–75 season, he struggled to finish out his own acting career with bit parts and guest appearances on shows like *Wonder Woman*, *Police Story*, *CHiPs*, and *Matlock*.

Purefoy said Hollywood wasn't interested in hiring a Black stuntman and would instead "paint down" his white counterparts for the role. The Black Stuntmen's Association was formed in 1967 and Cloud, whom Purefoy met when he first arrived, made a name for himself on movie and television sets as a stunt coordinator and could have easily found Purefoy work.

Purefoy wanted to be a movie star like Jeffries, and when that never happened, the North Carolina cowboy left California and was back on the road. In time, he performed with U2Rodeo and the Bill Pickett Invitational Rodeo along with the Pan American Circus and UniverSoul Circus. As a member of the Trick Roping Association, he performed throughout the United States and was honored by the group on several occasions as the best-dressed cowboy.

Years later, he performed at the Gene Autry Museum in California, where he finally met his hero, Jeffries. The two entertainers were part of a national broadcast hosted by Peter Jennings that honored Jeffries for a career spanning fifty years as a singing Black cowboy.

"He was kind of broke then," Purefoy recalled. "He told me he lost all his stuff in a landslide."

Purefoy eventually settled in Kansas City, where he has been a regular performer at the American Royal since the 1980s—an annual livestock and Western show that has been in existence since 1899. Once in Kansas City, he married a schoolteacher he had met back when he was stationed in Valdosta, Georgia, and quickly became a local celebrity. Purefoy could not even attend church without waving and shaking hands with everyone in the congregation, "because I'm an entertainer in Kansas City, plus I'm a photographer, so I'm at a lot of places."

"I have more ordinary people—John and Jim from the street—those are the ones that come up and tell you how they appreciate you," Purefoy said.

They knew him from rodeos and county fairs, festivals, carnivals, and, in later years, civic events and school visits. Well into his sixties, he would stand atop one and sometimes two horses that he trained to jump through an enlarged loop, while he did all of his fancy tricks with ropes, whips, and guns. He taught his horses to dance and march. They walked on their hind legs and would fall over and play dead on command. Like the rope tricks themselves, he would spend hours working with his horses every day.

Purefoy is in his eighties now. He still makes public appearances, which are mostly limited to community events, schools, museums, horse shows, and small-town parades in Kansas City and the surrounding area. He performs a limited number of tricks, but nowadays his show is more about educating audiences. Purefoy mostly shares stories about the forgotten history of Black cowboys and his own rise to fame as the self-proclaimed Lord of the Lasso.

5

Willie Thomas Sr. and Harold Cash

If there is no struggle, there is no progress.
—FREDERICK DOUGLASS

RICHMOND AND LA MARQUE, TEXAS

The stories of the late Willie Thomas Sr. are what legends are made of.

There are two versions of the first and only time Thomas entered a rodeo in Lake Charles, Louisiana, back in the early 1950s. They both end the same way.

In one version, it wasn't until he was in the bucking chute warming up his bull rope on the back of a big-horned, brindle-colored bucking bull he randomly drew that its owner noticed the color of Thomas's skin. He was Black. The brim of his cowboy hat had been pulled down low to shield his face, so it wasn't until the man saw Thomas's black hand reach up and grab the tail of his rope and pull it tight across his riding hand that the stock contractor realized his bull was matched up with the only Black bull rider in the draw that night.

As the man finished cinching up the flank strap around the bull's back hips, he leaned over Thomas's left shoulder and addressed him as *boy*. In no uncertain terms, he told Thomas if he didn't buck off, he had better jump off that damn bull or he would "shoot his Black ass off" before the timekeeper had a chance to blow the eight-second whistle.

Thomas calmly finished tying his riding hand into his rope and, without turning to face the contractor, told him, "You better get your gun ready . . ."

Then he reached up to push his hat down tight around his head. He didn't want it coming off during the ride. Thomas, who lost his left eye when he was five and had it replaced with a glass replica, never saw the man when he added, ". . . because this one's already rode."

In the other version, the verbal confrontation took place beforehand.

In either case, eight seconds later, Thomas did not pound his chest, victoriously throw his hat across the arena, or even wave to the crowd—many of whom did not realize they were standing on their feet and cheering for a Black man.

When the dust settled, he unassumingly picked up his rope and hustled behind the chutes, took off his chaps and spurs, threw them in his gear bag and was rolling up his rope when he was told he needed to leave.

Based on his score, Thomas would have placed second.

He asked about his money and was told there was not going to be any for him.

Instead, after some salty language, two men told Thomas, "You're lucky to be leaving here, and don't you ever come back."

They escorted him 34 miles west on Interstate 10 just to make sure he crossed the border into Texas and went back to wherever he came from. Thomas drove another 110 miles all the way to Houston, and for the rest of his life—Thomas died April 24, 2020, at age ninety—whenever he retold that story, it ended with him saying, "I never went back."

Willie Thomas Sr. was born in Richmond, Texas, on January 30, 1930, and raised nearby on the A. P. George Ranch, where his parents—Johnnie and Josephine—had been living and working since 1925. His daddy had a house on the property.

The second of four children, Willie dropped out of school in the fourth grade and, by the time he was twelve, was working alongside grown men. Whenever they would finish feeding the cattle, young Willie would jump from the feed wagon onto the back of a bull, where he learned how to ride without even using a rope. At sixteen, he was put in charge of overseeing more than five hundred head of beef cattle.

The George Ranch would also provide livestock for local rodeos. Willie and his younger brother, James, would ride along, and those jackpot events were really their introduction to rodeo.

Two years later, at eighteen, Willie started competing, but without anyone to serve as a mentor or teach him the fundamentals of bull riding, he had no idea he was putting his rope on backward. He also taught himself how to ride in the bareback competition just by watching others.

His first event was in Hempstead, Texas. The entry fee was only $3. Then came Prairie View, followed by the famous Diamond L Ranch on South Main in Houston, where they held Black rodeos on Sunday afternoons. He started riding at Diamond L in 1948.

In 1953 he entered his first pro rodeo in San Antonio.

He was still riding with his bull rope on backward, but much like the incident in Lake Charles, there are a few versions as to how San Antonio played out. There are those who say he won the bull-riding event, while others claim he finished second. There's no record of the event—only fading memories—but logic says there is no way both judges marked him high enough to win the event, much less place in the average and win money.

But one aspect of the decades-old story has been consistent for nearly seventy years. Hall of Fame cowboy Jim Shoulders was fascinated by how well Willie rode.

Shoulders had four re-ride bulls that none of the cowboys—regardless of their ethnicity—wanted to get on, so after the event Shoulders offered Willie $10 for each of the four bulls he successfully rode for eight seconds.

Willie went home with four ten-dollar bills in his pocket.

Soon after, there was an incident in Arkansas.

Without consulting the Negro Motorist Green Book—an annual guide published from 1936 to 1966 to help Black travelers with friendly motels, restaurants, and gas stations—Willie was left to spend the night in his car after a motel manager refused him service because he was Black. He drove to the rodeo arena and tried to spend the night in his car, but it was so uncomfortable that he wound up sleeping on the bleachers.

Then came a return trip back to San Antonio when Willie rode his bull well past the qualified eight seconds, but the timekeeper would not blow his whistle until after Willie stepped off his bull.

He was marked with a no score even though onlookers said Willie had ridden for almost fourteen seconds. Afterward, it has been said that rancher and stock contractor Zeno Farris confronted the timekeeper—telling him that he ought to be ashamed of himself.

Willie said nothing.

Discouraged by how he was treated, it was more than a year before he competed at another professional rodeo. When he returned—in 1956—Willie was known for telling judges, "You might cheat me, but you won't buck me off."

San Antonio would not be the last time Willie was cheated.

Bobby Steiner was eleven years old and ten years from becoming the 1973 world champion bull rider when his father, Tommy, produced a rodeo in McAlester, Oklahoma.

Willie drew a red bull with big horns that had #31 on its ear tag. That bull was one of Tommy's best and had been selected for the NFR a year earlier.

"Willie Thomas spurred the shit out of him," recalled Bobby, but one of the judges claimed Willie slapped the bull with his freehand. "My dad went, 'What do you mean no score?'"

Bobby overheard the judge tell his dad, "He slapped him."

Tommy confronted the judge, who told him, "Well, he's Black, isn't he?"

"And my dad said, 'You'll never work for me again,'" Bobby recalled. "It was one of the great bull rides."

Willie didn't cuss or say one word. He just smiled and went on.

"I'll never forget that," Bobby said. "After they saw how good he was, the people that were racist, they got over it."

Bobby was not alone in his assessment of Willie. Donnie Gay, an eight-time world champion bull rider, remembers Willie as "probably the best Black bull rider, maybe ever." Bubba Goudeau, another tough son of a bitch in his own right, agreed.

And then there's Pete Logan, a Pro Rodeo Hall of Fame announcer who lent his voice to events at Madison Square Garden a record ten times. Before Logan died in October 1993, Bobby sat with him at a restaurant and Logan told him Willie Thomas and Harry Tompkins were two of the all-time greats.

"I never heard him give compliments," said Bobby of his last conversation with Logan. "It's like, damn, at that time, I thought maybe I was the only guy that felt Willie Thomas was over-the-top great, but for Pete Logan to say that was incredible. . . . Willie needs to know that Pete told me that."

Harold Cash made sure he knew it.

Willie not only made a great impression on his white counterparts, but he also was an incredible influence on other Black cowboys—namely Freddie "Skeet" Gordon and Cash.

Gordon grew up with Willie on the A. P. George Ranch and later traveled with him to pro rodeos in New York City at the old Madison Square Garden and Boston, where Willie won another rodeo at the famed Boston Garden. In addition to New York and Boston, Willie won pro events in Harrisburg, Pennsylvania, and Waco and Austin, Texas. He won twenty pro buckles in all.

In the later years of a career that lasted until 1969, Willie befriended and became something of a father figure to a kid named Cash.

Harold Cash was the third of eight children born to George and Cora Lee Cash on December 26, 1948.

They lived in La Marque, Texas, where Harold attended school and would eventually graduate from Lincoln High School before going to Prairie View A&M University. Beginning at age five, he spent his summers with his paternal grandfather on his farm eighty miles west in Kendleton.

His grandfather grew corn and watermelon, had one horse and a few cows. He was not a cowboy, but he loved rodeo. Harold was nine when his grandparents introduced him to Black rodeos, but after they passed away, it was another five or six years until his mother's brother opened a rodeo pen at Menotti's Arena in Dickinson, Texas.

That's where he first saw Willie Thomas.

Thomas was not only the best rough stock rider entered in the rodeo, but Cash also thought he was as good or even better than any of the professional cowboys he saw competing on television at the Calgary Stampede. Seeing Thomas in person reminded him of the time his grandparents had taken him for barbecue and he overheard two cowboys talking about Thomas.

One said to the other, "That nigger won't ever win a world championship."

That comment stuck with him, and now, in 1967, after seeing Thomas and meeting him, Cash was ready to pursue his own career. His first event was at the same rodeo his grandparents had taken him to all those years ago—the S. P. Picnic Grounds in Kendleton.

He rode bulls and bareback horses in the Southwestern National Cowboys Association and went nearly an entire season without winning any money, until the final event.

It was 1969 by the time he teamed up with Thomas, who was in his last year as a pro. They took a liking to one another and Thomas showed Cash "the tricks and trade of rodeo" and even gave Cash one of his buckles to wear.

They were competing in the All-American Rodeo Association, which Cash co-founded with other fellow Black rodeo cowboys from Houston and the surrounding Gulf Coast region of Texas, and the protégé would split his winnings with Thomas.

"Willie was my coach and he was my mentor, so when I won, he won," said Cash, who knew Thomas was too old to still be competitive but had a family to support. Cash, who drove them as far north as Okmulgee, Oklahoma, never once asked Thomas to help pay to gas up his 1966 442 Oldsmobile or later his '73 Grand Prix.

Cash added, "We got tight. He was like a father to me."

But Cash was on his own when he traveled to the likes of Denver, Chicago, and Washington DC, where he experienced the greatest moment of his career at RFK Stadium in 1981.

Cash was en route to winning his second bareback title in three years for the All-American Rodeo Association (which is not the same as the American Rodeo Association). He had won the title in 1979—Thomas proudly wore Cash's buckle for the first couple weeks before trading it back with him—and missed out on winning again in 1980 by a mere $19. In 1981 he took a detour to the East Coast for a rodeo produced by Thyrl Latting.

In the pre-internet era, it was common for rodeo cowboys to show up at an airport to buy a plane ticket for the same day. Cash drove to Houston's William P. Hobby Airport a week beforehand to assure himself a direct flight to DC, but it was not until he arrived with his brand-new gear bag that he realized Continental Airlines had sold him a ticket that actually flew out of Houston Intercontinental Airport.

First, they wouldn't check his bag, saying they did not fly to DC.

It was not until another airline attendant overheard the conversation that she was able to explain to Cash what had happened. She asked, "Where you going?"

"A rodeo," he replied.

Confused, she said, "A Black cowboy?"

"Yes," he said, and by then it was too late for him to drive the twenty-four miles that separated Houston's two airports, so the attendant rebooked Cash on a flight to Baltimore.

Back then, there was not a designated taxi line, so he hailed one on his own when he arrived.

"Where you going?" the driver asked.

"Washington DC."

The driver was hesitant to make the hour-long commute and asked him what he was doing in DC. Cash told him he was competing in a rodeo at RFK Stadium. Like the Continental attendant earlier that day, the driver said, "A Black cowboy?" and then agreed.

By the time they arrived at the stadium and Cash found his way inside, Latting had no choice but to turn his horse out. Cash got in the arena in time to see his horse run through the out-gate. Latting apologized, but he knew, to hold it any longer would have been playing favorites. Cash took a no-score in round one.

The next day, in round two, Cash drew a horse named Playboy.

"You were going to win some money if you could stay on him," Cash said.

Playboy was a big, strong bucking horse with a list of cowboys he had thrown off that was much longer than the list of those who had made a qualified ride.

Thomas was not traveling with him, but Cash harkened back to a valuable lesson the old man shared with him on their first trip together: "Don't set your rigging so tight on them big horses. They strong, and they gonna take it from you."

That's exactly how the ride played out.

"Playboy rode me," joked Cash, when addressing just how difficult it was to make the whistle and how close he was to legitimately falling short. "If I was good, I would have won first on him. He was a first-place horse. . . . He rode me, but I held on. That was the thrill of my life."

In 1999 Myrtis Dightman Sr., the first African American to qualify for the NFR, wrote a letter (with the help of his son, Myrtis Jr.) to the Rodeo Cowboy Hall of Fame.

In that letter Dightman Sr. asserted that he was only able to influence Charlie Sampson, the first African American to win a PRCA world title, because Thomas had done the same for him when they met in 1956. Dightman Sr. referred to Thomas as a "dynamic cowboy" and said of his longtime friend, "He did not receive what he was entitled to while rodeoing."

Like Dightman Sr., Gordon also provided a letter. He wrote about Thomas's travels to educate young people about agriculture and rodeo and described him as "a magnificent driving force to persuade our young people to consider the sport, set goals, and be proud of their decisions."

In a handwritten letter, Harry Tompkins, who won eight PRCA world titles in a twelve-year span and, in 1979, was himself an inductee into the Rodeo Cowboy Hall of Fame, detailed how he had personally witnessed Thomas and other Black cowboys being treated unfairly and that Thomas "rode as well as 90 percent of the ones that rode." Referring to him as a gentleman around rodeo and a good citizen, Tompkins wrote, "I recommend Willie Thomas be honored with the best of them."

Unfortunately, he was never included among his peers inducted into the Rodeo Cowboy Hall of Fame. Thomas was inducted into the Texas Rodeo Hall of Fame (2004) and later the National Multicultural Western Heritage Hall of Fame in 2008. Cash followed two years later in the latter Hall. Thomas was posthumously inducted into the Bull Riders Hall of Fame in 2021.

Bobby Steiner stopped short of saying Thomas would have been a world champion had he "just hit the road hard," but he is certain of one thing: "Willie Thomas was an unbelievable bull rider. I'm not just talking about good. He was incredible."

6

Bailey's Prairie Kid (aka Taylor Hall Jr.)

Character, not circumstance, makes the man.

—BOOKER T. WASHINGTON

BAILEY'S PRAIRIE, TEXAS

Taylor Hall Jr. was sitting up in a saddle with his daddy, Taylor Sr., and sorting cattle before long before his earliest memories.

He was not even a year old when his mother, Irma, became pregnant with her fourth of ten children. She stayed home and looked after a pair of toddlers, while Taylor Sr. packed his firstborn son in the saddle with him, tucked a warm milk bottle in his chaps, and rode out into the pasture. They followed a dirt road—today it's Farm Market Road 521—for another five or six miles out to Stanger Ranch, where Taylor Sr. would tie his horse up under an old oak tree.

With his son's little legs sticking out to either side, he would push him in tight under the front of the saddle horn, so Taylor Jr. was facing the back of the horse. If he started to lean too far backward, the horse's neck was there to hold him upright.

His daddy's ol' horse took care of him from the time he was a baby until he was able to handle a horse of his own, as young as four or five.

"That old tree is there now," recalled Taylor Jr., who is still horseback and cattle ranching on the same land, "but it's kind of dead like."

"The whole time they working them cattle, cutting them cattle, you know, separating them cattle, they be keeping an eye on me too over there tied to that tree. That really is the truth. That happened to me."

In the almost ninety years since—Taylor Jr. was born February 15, 1932—that dirt road was covered and packed tight with crushed shells that left everything covered in white dust whenever the wind blew before eventually being paved.

But back when it was just a dangerous dirt road, Taylor Sr. used a couple of his mules to pull folks out who did not know enough not to drive down that road when it rained.

"Like a wrecker that runs down the highway and picks people's cars up, he was like that way. That's what my daddy would [do] when it rains," said Taylor Jr., "for something like four, five dollars [for a day's work]. That was pretty good money back in them days."

Taylor Jr. has been riding horseback and working ranches in that part of Texas ever since.

He appreciates the life he's had along with the lessons and skills passed on by his namesake, but perhaps more important to him is the respect he's been given as an authentic working cowboy.

"I appreciate it right to this day," Taylor Jr. said. "I really do. Back in that time, they gave me a lot of respect and I appreciate it. Sure do."

In addition to two older sisters, Taylor Jr. has two younger sisters and five younger brothers. They were raised on the coastal prairie in the "little bitty community" of Bailey's Prairie, Texas, which was established in 1818, incorporated in 1967, and has yet to reach a population of a thousand people.

Their mama raised the children—Leana, Annie Mae, Taylor Jr., Caesar, John, Herman, Sherman, Mike, Phoebe, and Mary—while their daddy was a ranch hand who mostly worked at the Stanger Ranch. Mr. Russell—Taylor Jr. said he never knew the man's first name—tasked Taylor Sr. with breaking wild horses and training them to become ranch horses.

Once Taylor Jr. could walk and talk, old Mr. Russell would drive past the oak tree and put the toddler in the front seat of the truck with him and drive into town. Matter of fact, there was always someone to look after him until he was old enough to ride a horse on his own. Taylor Jr. was only four when his daddy helped him saddle up a horse and he rode along on his first cattle drive.

"My daddy, he—well, let me get it together now—when I growed up a little bit, he sent me to work for the Munson's," said Taylor Jr. "That's another ranch. I was about ten years old when I went there."

He admits he did not get much of an education because he had to help feed a family of twelve.

"After I went to work for them, I didn't get much schooling, but I didn't give up. Whatever I had in mind to do, I didn't give up on. I done that. Yeah. Working around them ranches, whatever they asked me to do—I done that."

He would chase behind a mule baling as many as seventy to eighty bales of hay each day. He also used the same mule to haul Black schoolchildren in a covered wagon to a one-room, segregated schoolhouse in nearby Snipe.

Growing up the way he did—he worked for the Munson family until he was in his early eighties—a work ethic was second nature. He didn't learn or develop it as he got older; it came naturally to him. Taylor Jr. did not know any different.

He is still like that today.

At eighty-eight, he went on a three-day cattle drive between Victoria and Corpus Christi, Texas, and then went right to work on another ranch outside Bay City. There are not many working cowboys still alive today who came of age in the 1930s like Taylor Jr. did.

"I'm still riding a horse and doing like I always do," Taylor Jr. said. "I might not be quite as fast, but I saddle a horse and do all I ever done."

He added, "I growed up thataway."

As a teenager, Taylor Jr. branded himself Bailey's Prairie Kid, and his friends and fellow cowboys began calling him Bailey as well. "There was a lot of cowboys that rodeoed right along with me that didn't even know my real name. All they knowed was Bailey."

He created an unforgettable image.

He's known for wearing a white, long-sleeve, button-down shirt with a necktie embroidered with the initials B.P.K. To this day, he keeps a freshly pressed shirt hanging in his truck along with two or three extra ties. Yet, unlike other cowboys, he would shove his cowboy hat in his rigging bag, which was a potato sack he tied off at the top with twine.

However, he might be best remembered for the cigar he puffed on while competing.

"Every time he would spur his feet into the front end of the horse," said Bill Putnam, a professional bull rider who later founded The Bull Riding Hall of Fame, "he would blow a puff of smoke."

Putnam added, "That paints a picture that is pretty colorful and unique. That's something you don't see in rodeo anymore."

Bailey was not only stylish on the backside of an animal, he loved colorful cars, especially his light-blue 1939 Chevy pickup with red trim and a matching horse trailer. He bought the truck a few miles south of Amarillo in Wayside, Texas. It had knee-action springs that made for a rough ride bouncing up and down with the slightest bump in the road, but Bailey drove it for years—make that decades.

"He was quite a celebrity," Putnam said.

Bailey was the sharpest-dressed cowboy at his very first event in Bay City, where he competed alongside adults. At fifteen, he had no experience, no driver's license, and when his daddy found out he had "slipped off" on his own to Bay City, "it really surprised him. . . . He didn't care as long as I worked cows."

He was a teenager when he fostered a newfound passion for rodeo, "but had to get the work done" first. He found his way to T Diamond Ranch in West Columbia, Texas, as well as Clute, Pasadena, Rosenberg, Baytown, Giddings, Victoria, Fort Worth, and Dallas.

But the weekly events at the Diamond L Ranch Saloon on South Main on the southside of Houston from the late forties through the sixties and seventies were legendary. Those were especially great rodeos on Sunday afternoons, filled with rodeo lore—loud music, lots of beer and barbecue, shooting dice, and more loud music. And inevitably someone would shoot off their guns as if they were fireworks on the Fourth of July.

"It got pretty wild and pretty Western," Putnam said. "It was not unheard of for there to be some gunplay or some knife play and it got pretty rough, but it was . . . good times and top bucking stock and top cowboys to go with it."

Prior to going to prison for murdering his daddy, allegedly by hitting him in the head with an axe, O'Neal Browning was the best saddle bronc rider at the Diamond L. By the time Browning got paroled, Bailey was the best there, and Browning "wanted to match up with me real bad."

One Sunday afternoon, Jerome Sweeney, owner of the Diamond L, made it happen when he bet another man $150 there was no way Browning would beat Bailey.

Browning, who had been featured in *Ebony* for a profile of prison rodeo, barely cleared the bucking chute when his horse threw him straight over its head. On the inside of prison walls, Browning had won the top hand buckle seven times in the 1950s and '60s, but on the outside—at least, on this particular day—the top hand was Bailey's Prairie Kid.

"When they opened the gate, Bailey was scratchy," said Bubba Goudeau, a rough stock rider who was as much a working cowboy as he was a rodeo cowboy. "I mean you talk about a bronc ride. He was puffing on that cigar every jump. He let O'Neal Browning know he was the bronc-riding king now."

They blared Johnnie Taylor's biggest hit "Who's Making Love (to Your Old Lady)" so often it became an unofficial theme song. Ironic, considering Browning killed his daddy after finding out he had slept with his girlfriend.

Browning, who lost the thumb on his riding hand when it was snapped off after being caught in a loop as he dallied a rope around his saddle horn, was not long for the free world. Shortly before being sent back to prison, he told Harold Cash, "It's hell out here in the free world."

"I never did heard from him after that," Bailey said.

Putnam called the Diamond L events, which were predominantly Black rodeos, "a storied association," but among the white cowboys there was Goudeau, a self-described hobo who competed anywhere and with anyone—regardless of ethnicity. Quite frankly, despite not being Black, Goudeau loved the Diamond L and competing with Myrtis Dightman, Willie Thomas, Freddie Gordon, and Bailey's Prairie Kid.

Bailey and Goudeau developed quite a friendship.

Goudeau would drive all night to get there and then look for Bailey's station wagon—neither of them can seem to remember the make or model—which was easily recognizable because of the air conditioning unit hanging out the back window. It was an oversized house unit that Bailey swiped from an old, broken-down Chrysler he found. He had it "wired up and taped up some kind of way."

"I never had no problem with it," Bailey recalled. "I remember that just as plain as daylight."

Goudeau has a different memory he likes to recount.

"Bailey's Prairie Kid used to bring me barbecue armadillo every Sunday for years and years," recalled Goudeau, who laughs at the memory of Bailey keeping his cowboy hat inside of his rigging bag and pulling it out with his other gear. "Had that armadillo wrapped up in tinfoil and I never eaten anything better."

Early each week, Bailey used to go out behind his house "and plug me some armadillos" with a .22 and then "bring 'em back to the house, clean 'em and wash 'em down real good, put 'em in the icebox and cool 'em down and get ready to put 'em on the pit."

He'd wrap balls of armadillo meat in tinfoil and then fold it all up in a tablecloth or an old sugar sack to keep it "milky warm" until it was time to eat.

After starting his career locally, Bailey began competing in the Southwestern National Cowboys Association.

Sweeney, owner of the Diamond L, knew Bailey would do well at pro rodeos, so he bought his RCA permit and paid Bailey's entry fees. His first RCA event was in Duncan, Oklahoma. Sweeney, a former bull rider who had both legs amputated above the knees, bought Bailey a plane ticket, but when Bailey refused to fly—"that's just how green I was"—Sweeney arranged for Freddie Gordon's older half-brother to haul him up to Oklahoma.

Bailey won the bull-riding event, or as he recalled, "Yeah, I tore 'em to pieces."

That bull jumped from the chute and kicked so high he buried his nose in the dirt. Afterward, even the judges marveled at how the bull didn't tip over. Following three days of competition, Bailey split his winnings with Sweeney.

"The people who was promoting the rodeo, they cut his money out and mailed it to him and then paid me the rest right there," said Bailey, who felt it was fair to pay Sweeney 30 percent of whatever he won at RCA events he would not have otherwise entered.

He rode at RCA events in Chicago, Philadelphia, and both Boston Garden and Madison Square Garden in New York. He drove with other Black cowboys to those events and it was not until 1971 that he boarded a plane from Houston to New York for the first all-Black rodeo in Harlem. When they arrived at the baggage claim area, he watched as the others had to look at all the tags because so much of the luggage looked the same. Everything Bailey brought along was still tied off in that old sack of his.

"Let me put it together now," he said, trying not to confuse the pro rodeo at the Garden with the all-Black event at Downing Stadium on Randall's Island in the middle of the Harlem River. "It's been so long, you know, I can't think like I used to."

A moment later, he said, "Cassius Clay was there. You know him? The famous boxer."

By then, Clay had already assumed the name Muhammad Ali and was paid $5,000 to lead a parade on horseback from the Apollo Theater to the stadium, which was three miles away. Ali became enamored with the Black cowboys and stayed well beyond the time he had agreed to. At one point, he even climbed in the bucking chute and sat on a tamed, aging brahma bull.

"'Don't let that sucka hurt me,'" said Bailey, laughing at the memory of Ali in the bucking chute. "I never will forget that—'don't let that sucka hurt me'—he say that."

Looking back at it now, Bailey's own greatest success came from winning six titles in the SNCA starting in 1966 when he claimed the saddle bronc title. Two years later, he won the bareback title and then back-to-back steer-wrestling titles in 1972 and '73. In '75 he won a bull-riding title and then proved just how handy he was when he won the all-around title in 1978.

To a lesser extent, Bailey's brother Mike—known to many as The Sundown Kid—also competed, and years later, like his father, Taylor Hall III competed under the moniker Cold Duck Kid.

Bailey was inducted into the Texas Rodeo Cowboy Hall of Fame in 2001 and, in 2019, was inducted into the National Multicultural Western Heritage Hall of Fame along with James Pickens Jr. and Lu Vason, founder of the Bill Pickett Invitational Rodeo. Although those honors didn't come until much later in his life, and he recognizes the impact of racism throughout his career, Bailey felt that he had long since earned the respect of fellow rodeo cowboys regardless of their ethnicity.

"We done what we done," he said, "and what we done, we still got along."

Even when he and other Black cowboys had to wait to compete until after the spectators had left the stands following the event, Bailey said, he and his white counterparts, "still didn't let that separate us. We still got together and socialized."

He was then, and to this day, remains a consummate gentleman.

He addresses everyone as sir and ma'am—"That's just how I was raised"— and is quick to point out, "Like I say, I didn't leave too many enemies on the road. If I couldn't make friends with them, I kept a-walking."

7

Myrtis "Jackie Robinson of Rodeo" Dightman Sr.

Some people would view Jackie Robinson as a very safe African American, a docile figure who had a tendency to try to get along with everyone, and when you look at history, you learn that he has this fire that allows him to take this punishment but also figure out savvy ways of giving it back.

—CHADWICK BOSEMAN

CROCKETT AND HOUSTON, TEXAS

Seven times Myrtis Dightman Sr. qualified for the NFR. He was the first African American to compete as an alternate at the season-ending event (1964) and the first to qualify (1966). He traveled with legends and icons in the sport of rodeo while influencing and mentoring others on their way to greatness—none more so than Charlie Sampson, the first African American to win a world title in the PRCA.

Whether he fully understands his legacy or not, Dightman appreciates the attention and the nickname he earned: the "Jackie Robinson of Rodeo."

Nearly fifty years after retiring from riding on the backside of a bucking bull, his story would not be any more impactful had he won the elusive gold buckle of a world champion. Like Robinson, it's what Dightman has meant off the dirt and away from the rodeo arena that makes him more than a pioneer in his sport.

Faith has been deeply woven into the fabric of the cowboy culture for as long as Americans—white, Black, Hispanic, or otherwise—have headed west to raise cattle, rope calves, or, in Dightman's case, ride bulls.

Faith always has been at the center of Dightman's life.

Looking back, that's why he's at peace.

"I had a goal I was trying to reach," he said, "and I wanted to see, could I do it? I reached the goal. I never were the world champion, but I been a world champion as a man."

Myrtis Dightman Sr. was born on May 7, 1935, on a four-thousand-acre ranch located three miles outside of Crockctt, Texas. His father, O. D. Dightman, was a ranch hand for Karl Leediker, while his mother, Ada Lee, worked picking cotton. Myrtis and his four siblings were raised in a house that did not have electricity but was filled with faith and a family that looked out for each other.

O.D. had his son riding solo on the back of a horse by the time he was two. At ten, he was helping his father with ranch work. The stronger Myrtis got, the more he could help his old man, which meant he only attended school when it was convenient. Myrtis finally dropped out in eighth grade. Or in his case, he simply stopped going.

Though he fondly recalls memories of the Leediker family and is grateful for the opportunity they provided his mother and father, at seventeen, Myrtis moved two hours south to Houston.

It was 1952, and he was in search of something more than being beholden to work for a white landowner. He found a series of odd jobs and earned his own way. At the same time, he was a cowboy in a city and was looking for other cowboys to befriend when he met James Francis Jr.

Together they would attend rodeos. If the event was not sanctioned by the Southwestern National Cowboys Association, which was similar to baseball's Negro Leagues, they were hard-pressed to find Black cowboys competing.

In '56 Dightman and Francis talked about the fact that there were no Black cowboys taking part in the historic trail rides that kick off the annual Houston Livestock Show and Rodeo. Prior to the 1957 trail ride, Dightman and Francis partnered with Prairie View A&M University—a historically Black college—and founded the Prairie View Trail Riders Association.

It was the first Black association of its kind in Texas and, likely, the first in the country.

That year, they became the first Black trail riders allowed to chart an eighty-seven-mile trail that now draws as many as a hundred and fifty participants on horseback and in wagons.

The rest of the year, Dightman began fighting bulls on the weekends. He worked every kind of rodeo—amateur and semipro events and, eventually, professional rodeos.

Almost immediately, it was apparent that Dightman was athletic and catty and, perhaps, more importantly, he proved to bull riders—both Black and white—that he was fearless when it came to protecting them.

He developed a well-earned reputation as a modest cowboy who kept to himself, even when he decided to transition to bull riding. It was unconventional for a twenty-five-year-old with no experience to start riding bulls, much less with the goal of doing so at the highest level of competition.

Bull riders and rodeo producers were generally accepting of him, but that was not always the case with stock contractors and judges. Less concerned about whether or not he was scored fairly, his family and closest friends were rightfully worried about a Black man traveling alone at the onset of the 1960s—especially Dightman, who could not read or write much beyond signing his own name. That meant he could not even consult the annual Negro Motorist Green Book.

His then wife, Fannie Mae, said she had tried teaching him how to read, but he struggled with kindergarten-level books. In those first years, he was oftentimes sleeping in the backseat of his Chevy Impala.

Despite the challenges, Dightman was driven by something his mother had said to him years earlier: "Other people can never give you happiness. It comes from within. God gave it to you, and nobody can take it away unless you let them," according to a *Sports Illustrated* article.

After a year of learning the craft from Willie Thomas, Bailey's Prairie Kid, and Freddie Gordon, Dightman joined the RCA in time for the 1961 season. Francis paid his $50 membership fee.

Strong and humble is how Dightman is remembered, even in those early days. In the rare instances when a bull managed to get the fundamentally solid Dightman out of position, he could hang out away from his riding hand a lot further than most other bull riders. He might not have earned all the points he deserved, but he was determined to make the eight-second whistle more often than anyone else.

Don Gay, who grew up watching Dightman and other Black riders come to his father's weekly rodeo in Mesquite, and later won eight PRCA world titles, described Dightman as being tougher than boot leather.

When it came to strength, Bobby Steiner, who won a world title in 1973, pondered, "I don't know if you know any people who can do one-arm pull-ups, but it ain't very many."

Dightman could.

And he took great pleasure in proving he could.

That was him. He loved a challenge.

In 1964 he committed to competing full time, but at season's end, he was seventeenth in the world standings. He would have missed the NFR by two spots had it not been for late-season injuries to Carl Nafzgar and Bernie Johnson. He added less than $250 to his season total, and with a wife and now five kids at home, it's a good thing he made some guaranteed money as a rodeo clown. When he was not fighting bulls, he would even offer to help wrangle steers and bucking bulls in the back pens for extra money.

He had also been driving a truck part-time since '61, and in 1965 he took the year off from rodeo and went full time as a diesel driver.

Ultimately, as Dightman told the Associated Press, he was focused on becoming "the best bull rider in the world, instead of being just the best Black bull rider." The sabbatical lasted only one year before he returned to competition in time for the 1966 season.

His love of rodeo cost him his marriage.

That year, he became the first Black cowboy to compete in the Houston Astrodome. He won the opening round, and as legend has it, the lights went out while he was riding in one of the later rounds, leading to a cartoon in the following issue of the *Rodeo Sports News* with a caption that read: "Hang in there Myrtis, we'll get those lights back on!"

Shitty scores and blown circuit breakers could not stop him. In July he managed a top five finish at the Cheyenne Frontier Days Rodeo in Wyoming and became the first Black cowboy to ever be ranked No. 1 in the world and, ultimately, the first to *qualify* for a trip to the NFR. He finished the season eighth in the world.

The next year was a tumultuous one for America—with racial divide and opposition to the Vietnam War tearing the country apart—but for much of the 1967 season, it was a three-way dogfight between Bill Stanton, Dightman, and Larry Mahan, a young twenty-three-year-old hippie from Oregon.

Stanton and Mahan had their own planes, while Dightman drove himself to eighty rodeos as far west as California and as far north as Chicago. In June 1967, Pulitzer Prize–winning sports columnist Red Smith famously compared and mostly contrasted the careers of "independent athletes" Myrtis Dightman and PGA golfer Jack Nicklaus, who won a record eighteen Majors.

Though he was seriously contending for a world title or, perhaps, because he was a serious contender, Dightman was unable to escape the racial divide. At a rodeo in Little Rock, Dightman was kept from entering the Civic Center, which did not allow Negros, until Woodie Cone rode up to the top of a loading ramp and positioned his horse between Dightman and a security guard. He motioned for Dightman to enter. When the guard resisted, Cone told him he would whip his ass across the parking lot if he tried to prevent Dightman from getting on his bull.

When the trio finally arrived in Oklahoma City for the NFR along with twelve other top fifteen bull riders, the pressure was on Stanton not to lose the title, much less give it up to a Black cowboy.

Stanton ultimately won.

Mahan was second, and Dightman, who won the final round of the event, finished a career-best third in the world standings. Dightman was disappointed and frustrated about not winning the title. When he asked Freckles Brown what more he needed to do, the hall-of-fame bull rider is said to have told him to keep riding like he has been "and then turn white."

The next year, Dightman traveled with Bobby Berger, who, like Stanton and Mahan, piloted his own plane. They also would room together at a time when a lot of other white cowboys would never think of sharing a room with a Black cowboy, especially not in a year that saw Martin Luther King Jr. assassinated in April and then presidential candidate Bobby Kennedy gunned down in June.

Even Mahan took a liking to Dightman. Aside from his competitive nature, Mahan liked Dightman's positive disposition, and he would oftentimes offer Dightman one of the three extra seats in his four-seat Piper 250 Comanche.

Mahan and Dightman were in Dallas with Clyde Vamvoras, who would go on to win his second consecutive bareback title later that year, with plans to compete in San Diego. Mahan was going to need to make one stop, so he made plans to refuel in Wick, Texas, near the southeast corner of New Mexico.

As they approached Wick, Mahan lowered the landing gear, but the indicator light failed to come on. He did a flyby to have whoever was in the control tower take a visual to see if his landing gear was down in the locked position. It was down, *but* they could not tell with any certainty whether it was in the locked position or not. Mahan flew fifty miles back in the direction they came from to Odessa, with the gear down and possibly wallowing in the wind.

After a couple of flybys, the air traffic controller looked through his binoculars and determined it was safe to land. Mahan circled the airport a few more times while fire trucks were moved into position.

Dightman was up front, sitting white-knuckled in the copilot seat.

Vamvoras was in the back sleeping, so Mahan hollered for him to wake up and get his boots on. "We might have a little problem here," said Mahan. Unlike Dightman, Vamvoras was unfazed. He slipped his boots on and caught several more minutes of shuteye, while Mahan prepared to land.

Then came the okay from the tower.

Dightman had yet to say a word, much less let go of his seat, when he anxiously asked, "Are they sure they don't want us to fly by one more time."

Everything worked out just fine when they landed. It had been a wiring problem. Maintenance had it fixed in thirty minutes. Back in the air, Dightman did not feel any better when Mahan assured him, "You can belly those suckers in, and chances are 99 percent of the time you can walk away from it."

Mahan still laughs.

Dightman, well into his eighties now, still shakes his head at Mahan's casual demeanor when it comes to the possibility of crash-landing. Then again, the first time Dightman ever flew with Mahan, he did so unsure of what to expect. At one point, as they flew over West Texas into New Mexico, he saw a pack of wild dogs and thought to himself, "They could push me out and my mama and family would never see me again."

Dightman finally laughs.

Mahan winks.

While the eight-time PRCA world champion was unbothered by Dightman's ethnicity, Dightman knew to avoid the South—namely Louisiana, Alabama, and Mississippi. Mahan, on the other hand, could not understand why Dightman refused to fly with him to Jackson, Mississippi.

"Jackson was awful. Mississippi was awful. There's the world, there's the South, and there's Mississippi," explained Ryan Jones, a historian at the National Civil Rights Museum at the Lorraine Motel in Memphis. Jones echoes William Faulkner, who once said, "To understand the world, you must first understand a place like Mississippi."

As bad as it would have been for Dightman, it would have been worse for Mahan.

"I don't know if [Mahan] realized what he [would have been] sacrificing," said Beverly Robertson, former director of the National Civil Rights Museum, "subject to sacrificing his own life."

In any case, travel was made easier by flying—Dightman was able to compete in more than one hundred rodeos that year—but he still finished fourth and never seriously contended for a world title in his final three seasons.

It has often been reported that Dightman won the Calgary Stampede in 1971, when in fact, a year earlier, in 1970, he received the Guy Weadick Award given to the Stampede competitor who best embodies what the cowboy stands for. That year, he finished thirteenth with merely $12,134 won at the end of the season.

In '71 he won the Cheyenne (Wyoming) Frontier Days Rodeo, but he missed the NFR for the first time since 1966.

That year, he appeared as himself in the film *J. W. Coop.*

Cliff Robertson, who wrote and directed the film, personally cast Dightman after meeting him at a rodeo in Oklahoma. He was so smitten by Dightman that he wrote the part into the script. Dightman, who was never one to pay attention to movies or television, had no idea who Robertson was even though he had won the Academy Award for Best Actor in 1968.

By 1972 Dightman's focus on bull riding had waned. He had other interests. Once again, he was paid to ride bulls in the Sam Peckinpah–directed *Junior Bonner*, which starred Steve McQueen and rodeo legend Casey Tibbs. He still flew to a few rodeos, drove to some, and hitched rides to others and then retired—save for a handful of Old Timers Rodeo Association events, from 1984 to 1988, which is when the Jackie Robinson moniker took hold.

For Dightman, the name means a hell of a lot more than being the first, as is typically the case when anyone is tagged with being "the Jackie Robinson of . . ."

Though they never met, and Robinson likely never even knew who Dightman was, their connection goes beyond their athletic abilities. It is about strength of character, about being the right man at the right time.

"Where talent meets tenacity is the unique quality that people like Myrtis and Jackie share," said Dr. Yohuru Williams, dean of the College of Arts and Sciences and founding director of the Racial Justice Initiative at the University of St. Thomas. "And then also this sense of . . . personal identity that allows them to transcend the great racial animus that clearly they were going to face in the process."

Only in recent years has Dightman received the recognition he has deserved for decades.

He's been inducted into every imaginable hall of fame open to cowboys and rodeo athletes, beginning with the Rodeo Hall of Fame in Oklahoma City, yet he is admittedly annoyed that it took until 2016 for the PRCA to enshrine him into the Pro Rodeo Hall of Fame in Colorado Springs.

His ex-wife, Fannie Mae, has always been proud of his accomplishments, but she's thankful he lived long enough to finally experience the recognition he deserved all those years ago, even though back then, "it wasn't worth it" to her in terms of the sacrifices they made as a family. Myrtis Jr., the oldest of their five children, spent part of his childhood living with his grandmother, Ada Lee, and would see his father on occasion when he was not at a rodeo. His siblings saw little of their father, though Fannie Mae described Myrtis Sr. as a great provider.

"There was not a time he didn't see to it that me and the children were taken care of," she said. "He's a good man and I want to see well for him."

Ultimately, Dightman overcame the temper of the times.

He is generally reserved with his thoughts and oftentimes needs to be pushed and prodded when it comes to sharing the wisdom of his life experiences. Even then, while sitting at the dining-room table in his girlfriend's Houston home, Dightman deflects the attention. "The Lord got me like this. The Lord been taking care of me. I tell everybody, put God first and everything will work out. I know the places I been and the things I done; it had to be the Lord."

Freddie "Skeet" Gordon

The most important thing to me is the friends that I made.
—BILL RUSSELL

SUGAR LAND AND RICHMOND, TEXAS

Freddie "Skeet" Gordon was never made to feel as unwelcomed as he was the one and only time he went to a pro rodeo in Liberty, Texas.

After making the seventy-mile drive from Richmond, he parked his car, grabbed his rigging bag from the trunk and walked to the main gates. He was checking in when a local police officer approached and informed him that he could not enter unless he bought a ticket to sit in the grandstands.

Gordon pulled a day sheet from the program and pointed to his name among all the contestants listed. The officer shrugged his shoulders and shook his head no.

Gordon was not the only Black cowboy entered. There were five or six that day, but he was the only one at the gate. And he was made to feel as though he was less than human.

"They didn't let me go in," remembered Gordon, until one of his white counterparts—in the more than seventy years since, he's forgotten who it was—spoke up on his behalf. "Some cowboy—coming in or coming out—told them who I was, and they let me on in."

He added, "A man is not supposed to go through all that."

It's a damn good thing it was an RCA event and that he had entered under his real surname of Gordon or he would have most certainly been turned away had he entered under his alias—Freddie Richardson.

From the time the RCA was founded in 1936 until the labor laws were challenged in the 1980s, they prohibited RCA card holders from entering non-RCA events. However, by the 1950s, it "got to where, if it was 'all-Black,' you could enter," according to Gordon. Otherwise, any contestant—regardless of ethnicity—who entered a non-RCA event would be prohibited from competing at future RCA events for as long as a year, and those who were found to have violated the rule multiple times could be banned for life.

Gordon would enter RCA events and Black rodeos under his given name—Gordon—but was known to use Freddie Richardson—the same last name of his half-brother and mentor Sherman Richardson—whenever he entered mixed rodeos with white and Black contestants that were not sanctioned by the RCA.

At the time, Liberty was one of the smaller and lesser-paying RCA events.

Once inside, he and the other Black contestants had to wait by themselves behind the chutes until after the event was over with. They rode after the spectators had gone home, and coincidentally, none of them drew a bull or bronc worthy of an event-winning score.

"That was a bad feeling right there," said Gordon of the bitter taste it left, never mind the fact it was not even one of the better-paying rodeos for his white counterparts.

"We never did go down there anymore. That was one of the baddest ones. I had some more like that, but that was the baddest one right there."

Freddie Gordon was born October 13, 1935.

Though he and his older siblings shared the same mama—Freddie had a different daddy from them—and was raised in a home along the southwest corner of Houston in Sugar Land. Unlike a lot of other ranch kids, Gordon attended school regularly but was not happy about having to walk about a mile to and from school every day.

When he was not in school, he spent a lot of time with his older brother, Sherman Richardson, working on a ranch in nearby Richmond. From branding cows and feeding cattle to mending fences, Gordon "done it all" at a young age.

"Whatever they do on the ranch, we done it," Gordon said. "If you love something, it's easy for you. It was a good living. It was pretty nice, and I wish I had me a ranch now."

It was there that Sherman sparked his younger brother's interest in rodeo.

"If it wasn't for him, I wouldn't have gotten into this rodeo business," said Gordon, who learned how ride rough stock from Sherman.

Sherman had been competing since 1946 or '47. He won the first all-around buckle ever handed out by the Southwestern National Cowboys Association. Though the RCA (and later the PRCA) never barred Blacks from competing, Jim Crow–era laws often prohibited Blacks and whites from competing in the same rodeos.

The Southwestern National Cowboys Association was a minor league of sorts for the RCA and featured the best of Black rodeos along the Gulf Coast of Texas.

Despite various newspaper accounts stating otherwise, the association was never known as the Southwestern Negro Cowboys Association in the 1940s or the 1950s.

Gordon has no recollection of "Negro" ever being used. Neither does Bailey's Prairie Kid, Myrtis Dightman, or Tex Williams, whose father, Collie "Big Preacher" Williams, was a co-founder and the association's first president. Bobby Jackson, another of the association's past presidents and successful Black rodeo promoter, also confirmed with Harold Cash, who competed in the association during his own pro career, that some local white rodeo promoters and media members "replaced National with Negro" or even "Nigger" as a way of discrediting the competition as being less than its white counterparts.

In 1952 Gordon left school in the eleventh grade and moved from Sugar Land to Richmond with his brother. Gordon was seventeen when he started his rodeo career in the SNCA.

His first pro event was in Mercedes, Texas, where he won the bull riding.

Like Bailey's Prairie Kid, Gordon always wore a freshly pressed, white, long-sleeve, button-down shirt. In addition to being nicely dressed, Bubba Goudeau, a white counterpart from Louisiana, who saw Black cowboys as his equal when it was not always fashionable, said Gordon was "as good a guy as you would ever want to meet."

While everyone has heard of Willie Thomas, Bailey's Prairie Kid, Dightman, or Calvin Greely Jr.—all of whom were from the greater Houston area—Gordon and his good friend Clinton Wyche were often overlooked by those who weren't around to see them compete in the 1950s, '60s, and '70s or were not from within one hundred miles of Houston.

Gordon is every bit the working cowboy and rodeo cowboy as any one of the others.

"Along the Gulf Coast, you have a much higher percentage of Black cowboys than out on the Panhandle [of Texas], where you would only have a handful," said B. Byron Price, who previously served as executive director of the National Cowboy and Western Heritage Museum in Oklahoma City.

Houston is "a good example of where that tradition runs deep," added Price.

Throughout his career, Gordon was an all-around cowboy who competed in all three rough stock events—bareback, saddle bronc, and bull riding—as well as steer wrestling. Entry fees were only $5 per event. "Back then, you didn't win a lot of money [from one event]," reasoned Gordon on competing in multiple events, "so if you in three or four events, you might do pretty good."

He was better than good.

In 1956 and again in 1957, Gordon won the bull riding and all-around titles in the SNCA.

He had become an RCA cardholder in '55 and traveled to New York for RCA rodeos held in 1956, '57, '58, and '59 at the old Madison Square Garden. He was only twenty years old the first time he drove east along with Willie and James Thomas, Marvel Rogers, Jimmy Gibson, C. L. Mathews, Clarence Gonzales, and his brother Sherman. At the time, it was the biggest rodeo in the world and spanned twenty-two days at the world's most famous arena.

"I wanted to go to New York," said Gordon, who admitted that, in 1956, he was scared and overwhelmed by the considerable amount of people on the streets of Manhattan. "I didn't want to stay in these local rodeos. I wanted to get better, so I could go to different places and make a little more money, too. You could always pick up some money there."

As a boy in Texas growing up without a television, Gordon had never even dreamed of competing in places like California—Salinas and Redlands—or

New York, much less twice winning the wild-horse race at Madison Square Garden in 1957 and again in '58.

Both years, Gordon was teamed with Gonzales and a white cowboy named Bill Monroe. It was one of the few rodeos where Black cowboys felt like the spectators treated them better than their white counterparts. Fans, especially young kids, had never seen Black cowboys on television.

On several occasions, he was asked where he kept his six-shooters.

"I would tell 'em, 'Not all cowboys have pistols,'" said Gordon, who chuckled at the memory. "They didn't know. They had only seen the white cowboys on TV. They had a few Black ones back in the day, but they had never seen a Black cowboy in person."

Beginning in 1958, Gordon was a regular in Mesquite, Texas.

In May of that year, Pro Rodeo Hall of Famer Neal Gay partnered with several others to produce the Mesquite Championship Rodeo—a weekly rodeo on Saturday nights that continues today.

Gay's son, Donnie, who went on to win eight PRCA world titles in bull riding, was five at the time and would often spend the evening hanging around Gordon and the other Black cowboys who had driven up from Houston.

"He was comfortable to be around," said Donnie, who still remembers Gordon always looking whoever he was speaking to directly in the eyes. "I was disappointed when he didn't enter [my daddy's] rodeo on Saturday night."

When Gordon was there, which was damn near every weekend, he would win the bull riding just about any time he made the whistle. Whenever Gordon or the others were unfamiliar with a bull in the draw, they would ask Donnie, who would know all the patterns and tendencies of his daddy's bulls.

Neal Gay and Jim Shoulders, known as the Babe Ruth of Rodeo, had some of the toughest bucking stock in all of rodeo. Gordon was one of the few bull riders—white or Black—according to Donnie, who was never intimidated by whatever bull he drew that night.

"He'd get one away from his hand and just spur one down," Donnie recalled. "He was kind of a strength guy. . . . He woulda done just as well as Myrtis had he gone full time."

Dightman was the first Black cowboy to compete in the NFR in 1964.

Gordon and Wyche would often ride together to Mesquite and show up Sunday afternoons for the weekly rodeo at the Diamond L Ranch Saloon.

Wyche, who generally preferred to stay close to home, was just as good as the others. In fact, he won the SNCA bull-riding titles in 1966 and '68.

"Everybody knew he was the best," said Larry Callies, a rodeo cowboy from El Campo, Texas, who, in recent years, founded the Black Cowboys Museum in Rosenberg, Texas. "Clinton didn't talk. He didn't brag and he didn't have to."

Gordon followed Wyche by winning his third bull-riding title in 1972—a year after he competed at the American Black Cowboys Association's first all-Black rodeo in Harlem—and a fourth and final title in 1974 before retiring from rodeo in 1979.

An image of Gordon competing in Harlem was forever captured in a dramatic photo of him on the movie poster for the documentary film *Black Rodeo*, a cult classic featuring Muhammad Ali and Woody Strode filmed at the seminal all-Black rodeo held September 4, 1971. An image of Gordon riding bareback with his left free arm held up high and both legs kicked out to either side was superimposed above the New York skyline and made to look as though Gordon was jumping over the Empire State Building.

Gordon, who placed second in bareback and won the bull riding in Harlem that year, saw the film at a premiere that took place at a drive-in theater in Houston in May 1972. He had no idea he was going to appear, much less be prominently featured on the movie poster, and likewise was equally surprised, years later, when he saw the DVD packaging.

Still, he didn't watch the film again until decades later.

After retiring, Gordon focused on his family and a twenty-plus-year trucking career with the Kroger grocery chain. He has four children from his first marriage, and he married his current wife, Martha Jackson, in 2001.

His career went largely unrecognized until he was inducted into the Black Go Texan Gala at the Houston Livestock and Rodeo (1995), National Multicultural Western Heritage Hall of Fame (2011), and the South Central Texas Rodeo Ring of Honor (2019), along with Wyche, Thomas, and Bailey's Prairie Kid.

As celebrated as he's become in recent years, Gordon remains as unassuming as he was a half-century earlier.

Ernest "Bud" Bramwell Jr.

Each and every one of you has the power, the will, and the capacity to make a difference in the world in which you live in.

—HARRY BELAFONTE

Heather Atlas Crow admits she doesn't know much about rodeo.

She knew her father, Ernest "Bud" Bramwell Jr., was a well-liked man, who left the familiarity of his home state of Connecticut and moved to Oklahoma to pursue his passion and dream of becoming a rodeo cowboy. She knew he had been on the rodeo team at Oklahoma State University, that he had been the president of the American Black Cowboy Association, won some rodeos and a few titles and had a handful of buckles—but she knew little else.

"It's funny," she said. "Kids are probably a little self-absorbed in their relationship with their parents and don't really stop to ask, who are you? What have you accomplished in your life?"

So in 2012, at thirty-seven years old, Crow wanted to know more about a time in her dad's life "he never talked about." In celebration of his seventy-fifth birthday, she spent months collecting and printing out articles and speaking to "old-timers who were stretching their memories" of her father and his famous apple pies and steer-wrestling titles.

Even Bramwell had not talked about those days for the better part of thirty years.

"I didn't actually realize the extent of any of it," said Crow, who lives in California.

She put everything in a scrapbook and mailed it to her father. They were on the phone together when he opened it.

"He's not one to share, but I think it touches him to see some of the memories and the reminders of what he's done," she said, "and how far other people have come because of what he did back then."

This is the story she uncovered.

Ernest "Bud" Bramwell Jr. was born July 25, 1937, in Stamford, Connecticut.

His father was a contractor who owned apartment houses and had a business that provided interior painting and wallpapering services. The elder Bramwell enjoyed horseback riding, but for him, it was more of a hobby than a passion. He often would take his kids—one son and two daughters—along with him.

"That's how we started," said Bud, who was ten years old at the time. "We rode for six or eight months and then I was the only one that kept it up. From there, I was able to talk my parents into buying me a horse."

He was described as a horse-crazy kid, and even though it was not nearly as expensive as it is now to board a horse, the $50-a-month fee was a big sacrifice for Bramwell's parents. But they saw his commitment. It is a part of who he has always been—devoted, loyal, responsible and faithful. As a teenager, he entered into a contract with his father, pledging never to smoke, drink, use drugs, or curse. He never has, and now in his eighties, the agreement is framed and still hangs in his living room.

That's the type of kid he was and the man he's become.

In high school, Bramwell played football—he was a three-year starter on the varsity team at defensive end and tight end. He also ran track.

He had not yet graduated from Stamford High School when he met a guy who owned some roping calves. Bramwell would go out to his place an hour north, in Bethany, two or three nights a week and learn to rope calves.

He attended college for a year in Massachusetts and another year at Colorado State University before transferring to Oklahoma State University on a rodeo scholarship. The eighty-five-member team competed at college rodeos in Texas, New Mexico, Arizona, and Oklahoma as an Intercollegiate Rodeo Club.

That was 1957, and Bramwell earned a bachelor's degree in animal science and a master's in nutrition.

"I had come out two or three times on trips buying a horse or buying a horse trailer," Bramwell said of Oklahoma. "I had been a few times, so it wasn't a complete culture shock. It's a big difference. I saw more cowboys there. Everyone had a rope and so there were plenty of places to practice."

For a city kid from back east, Bramwell loved the heat, the dirt, and flat landscape.

In Oklahoma he met rodeo cowboys who had grown up competing and took it a lot more seriously than anyone else back at home.

He proved to be an all-around cowboy who developed expert-level horsemanship skills and was mighty handy with a rope. In those days, he would steer wrestle, calf rope, team rope, and even ride rough stock—bucking horses and bulls.

Bramwell entered a handful of college rodeos and would compete at a series of Black rodeos in places like Drumright, Boley, Seminole, and Okmulgee, Oklahoma, and then, in 1962, he met the minimum money earned to fill his permit with the RCA (which later became the PRCA), became a full member, and entered his first pro event in Fort Worth, Texas.

While taking a year off from OSU, Bramwell, who was one of only fifteen Black cowboys among the more than 4,500 professional cowboys in the RCA, was staying with Ralph Stone in Marlo, Oklahoma. He and Stone had a deal: Bramwell would work every other day on Stone's ranch and practice bulldogging on the off days. It didn't take long for Stone to realize the kid was pretty good, so he offered to pay the entry fee for Bramwell to compete in Fort Worth.

It was common for bulldoggers to ride someone else's horse and then pay the owner 25 percent of whatever they won. Stone reached out to Aubrey Rankin, who was hauling a horse around for C. R. Boucher to ride. Boucher had won the average at the NFR in 1961 and the world title in 1964. Stone described Bramwell as a real talented kid that was working for him.

When Bramwell arrived at the rodeo, he introduced himself to Rankin.

"Well, the guy went to stuttering and stammering," Bramwell recalled, "and said, 'Oh no,' I couldn't ride him because he didn't know I was Black when Ralph called him on the phone. I got there and he refused to let me ride the horse."

Bramwell didn't know anyone in Fort Worth.

He asked two or three people to no avail before he met a guy from Illinois, Howard Cox, who said Bramwell could use his horse. A few hours later, Bramwell won the steer wrestling.

"At that time, that was the largest day-money ever won at a pro rodeo and first Black [cowboy] who ever won a pro rodeo," said Bramwell, who placed in one round and won the average on two steers. He pocketed $3,500, which is like winning $29,980 in 2020, and didn't think anything of it.

Winning was not about making a racial statement so much as Bramwell simply wanted to win. But it was a monumental moment for Black rodeo cowboys.

He shared the same story with his daughter, who included the anecdote in the scrapbook she gave him. "My blood would boil," said Crow, who was taken by how unfazed and undaunted her father was by how he was treated. "Even though it was so long ago, I just got mad. . . . It's really a testament to who he is."

Today, Bramwell still laughs about what happened and offers, "That was the old days."

"The younger kids don't know, but some of the older guys remember when I won [Fort Worth]," Bramwell continued. "I was reading some articles on some football players and baseball players and some [kids today] don't even know who Jackie Robinson is. If some of those kids knew the struggle some of the [Black cowboys had] in the early days, they would look at it a little different, but they just think about the money now."

Being from the East Coast, Bramwell had never been to a segregated restaurant until he was out on the road with Calvin Greely Jr. and Myrtis Dightman, a couple of legendary Black cowboys from South Texas. They pulled up to a restaurant in a small Texas town they were just passing through and Bramwell was the first out of the car and was making his way to the front door when Greely and Dightman called out his name.

He turned back and Greely said, "*You* can't go in there."

It never occurred to Bramwell that he would have to go around back to get a sandwich simply because he was Black. That was the first and last trip in which Bramwell was going to subject himself to that kind of discrimination.

"I just always decided if I couldn't go somewhere to eat, I would pack enough lunch with me so I wouldn't have to go to a restaurant and eat around the back," said Bramwell, who traveled with a cooler from then on. He was not okay with it, but he was not about to give them his money either.

Then came a trip to Lake Charles, Louisiana, which was part of the Southeastern Circuit, which is where Willie Thomas had run into trouble a decade earlier. Bramwell was entered in the steer wrestling. He was sitting on the back of the chutes with the other cowboys—all of whom were white—when a local police officer approached and told him he could not sit with the white cowboys, especially within view of the spectators.

"Well, I'm entered in the deal," said Bramwell, thinking it was just a misunderstanding.

The officer replied, "This is Louisiana, and you can't sit there with these other guys."

Bramwell had heard stories about Black cowboys having to compete earlier in the day—during the slack—or afterward when the fans had long since gone home, but he was taken by surprise when he was told he could not even sit and watch the rodeo with his white counterparts.

Much of the Southeast was segregated; in Louisiana, Black athletes were not allowed to play on the same team as white athletes, and at least in Lake Charles, the authorities felt that was also true of rodeo events—even at the professional level. Not wanting to make a scene, Bramwell complied. When the producer of the rodeo, Tommy Steiner, heard about what had taken place, he was not happy.

"He said, 'Listen Bud, you're entered here, and you can compete whenever you want. If you want to run after the rodeo, we'll run you after the rodeo, but if you want to compete during the rodeo, you can compete during the rodeo,'" recalled Bramwell, who said knowing Steiner took up for him, "Made me feel pretty good."

Bramwell had been competing in three or four and sometimes five events at a single rodeo in order to make a decent living. The racial animosity he and other Black cowboys faced is what ultimately led Bramwell to choose timed events—bulldogging and calf roping—versus judged events, where Black cowboys were not always judged fairly.

"They cannot argue with the stopwatch," said Bramwell, who even recalled a judge from Florida not treating him fairly at a weekly pro rodeo in Cowtown, New Jersey. "They'd open the gates and they just mark you zero. They wouldn't even look at you, so I quit riding bareback."

In the late 1960s Bramwell used the skills he learned from his father and oversaw the construction of a rodeo arena in Langston, Oklahoma. A lot of the wood was milled from telephone poles that were donated, and more than thirty people helped with the construction. Afterward, Bramwell and Cleo Hearn, whom he met while they were at OSU together, helped to interest locals into forming their own Langston Round-Up Club that would later produce annual Black rodeos.

About that same time, Arthur Moore, a longshoreman from New Jersey, reached out to Bramwell and Hearn. He came to visit in August 1967 and was interested in Bramwell and Hearn rounding up enough Black cowboys to host an all-Black event in New York.

Ultimately, it was George Richardson—a controversial Newark councilman and recovering heroin addict, who co-founded the marketing firm Periscope and Associates with his wife, Ingrid Frank—who worked with Bramwell, Hearn, Marvel Rogers Sr., and Charles Evans to bridge the Black trailblazers with modern-day Black rodeo cowboys for what became the most important Black rodeo of all time. It took place September 4, 1971, in Harlem.

The four Oklahoma cowboys went on to form the American Black Cowboy Association. Bramwell won a coin flip between he and Hearn and became the association's first and only president.

"We came within a whisker of getting in Madison Square Garden," said Bramwell. Instead, a series of three events in 1971 concluded with the Harlem event at Downing Stadium on Randall's Island situated in the middle of the Harlem River.

Four days after the Harlem rodeo, Bramwell was quoted in the *Des Moines (IA) Register*, "It's important that Black people, kids especially, be aware that their people helped settle the West." That same story was syndicated nationwide and appeared in the *Arizona Republic* under the headline "Black Rodeo Excites Harlem Kids."

Earlier that year, Bramwell told the *Detroit Free Press*, "You talk about cowboys, and most Black children think about white people."

The American Black Cowboy Association, which used the all-Black rodeos they produced and promoted as a means of educating Black America, produced their first event in 1970 and a final event on July 20 and 21, 1973, at the Freehold (New Jersey) Raceway.

By then, Bramwell was living in Upstate New York and for the last decade of his career, he competed full time in the newly formed First Frontier Circuit—one of twelve regions in the PRCA. It was there that he experienced, perhaps, the greatest personal success of his rodeo career.

He dominated the competition by winning the steer-wrestling circuit championship in 1975, '76, and '77 and one more time in 1984. And Bramwell proved his all-around skills by winning the all-around circuit championship in '75, '77, and '78. In addition to his two First Frontier Circuit titles in 1977, he also was the all-around champion for the season at the weekly Cowtown Rodeo down in New Jersey.

Bramwell's father died in 1978.

During the final seasons of his career, he was competing at about thirty rodeos a year and transitioning to a new career by taking over the family business managing apartments and building homes. He was splitting his time between Upstate New York, where he met a doctor who hired him to build him a new home in Africa, and Norwalk, Connecticut, where the family's real estate business was based. He made three trips for two weeks at a time to the Republic of Ghana—"I liked it there"—before plans fell through to build more homes in the West African country located along the Gulf of Guinea and the Atlantic Ocean to the south.

These days, he's living in Stillwater, Oklahoma, with his longtime partner, Darlene Crowley, whom he met at a rodeo back east. She still runs barrels and Bramwell operates an aquatic treadmill for horses, a modern therapy that he "kind of stumbled into" when the mother-in-law of a cowboy he used to rodeo with bought a farm and discovered the machine in her garage.

Bramwell uses it to condition or rehab horses of all types—ranch, trail, or barrel racing—and said, "It's really been a blessing. I've had some good years" being hired to work horses back into shape. It's ironic that it took more than fifty years for Bramwell to put his animal science degree to use. He laughed, "Yep. You never know."

Prior to December 2019, when Bramwell was honored as the inaugural recipient of the Forgotten Trailblazers Award at the annual Legacy of the West Gala in Las Vegas, he had not been recognized by any of the rodeo or cowboy halls of fame.

Like most other Oklahoma cowboys, Bramwell has never gotten the recognition he deserves. He's okay with how it worked out—mostly because he knows the impact he has had, although he is too humble to brag about it.

"It's been a good life," concluded Bramwell, who smiled and laughed. He does that a lot.

10

Nelson Jackson Jr.

I cannot accept failure. Everyone fails at something, but I cannot accept not trying.
—MICHAEL JORDAN

BIXBY AND TULSA, OKLAHOMA

When Nelson Jackson was a teenager, he and his younger brother played baseball on Sunday afternoons with adults.

Their father, Nelson Sr., was the coach. It was the mid-1950s and he was harder on his boys than he was the rest of the team. He taught them how to do things the *right* way and, despite the age difference, expected them to play error-free ball.

One game was played against a mostly Native American team at a church field near Turkey Mountain. Nelson Jr. struck out. As he made the slow walk back to the bench, he was expecting to get an earful from his father. Only this time, Nelson Sr. didn't say a word. He didn't mention it on the drive home or the next day or the day after.

It was not until Wednesday evening that he asked his son, "How'd you do?"

"Not good," Nelson Jr. replied.

"How'd that guy struck you out?" he asked.

Nelson Jr. shrugged his shoulders as if to say, "I struck out."

"I'm going to tell you one more time how to hit the ball," said Nelson Sr., who then explained to his son that by swinging down at an angle, his bat had to be in perfect time with the ball's arrival. He wanted his son to swing his bat parallel to home plate and said, "Get that bat down here behind you and if you can catch a ball then you can hit it."

Until that moment, the younger Jackson never realized his father knew so much about baseball. All these years later, he still doesn't know when, where, or how the elder Jackson learned what he knew.

Nelson Jr. mostly played first base and shortstop, but he filled in wherever he was needed depending on who showed up—most of the players were married, with kids, and often had to miss because of family commitments. On rare occasions, Nelson Jr. even pitched a few innings.

"I didn't realize this until way later," said Nelson Jr., "but my dad was hard on us playing ball because that was the foundation that things gotta be done a certain way. It can't be what feels good or you're comfortable with. You gotta do what it takes."

Those were life lessons meant to be applied beyond the ballfield. Their father was teaching them that if something is worth doing, then it's worth doing right. Getting better was not simply about spending more time than everyone else practicing, it was about practicing *perfection*.

Doing it the right way was, "doing it an exact way. Not almost," explained Nelson Jr.

His father has long since passed away and Nelson Jr. has not played ball since he was a teen, but he has spent the past seven decades pursing perfection in rodeo and other endeavors.

Nelson Jackson Jr. was born December 11, 1940, and raised just outside of the southwest corner of Tulsa, Oklahoma, in the little farming community of Bixby.

His father's farm did not have running water or modern farm equipment until the younger Jackson was a teenager. As soon as he was big enough to work in the fields (before he was even ten), Nelson Sr. groomed his firstborn son to follow in his bootsteps as a horse-pulled plow chaser.

When Nelson Jr. was not tending to the fields and harvesting crops, he was in the barn milking dairy cows by hand, twice a day.

It was hard work and he loved it.

"That's all we knowed," he said.

As a teen, Jackson was built much like he is today: tall, lean, lanky, and deceptively strong. He could do twenty-five one-arm pushups with either arm. He also was an exceptional athlete, who did a little boxing in the Tulsa area.

Gene Smith, an accomplished bulldogger from Stringtown, Oklahoma, recognized the combination would make Jackson one hell of a tough steer wrestler. He introduced him to the sport and the two started competing together around their home state.

Smith eventually became more of a big brother than a mentor, but he was often traveling fulltime and gone for weeks at a time when Jackson met Emmett Perkins at a laundromat near Booker T. Washington High School, where Perkins was on the rodeo team.

Perkins invited Jackson to a stable where he looked after a few horses not far from the school. Before that day, Jackson had never roped calves. But afterward, he and Perkins practiced every day. Just two years later, Jackson said, "They had to deal with me in competition."

He finished high school, and unlike his younger siblings who went on to college, Jackson became something of a rodeo legend in Oklahoma.

In Okmulgee—an all-Black rodeo produced by the LeBlanc family—Jackson won the all-around title seven times, including a stretch of four consecutive years.

But he really made a name for himself at an Easter weekend event in Checotah, Oklahoma. Jackson is not sure of the year—after fifty years, they all run together—but the event was no less memorable.

Jackson showed up having been told it was a calf-roping event. When he got there, he discovered it was a stand-alone steer-wrestling competition featuring world champions from the PRCA and the IPRA.

Initially he was not going to enter because he was wearing a short-sleeved shirt and "those steers had big horns," but it was a straight three-header with the lowest cumulative time being named the winner.

Jackson felt like it was an opportunity for him to prove himself against former champions.

Shortly after he paid his entry fees, a cowboy he didn't recognize gave him a hard time, saying he was out of his league entering an event against that kind of talent.

Jackson responded to the less-than-encouraging words with the second-fastest time in the opening round. He was 5.6 seconds. The winning time was 5.3, while third place was more than 7 seconds.

The same cowboy scoffed and said, "You won't be no five on this one."

"That steer don't know nothing about them damn buckles," Jackson cracked back.

Jackson had a little different bulldogging style than most. He'd ride up on the left side of the steer, jump down and when he reached across with his right arm, he would grab the far end of the horn from underneath and then grab the very end of the left horn like he was holding the handlebars on a bicycle. He'd use the leverage to his advantage.

"You got 'em in a bind, and you can really put the hurt on 'em," Jackson said.

He ultimately won the event with two times just over 5 seconds and a third time of 4.1 seconds. There were no other times in the four-second range all day, and according to Jackson, "There wasn't but three 5s and I had two of them."

In 1970, '71, and '72, he made his first and only trips east of the Mississippi River for a series of Black rodeos in inner cities including Baltimore, Newark and Jersey City, New Jersey, and Harlem, New York.

In Harlem, Jackson rode in a parade of Black cowboys on horseback alongside legendary fighter Muhammad Ali before winning the steer-wrestling event and placing in the top five of calf roping.

It was around that same time that Ben Johnson—a world champion team roper who became a Hollywood actor—invited Jackson to his annual roping held every Father's Day weekend in Osage County, Oklahoma.

It was an unusually long arena comparable to the one used in Cheyenne, Wyoming, and is large enough to fit more than one football field or twice the length of a typical roping arena.

Tom Ferguson was there competing. Ferguson was the first rodeo cowboy to win $100,000 in a single season and the first to surpass $1 million in career earnings.

Because of the size of the arena, Jackson brought what he called a real nice running horse. As fast as this horse was, he also was noticeably smaller than the other horses. He barely weighed 945 pounds compared to the 1,100–1,300 pounds the other horses weighed. Some of the pros who were not from Oklahoma joked, "What's that Black guy doing unloading a Shetland pony?"

One of them was so bold as to tell Jackson there was a good chance the calf would outrun his horse, to which Jackson informed him, "There isn't a calf in Osage County that can outrun me."

What the out-of-towners didn't realize was that Jackson's horse might have been small in stature, but he was the son of a son of world champion quarter horse Go Man Go. A couple hours later, Jackson won the second round with a time of 12.4 seconds, which is comparable to the winning times at Cheyenne, and the crowd knew it. They gave him a standing ovation as he trotted out of the arena.

Jackson always has proclaimed he was willing to compete against anybody, but a sleeping disorder that still affects him today kept him from doing a significant amount of traveling, especially those calling for overnight drives. He was forced to stay mostly within a few hours of home.

By this time, he also was married and supporting a growing family by shoeing horses fulltime, and in order to rodeo, he had to use money that he won.

In February of 1978, his pals Calvin Greely Jr. and Clarence LeBlanc took off to rodeo together in the IPRA. They invited Jackson to travel with them, but he did not take them up on their offer until early July. He only had $300. He spent one hundred of it buying an IPRA card and by the end of August—after just two months of a seven-month season—he missed out on qualifying for the IFR by only $700.

The '78 season was the closest Jackson came to qualifying for the IFR.

A few years later, he lost his longtime travel partner and close friend Chris Prophet. The two had very different approaches to rodeo. Jackson was focused on winning, while Prophet was often preoccupied with chasing women, which ultimately led to his death. A scorned ex-girlfriend confronted him in the parking lot of a Dallas apartment complex and fatally shot him in the chest.

Jackson had last seen Prophet at a rodeo in Waco, Texas, and forty years later, he's still not sure about the details surrounding his friend's death. In 1982 he was nearing the end of his own competitive career when the top-ranked PRCA cowboys arrived in Oklahoma City a week before the NFR.

Five of the top fifteen calf ropers were at a practice pen outside of town when the building's manager called Jackson to let him know they were organizing a last-minute jackpot roping later that evening. He and his son Mike drove over and brought a couple of young horses with them.

Jackson let the first calf get too big of a lead on him and took damn near 12 seconds to get his piggin' string tied around the calf's feet. But he settled down and was a blistering 7.2 seconds on the second calf to finish the night with the fastest time.

"Mike said them guys was so mad," laughed Jackson. "If it was two-head or more, I was going to get a check. I didn't care who was there. I'd rope with them guys."

Jackson made a handsome living shoeing horses and later, in 1990, he took an adult carpentry class in the evenings at Booker T. Washington High—a skill his maternal grandfather introduced him to as a young'un. He started his own business overseeing and managing the construction of large metal buildings and covered ranch arenas—something he still continues doing.

However, Jackson is understandably prouder of "being able to survive doing what I wanted to do and not have to punch a clock."

11

Cleo "Mr. Black Rodeo" Hearn

As a young Black boy, it made me proud to see Black leaders that did something amazing and made the world change.

—JOHN LEGEND

SEMINOLE, OKLAHOMA

President John F. Kennedy's order came down a few years after the grandmother of a soldier killed in the early years of Vietnam walked up to a Black member of the Presidential Honor Guard moments before the start of a funeral and slapped him across the face.

That soldier was supposed to be the first Black member to carry a casket in Arlington National Cemetery.

Never happened. Not that day.

"She didn't want no nigger holding the kid," recalled Cleo Hearn, who only learned of the story after he was one of seven Black soldiers named to the Honor Guard under orders from Kennedy, who "wanted to integrate the casket-bearing team, and I was the one they integrated it with. The first job I ever had was a drop job. We were in our blue and gold suits and I couldn't believe there was over three hundred photographers."

"It wasn't enough just to carry a casket, he was carrying the hopes of a community," said Lonnie Bunch III, founding director of the Smithsonian's National Museum of African American History and Culture.

"Things like the Honor Guard was really traditionally a bastion that allowed people to say tradition trumps change," Bunch added.

It was Hearn's third day on the job.

Six members of the Honor Guard, including Hearn, rode a bus out to the cemetery plot.

The casket arrived in an ambulance.

Hearn, who in 1959 became the first African American to become a professional tie roper in the RCA, was positioned in the center on the left side of the casket.

A so-called drop job differs from a full funeral service in that once the Honor Guard positions the casket above the burial vault at the gravesite, they turn and leave and are not present for the ceremonial 21-gun salute or the actual funeral. In this case, the family of the soldier would have had no idea that their loved one's casket had been carried by a Black member of the Honor Guard had it not been for the media coverage.

"The minute I stepped off of [the bus], they started taking pictures," Hearn recalled. "The army had to tell [photographers] to get back. We didn't have any idea what was going on. They told me when I got back, 'Hey, you just made history. It was an order from the president.'

"Man, I had no idea—no idea—why all the photographers were there."

That moment came thirteen years after President Harry Truman signed Executive Order 9981, which fully integrated the U.S. Armed Forces, becoming the first president to use such an order to enforce a civil rights issue. Now it was 1961 and Hearn spent the next two years as a member of the prestigious Presidential Honor Guard.

He knows what it's like to carry a casket in perfect formation across cobblestone walkways.

He also knows what it's like to stand at attention at the Tomb of the Unknown Soldier.

On the Fourth of July in 1962 and again in 1963—nearly one hundred years after the first military burial took place on May 13, 1864—Hearn's six-man team, of which he was the only African American, was assigned as many as seven funerals at Arlington National Cemetery and all of them were officers in the military.

"It got to be, as Black people called me, 'Cleo Hearn, the Show Nigger,'" said Hearn. "That didn't come out of a white person's mouth. That came out of a Black person's mouth. My own friends, 'Hey Cleo, you're a Show Nigger now.'"

He laughed.

Still laughs.

"Well, that's exactly what it was, because, like I said, I was the second one going into the cemetery and you could tell when they was burying one of the big boys," explained Hearn, who said his team was never assigned to carry an officer ranked below that of a major.

"He's making history and he realized he was making history," said Beverly Robertson, former executive director of the National Civil Rights Museum in Memphis, Tennessee. "There's a tremendous burden that you bear. . . . Someone who is a pioneer like that, often they will plow the ground, but they never really reap the benefits of the work they have done. People often never know what they have done."

While his friends and fellow soldiers may not have recognized the burden of being a pioneer, Hearn certainly did, and he accepted the responsibility that came with it.

"I got out of the army thirty-two days before Kennedy got killed," said Hearn, who was honorably discharged in late October and back in Dallas the weekend before Kennedy was assassinated on November 22, 1963. Matter of fact, Hearn was entered in the tie-down roping and steer wrestling at Neal Gay's weekly rodeo in Mesquite.

"Had I been in the army when Kennedy got killed, the Black guy on the left side of the casket would have been me, period. That was my job in the army. I was an Honor Guard casket bearer, carried over one hundred caskets in Arlington National Cemetery. It was like home to me."

Cleo Hearn was born May 3, 1939, and raised by Doc and Gertrude Hearn in Seminole, Oklahoma. He grew up at a time when the town's population peaked at nearly twelve thousand. School and sports were important in the

Hearn home. Doc graduated from Langston (Oklahoma) University and played semipro baseball in the Negro Leagues before becoming a father.

Cleo, who only dreamed of becoming a Black cowboy after a chance encounter with Marvel Rogers Sr., attended Douglas High School in Oklahoma City because of segregation issues in Seminole.

Like his father, Cleo was a hell of an athlete in all sports. Baseball was his best, but he stood out in football and had his heart set on rodeo. Growing up, Hearn could ride bulls and broncs. He could bulldog as good or better than anyone his age, but he wanted to rope.

"There were a couple of guys—white guys who could really rope—and I just started turning out calves for them," Hearn said, "just picking things up, and the next thing you know, I could rope good enough to be at the rodeo."

Initially, he would compete at youth rodeos as a teen—his first was in 1953—but, he recalled, "they wouldn't let me rope because I was Black."

Just twenty years removed from the nearby Tulsa race riots, it was all right for Hearn to bulldog, but the locals in his own hometown were not about to let him rope calves. In the 1940s, '50s, and even in the '60s, the thought of a Black cowboy having the horsemanship and roping skills to compete was incomprehensible—in the same way people at the time could not imagine a Black football player having the skills and smarts to play quarterback.

In 1956 Hearn took a bus from Seminole to Drumright to compete in his first rodeo—an annual all-Black event, where he won $112. Then came Shawnee, Boley, Okmulgee, and his hometown.

After graduating from high school in 1957, Hearn was recruited and initially attended Oklahoma State University on a football scholarship, but he was more excited to join the rodeo team. According to a one-page bio distributed to media outlets by the American Black Cowboy Association, "within the year, he exchanged his shoulder pads for a cowboy's piggin' string."

Hearn was recruited by the University of Texas–Austin, but he politely declined.

As it was, he spent only two years in Stillwater before finding his way down to Bandera, Texas, after meeting Ray Wharton—the 1956 world champion known as the "Mighty Mite" of tie-down ropers—at an event in Ada, Oklahoma.

Hearn knew that another Black cowboy, Calvin Greenly Jr., had gone to stay with Wharton. Greely introduced the two and Hearn asked if he could come down to his ranch. Wharton was headed out East for a three-week rodeo in New York at Madison Square Garden and another two weeks at Boston Garden.

"When I get back home," Wharton told him, "you call me and then come down to Bandera and start working for me, and we'll just go from there."

Wharton returned in early November. It was 1958. Hearn packed a bag, caught a bus, and headed to Bandera. Located in the Texas Hill Country, Bandera is known as the "cowboy capital of the world."

"It's a tough town," Hearn recalled. "But it was a real cowboy town."

He added, "Women would come down from everywhere. They'd have a good time in the saloons and everything. Bandera, it was the place to be, and at that time, it was very segregated. Hell, I lived down on the ranch and I'd go to town and everybody knew me because I worked for Ray. If I wanted to go anywhere for activities, [Wharton would tell him], 'Hey, man, take off this weekend and go over to San Antone, stay all night and visit around and do whatever you need to do.' You know, [south Texas] was still very segregated."

Wharton had a large ranch and every morning Hearn would saddle up a horse and ride around looking for calves, steers, cows, and other animals that might have gotten themselves hung up in the fence. Then he would saddle another horse and lead two others—one on each side of him—for as far as the horse would take him, stop, unsaddle one horse, saddle another, and keep riding.

The days were long and the work was hard, especially fully dressed in his long-sleeve shirt, chaps, and freshly starched jeans underneath the heat of the blistering Texas sun. But spending all his days with Wharton made it worthwhile.

They were together every day.

Wharton was not only impressed with Hearn's work ethic and horsemanship skills, but he also saw that his protégé was progressing as a roper. Wharton was the calf-roping director for the RCA, and according to Hearn, "He just signed the deal and I got in the PRCA and never went to a rodeo. I didn't qualify like everybody else."

Wharton offered to pay Hearn's entry fees for both steer wrestling and tie-down roping in exchange for half his winnings.

"I would have paid money," said Hearn of the priceless lessons he learned from being with Wharton.

In 1961 he was drafted and spent two years in the U.S. Army, but not before he competed at the Fort Worth Stock Show and Rodeo.

By the time Hearn left for basic training, he was already famously known as "Mr. Black Rodeo," and he was not about to lose two years in the prime of his rodeo career. After being named to the Presidential Honor Guard, Hearn would compete in various army rodeos in Virginia and oftentimes made the weekly 125-mile drive north to Cowtown, New Jersey, on Saturday nights.

His first time there, he made newspaper headlines and his fellow soldiers wanted to go along.

"The army cut three buses loose and took three busloads of soldiers to watch me," Hearn recalled, "and from that day on, I never paid another entry fee at a Howard Harris rodeo."

When he checked in with the rodeo secretary for Cowtown the following week and tried to enter for tie-down roping and steer wrestling, she slid his money back across the table and said, "Mr. Harris told me, 'Don't charge him any entry fees.'"

He added, "They took care of me."

There were plenty of Black cowboys who competed at Cowtown—in fact, Gene, Jimmy Lee, and Willie Ed Walker grew up and lived right there on the rodeo grounds—but during the grand entry, the announcer would feature Hearn and tell spectators he was a key member of President John F. Kennedy's Honor Guard at Arlington National Cemetery.

Harris would even pay Hearn some extra money to spend time signing autographs at the merchandise stand. Hearn was seen as a hero, and that was good for business.

Not everyone saw his success in the rodeo arena or his inclusion in the Honor Guard as heroic.

Hearn had heard a lot of praise for the barbecue joint across from the entrance on the barracks side of the base. He recalled a Saturday night in June 1963, when he placed in both events at the Cowtown Rodeo and drew a sizable check, so the next afternoon he took a couple of buddies to the restaurant.

The waitress brought out two glasses of water.

She put them on the table in front of Hearn's colleagues—who were white—and acted as if Hearn was not even at the table. She never took anyone's order. Instead, the owner emerged from the kitchen and said, "We don't serve niggers here."

Without missing a beat, Hearn replied, "I'm glad, because I don't eat 'em."

Hearn did not think it was funny, but in the face of the owner, he laughed and so did the other patrons. The other two soldiers with Hearn were embarrassed and uncomfortable with the situation, so they and Hearn stood up and left.

"I bet you half of the people got up and left with us," Hearn recalled. "That place became off-limits to all military and inside of ten days, he had to close down."

After returning home from the army, Hearn enrolled at his father's alma mater, Langston University, where he finished his business degree. Then he accepted a job he kept for thirty-three years with the Ford Motor Company–Southwest Division in Dallas, after appearing in a Ford tractor commercial.

He became something of a regular in Mesquite, Texas, where he first competed in 1958 prior to being drafted, at a series of all-Black rodeos in Oklahoma and became a semiregular at RCA events.

An all-around rodeo cowboy, Hearn ultimately favored timed events like tie-down roping and steer wrestling because the outcomes are determined by a stopwatch as opposed to the opinion and, perhaps, racial animosity of a judge. It made for fewer discrepancies. In January 1970 he became the first Black cowboy to win the calf-roping competition at a major rodeo, "when [he] busted 'em good" at the Denver National Western Stock Show.

He roped two calves in just 12.1 seconds and pocketed $3,491, which would be about a $24,000 payday in 2020.

A year later, in July 1971, he placed sixth out of more than two hundred ropers who competed at the Cheyenne Frontier Days Rodeo.

Two months later, he was a key player in producing the first all-Black rodeo in Harlem. Hearn served as vice president of the American Black Cowboy Association along with Bud Bramwell, Charles Evans, and Rogers, who twenty-three years earlier had inspired a passion for Hearn to become a cowboy. Together, along with the help of George Richardson and Ingrid Frank, they produced five all-Black events in New York and New Jersey.

"I brought about ten cowboys in each event that I knew," said Hearn, including his oldest son, Harlan. But it was an appearance by Muhammad Ali that largely added to the lore and legacy of the Harlem event.

"We always said we were going to do something else and he just got bigger and bigger and bigger. We never did get a chance to really do what we wanted to do, but Ali was typical Ali. He took his coat off and got in the chute with a bull."

A documentary, *Black Rodeo*, was released in 1972, and although it was critically heralded, it was not widely seen and thus did little to bolster the stature of the American Black Cowboy Association or Black rodeos. A year later, in 1973, the association dissolved.

Back in Texas, Hearn, who himself is half African American and half Native American, founded what would eventually be rebranded the Cowboys of Color rodeo series.

Cowboys of Color and the Bill Pickett Invitational Rodeo, founded by the late Lu Vason in 1984, represent the two most significant and much-needed Black rodeo circuits in the world.

In 1986, of the more than six thousand cowboys competing in the PRCA, only thirty-five were Black, according to an article in the *Del Rio (TX) News Herald*, which was in stark contrast to the two hundred Black rodeo cowboys the Associated Press reported were in the Dallas area the year Hearn founded the Cowboys of Color.

A vivacious personality—evident by his being tabbed the *first* Black cowboy to be cast as the Marlboro Man, according to Hearn—the business-minded cowboy knew how to promote his fledgling organization. His mission from day one, and it continues today, is to entertain and educate spectators regarding the history of Black cowboys in the Old West and the emergence of all-colored rodeos.

Today, Hearn has been producing and promoting his rodeos for well over fifty years.

"He's done a lot for the cowboys, especially the Black cowboys," said eight-time PRCA world champion Don Gay, who untied calves for Hearn as a young boy at his daddy's rodeo in Mesquite.

In addition to still producing as many as a dozen Cowboys of Color rodeos, it's worth noting that Hearn—who competed professionally for thirty-six consecutive years—was still roping calves at seventy-eight, when he injured his knee in the summer of 2017.

"Some things happened to me that I didn't plan," said Hearn, not of his injury but of his pioneering accomplishments. "I was just in the right place."

He concluded, "Of course, my dream is getting in the [National Cowboy and Western Heritage] Hall of Fame in Oklahoma City. That's *home* and I'm going to get there."

12

Glynn Turman

I have discovered in life that there are ways of getting almost anywhere you want to go, if you really want to go.
—LANGSTON HUGHES

HARLEM, NEW YORK, AND HOLLYWOOD, CALIFORNIA

For five days in spring 1992, the world held its collective breath as it watched much of Los Angeles burn in the wake of four white police officers being acquitted in the beating of Rodney King. By the time a dusk-to-dawn curfew was lifted on May 5, and some semblance of order was restored, the riots had left fifty people dead, more than 2,300 injured, and more than three thousand buildings either partially damaged or totally destroyed, according to various news reports.

King's beating had been captured by an amateur videographer. The acquittal of the Los Angeles police officers involved in King's controversial arrest touched off what the History Channel has since characterized as the most destructive civil disturbance of the twentieth century and is estimated to have caused more than $1 billion in damage.

The sustained rage and violence—which had not been seen in LA since the Watts Riots of 1965 resulted in thirty-four deaths—had less to do with King and more to do with a growing sentiment that the mostly white Los

Angeles Police Department and its scandalous police chief, Daryl Gates, had been racially profiling minorities, especially in inner-city neighborhoods like South Central LA, Watts, Compton, and Inglewood.

In its aftermath, Dr. Martin Luther King Jr.'s widow, Coretta Scott King, and her husband's friend and confidant Andrew Young—U.S. ambassador to the United Nations—called for a peace summit. They brought together civil rights and social justice leaders, well-respected Black actors and athletes and leaders from the city's rival street gangs, the Bloods and Crips.

King levied a stern challenge to all in attendance: Before leaving the summit, everyone had to not only promise to help bring peace and unity to their communities but also conceive an individual way to accomplish that promise.

Actor Glynn Turman, who owns a twenty-acre ranch north of Los Angeles, was among those at the gathering. He made a promise to develop a summer camp for kids that would introduce as many as one hundred inner-city kids to "a dose of fresh air and a different way of life" that included horseback riding.

Almost thirty years later, Turman described the annual Camp Gid-D Up and the work he's done with his foundation as "one of the highlights of my life."

Glynn Turman was born on the last day of January in 1947.

After his parents divorced, he and his mother lived in an apartment tenement in Harlem with two of her sisters and a brother-in-law. Turman was eight or nine years old when he and his mother moved to Greenwich Village in the mid-1950s.

The sisters remained close, which helped Turman learn how to get around Manhattan. A latchkey kid, he would return to Harlem to spend some days with one aunt or head to the projects on the Lower Eastside to be with the other. It was a lesson in independence that served him well years later on the rodeo trail and when his Emmy Award–winning acting career led him around the world.

But his true passion came to pass on the corner of 147th Street and Amsterdam Avenue.

Too young to venture out into the streets of Harlem on his own, Turman would sit on the stairwell of the fire escape and watch as mounted officers from the New York City Police Department would ride south on horseback down Amsterdam.

Seeing those big bay horses—brown bodies with black manes, tails, and lower legs—from afar was magical.

On rare occasions, Turman would wait downstairs and run alongside them from 147th down to 146th Street. He wasn't allowed to cross from one block to another on his own, but he would often steal an apple from an outdoor fruit stand to feed one of the horses while they waited to cross at the first corner. The risk of getting caught was worth the opportunity to interact with the horses.

He was amazed and fascinated by them, and even when he watched Roy Rogers or Hopalong Cassidy shows on television, his interest was less about the cowboys and more about the horses. A friend of his mother's once took him to a professional rodeo at Madison Square Garden. More than being a rodeo cowboy, he dreamed of one day owning a ranch and having horses.

Turman was popular and athletic but hated school and was chronically truant. In those days, the kids played a lot of stickball in the street around the corner from where he lived in the Village. They would break off a broomstick handle, grab a ball with a great deal of bounce to it, and wait for the street to clear of traffic. Turman had a passion for the game and enjoyed playing alongside his friends.

Turman's mother raised her son in an artistic community. They lived in a six-floor, cold-water flat with a shared bathroom in the hallway. His mom was friends with novelist James Baldwin and playwright Lorraine Hansberry, who arranged for the eleven-year-old Turman to audition for the Broadway production of *A Raisin in the Sun*.

He made his acting debut as Travis Younger on March 11, 1959.

Turman found himself on Broadway acting with Sidney Poitier and Ruby Dee and twenty-two-year-old Louis Gossett Jr. He was a preteen and, as such, was not aware of the historical implications of the landmark play, which took its name from the Langston Hughes poem "Harlem."

While he enjoyed the experience, he did not like the fact that his mother had pulled him out of public school and enrolled him in a private school.

"I wasn't very happy with that arrangement, because I wasn't a show business–minded kid," Turman said. "I would rather go to baseball practice than rehearsal."

Prior to his thirteenth birthday, Turman quit Broadway.

Without the responsibility of acting professionally, he could return to junior high and attend a public school. For the next six years, his grades were good enough to play on the baseball team and participate in theater. His drama teachers in junior high and high school cast him in the lead roles.

He also continued to play hooky. If he happened to have a quarter, he headed down to the movie theaters on Forty-Sixth or Forty-Second Streets. If his pockets were empty, he headed up to Central Park and offered to help a stable manager "shovel shit . . . if you let me ride a horse around the arena."

It was there that the teenager rode a horse for the first time.

When his mother found out where he was, she was not happy, but she supported his passion. "Instead of getting pissed off, she took me to a stable to horseback ride up in the Bronx—Pelham Bay Park," said Turman of the stable where he learned how to properly saddle a horse and ride.

Though he was too young to know any better, Pelham Bay is where Black cowboys like Bud Bramwell, Charlie Reno, and Steve Robinson regularly rode in the 1960s. More than fifty years later, those same legends don't remember befriending Turman, but each recalled how they would attract youngsters and adults of all ethnicities whenever they were around.

"It was a magical time," Turman said. "Sometimes, I've got to pinch myself to see how a little Black boy from a tenement in Harlem got to, I mean, I'm talking to you from my ranch. It's more than I could have ever imagined my life would be like."

By the late 1960s and early '70s, Turman was living in Los Angeles and was regularly guest starring on popular television series like *Peyton Place*, *The Doris Day Show*, *Hawaii Five-O*, and *The Rookies*. He also earned roles in a series of made-for-television movies and the cult classic film *Cooley High*. Then, in 1975, a year before he married Aretha Franklin, he auditioned with director George Lucas for a film called *Star Wars*, which would become one of the biggest films of all time when it was released in the summer of 1977.

Turman did not know it at the time, but he was up for the role of Han Solo, which would have made him a cowboy of sorts in a galaxy far, far away. Instead, the part went to Harrison Ford because Lucas knew in subsequent films there was a romantic storyline between Solo and Princess Leia and the famous filmmaker did not want the racial implications of a mixed couple to distract from the rest of the episode, according to the biography *Skywalking: The Life and Films of George Lucas.*

In recent years, Lucas confirmed the reason for the casting change when he and Turman attended a fundraiser together and Turman asked the iconic filmmaker whether the story was true or not.

Turman spent much of the 1970s away from the bright lights and stress associated with a career in Hollywood. He became one of the top ten horsemen competing in the Tevis Cup, a one-hundred-mile endurance race held annually since 1955. He has quite a trophy case chronicling his many accomplishments.

In 1984 Lu Vason, founder of the Bill Pickett Invitational Rodeo, called Turman and fellow actor Danny Glover to ask if they would serve as grand marshals on horseback and welcome the crowd at his Los Angeles rodeo.

Not being a contestant allowed Turman to get more involved. As the rodeo unfolded, he was on horseback as a pickup man during the rough stock events, did some hazing during the steer wrestling and helped the rodeo hands gather cattle.

Once Vason and his staff saw how skilled the actor was on the back of a horse, they asked if he would be interested in staying involved. When the Bill Pickett rodeo was in Atlanta, Turman was in Atlanta. When the rodeo made its way to Denver and Washington DC, Turman made his way there, too. Even today, he will make himself useful when he attends a Bill Pickett rodeo.

Turman was introduced to the competitive side of rodeo by a stuntman named John Sherrod, who also introduced the actor to Reginald T. Dorsey. Turman and Dorsey became fast friends while honing their skills as team ropers. They mostly competed in California and would sometimes travel to Arizona and Nevada.

At the time, Turman could be seen in a series of guest roles on everything from *The Paper Chase* and *White Shadow* to *The Love Boat* and *Fantasy Island* before taking another turn on the big screen in *Gremlins.* You could also see him on *T.J. Hooker, Riptide, The Twilight Zone, Matlock,* and *Murder She Wrote.* Then came a five-year run as Col. Brad Taylor on the television series *A Different World,* from 1988 to 1993.

1. The gravesites for Bill Pickett and his horse Spradley, whose grave is outlined with rocks in the upper right-hand corner, are located next to White Eagle Monument outside of Ponca City, Oklahoma. Courtesy of the author.

2. Eleven of the charter members of the Okmulgee Colored Round-Up Club in 1956. *Left to right*: Ernest Thigpen, D. P. Lilly, Larnell Williams, Willie Tate, John Grant, Frank Haygood, Roy LeBlanc, Ernest Bruner, Clarence Williams, Charles LeBlanc, and Alfred Nonnett. Haygood (*standing sixth from the left*) had recently returned to Okmulgee after playing baseball in the Negro Leagues for the Kansas City Monarchs. Courtesy of Kenneth LeBlanc.

OFFICIAL RODEO PROGRAM!

FIRST ANNUAL

All Colored RODEO

OKMULGEE, OKLAHOMA

August 25-26, 1956

Support the Businessmen and Merchants
Supporting Us.

First Annual Okmulgee All Colored
Championship

RODEO

AUGUST 25 & 26 TWO 8:00 P.M. NIGHT SHOWS

AT THE OKMULGEE ROUND-UP CLUB ARENA
• Located 1½ Miles North of Okmulgee on Wood Drive •
Sponsored by the OKMULGEE COLORED ROUND-UP CLUB, Okmulgee, Okla.
$600.00 ADDED MONEY—4 BIG EVENTS

CALF ROPING	BULL RIDING
$5.00 Entry Fee	$5.00 Entry Fee
STEER WRESTLING	BARE BACK BRONC RIDING
$5.00 Entry Fee	$5.00 Entry Fee

CLOWN – BILLY THE KID and his TRAINED MULE, ELIZA

PARADE, Saturday, August 25, 6:00 p.m.

BOOKS CLOSE 7:00 P.M. EACH DAY
For Further Information Call:
Roy LeBlanc 4094—D. P. Lilly 1958 or 4132—Henry Lyons 3977 or 3584-W
SECRETARY, Roy LeBlanc   PRESIDENT, Charles LeBlanc
ARENA DIRECTOR, Wesley Young
• IN CASE OF RAIN, SHOW HELD AT LATER DATE •
STOCK FURNISHED BY
CLAUDE ROBINSON, DRUMRIGHT, OKLAHOMA
PARADE MARSHALL, BRAD SIMMONS
ADMISSION: ADULTS $1.00 - CHILDREN 50c

3. & 4. Okmulgee Colored Rodeo program cover from 1956 and an advertisement from the same year. The annual event has been held every year since. Courtesy of Kenneth LeBlanc.

5. Freddie Gordon at the Houston Rodeo in 1965. Courtesy of Freddie Gordon.

6. Cleo Hearn and the Presidential Honor Guard. Courtesy of Cleo Hearn.

7. Notice the position of Myrtis Dightman Sr.'s left free arm. Like a stage actor, he is leaving no doubt his free arm is out away from his body and above the bull so as not to give either judge an opportunity to disqualify him for touching his bull. Courtesy of Ferrell Butler.

8. One of the rare times Myrtis Dightman Sr. was knocked out and found himself in the precarious position of being underneath his bull was in 1968 at the National Finals in Oklahoma City. Notice the "bullfighter" to the right of the barrel man is out of position. He is trailing behind the bull and doing little to help clear the bull out away from Dightman. Courtesy of Myrtis Dightman Jr.

9. Bud Bramwell competing at the Houston Rodeo at Sam Houston Coliseum in the 1960s. Hazing for Bramwell is 1957 world champion steer wrestler Willard Combs. Courtesy of Ferrell Butler.

10., 11., & 12. Tony Brubaker is a cowboy-turned-stuntman. His career in Hollywood began in the late 1960s—he doubled for Sidney Poitier in the Black Western *Buck and the Preacher*—and he continues working to this day. He most recently did stunts on the 2019 film *Harriet*. Courtesy of Tony and Sharon Brubaker.

13. Will Dawson was born in Alligator, Mississippi, raised in Detroit, and left home as a teenager for Los Angeles with dreams of becoming a cowboy. A regular over at El Fig Stables, Dawson would rodeo and work in the movie business—his last film credit was *D2: The Mighty Ducks*—before returning home to Detroit after being diagnosed with cancer. He famously appeared on the cover of *Sepia* magazine. Photos of Dawson are rare because most of his personal memorabilia was destroyed in a house fire. Courtesy of Sherral Clayton.

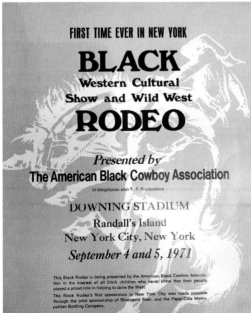

14. & 15. Cover and inside cover page from Harlem rodeo program in 1971. Courtesy of Bud Bramwell.

16. Marvel Rogers (*left*), George Richardson (*sitting*), Charlie Evans (*laying across bed*), and Cleo Hearn (*right*) meeting in Richardson's hotel room the day before the September 4 all-Black rodeo in Harlem. Courtesy Bud Bramwell.

17. A candid photo of Cleo Hearn during the all-Black rodeo in Harlem. Courtesy of Bud Bramwell.

18. Bud Bramwell (*left*) and Wayne Orme (*right*) discuss the first all-Black rodeo held in Harlem in September 1971. Courtesy of Bud Bramwell.

19. Marvel Rogers behind the chutes at the all-Black rodeo in Harlem. Rogers was born January 25, 1924, in Arkansas and raised in nearby Idabel, Oklahoma. He started to rodeo, at fifteen, as a calf roper and later, in the 1950s and '60s, rode bucking horses. Known as a lady's man, Rogers was famous for his well-starched, white button-down shirts and for smoking cigars while riding bucking stock. He would blow a puff of smoke every time the horse's hind feet would hit the ground and kick. Courtesy of Bud Bramwell.

PERISCOPE ASSOCIATES
Public Affairs Marketing and Promotion

Suite 6B
131 West 82nd Street
New York City, N.Y. 10024
TeVFax: 212-721-7366

A table-top photo book of pride and inspiration......

"MUHAMMAD ALI
at the
BLACK RODEO"
The Muhammad Ali America Doesn't Know
The America The World Doesn't Know

CHAPTER OVERVIEW

Foreword	**Muhammad Ali, A True American Hero** **by Kareem Abdul Jabar**
Section One	**Ali At The First Harlem Black Rodeo ('71)** **and in "Black Rodeo", the movie, ('72)**
Section Two	**Heroes Of Harlem's First Black Rodeo**
Section Three	**Real Heroes of America's Forgotten Black West**
Conclusion	**Reclaiming the Past To Build The Future** **by Major General Hugh Robinson (Ret.)**
Appendix	**How You Can Help**

Cover Photo of Ali on Horseback at 1971 Black Rodeo, in Harlem NY.
Photos From Documentary Movie Of This Event: "Black Rodeo"
Muhammad Ali Quotes From Same Documentary
Archival Photos And Historical Stories of Old West Black Cowboys and Heroes

20. Book proposal featuring Muhammad Ali and Black cowboys. The manuscript was never completed. Ali's then-manager Bob Arum said, at eighty-eight, that he could not recall Ali attending the rodeo in Harlem, much less reviewing the proposal, because too many decades had passed. Courtesy of Ingrid Frank.

FOR THE BENEFIT OF THE NEW JERSEY URBAN LEAGUES

Dear Youth Leader:

This summer, let's give our children a chance to see black cowboys!

Americans have always idealized the cowboy as a symbol of manhood and courage. But it has been a one-sided symbol because our history and story books have forgotten the black cowboy. We think it is very important for all our children to know that black and white cowboys rode together to help tame the wild west.

That is why we are bringing our BLACK RODEO to Freehold Raceway, in Freehold, N.J., on July 20 and 21...so that the people of New Jersey and the children in your group can see real black cowboys in wild, western action....so that they will learn that the settling of our western frontier was a joint effort by black, as well as white men and women.

In order to give more children an opportunity to see the black cowboys, we are having two special Youth Performances, at greatly reduced rates. Normal BLACK RODEO tickets range from $7 to $4, but for the Youth Performances all seats will cost only $2. In this way we hope that Sunday School Classes, Boy and Girl Scouts, Day Care, community Centers and other groups who work with children, whose parents could not afford to take them to the BLACK RODEO, will also have an opportunity to see black cowboys ride and rope and wrestle steer. It's a really great opportunity to give the children in your group an expanded view of our nation's western history. It is an opportunity we hope you will not want to miss!

Both Youth Performances will be held on Friday, July 20. one at 11 a.m. and one at 2:30 p.m. Performances will last approximately two hours, so that it should not interfere with your groups normal summer program schedule. There is, of course plenty of free bus parking at Freehold Raceway.

Please fill out the enclosed Reservation Form, and return it to us, with your check as quickly as possible. The reduced-rate Youth Performances were totally sold out in 1971, when the BLACK RODEO last appeared in New Jersey, so please get your orders in as soon as possible. We must distribute tickets on a first-come, first-served basis.

Sincerely yours,

Bud Bramwell

Bud Bramwell
President
American Black Cowboy Association

P.S. If your group can not attend the special Youth Performances because they are on a weekday, please phone us for our special reduced rates for groups of 50 or more, for the two Saturday performances.

N.J. RODEO HDQTRS: 455 Elizabeth Avenue, Suite 16-E, Newark, N.J. 07112 Phone: (201) 242-1961

21. Press release sent to Urban Leagues regarding event at Freehold Raceway in 1973. Courtesy of Bud Bramwell.

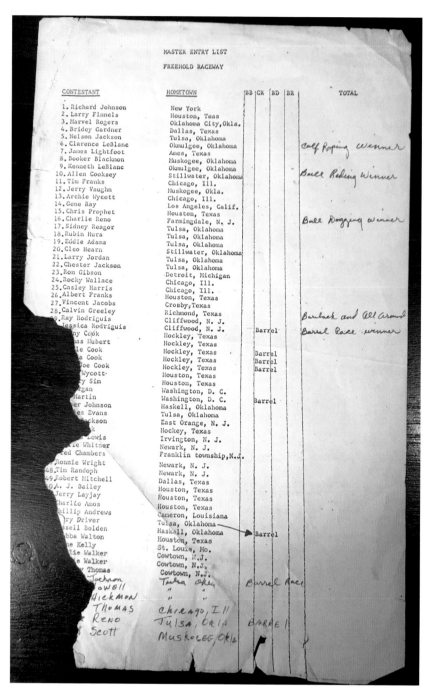

MASTER ENTRY LIST

FREEHOLD RACEWAY

CONTESTANT	HOMETOWN	BB	CR	BD	BR	TOTAL
1. Richard Johnson	New York					
2. Larry Finnels	Houston, Teas					
3. Marvel Rogers	Oklahoma City, Okla.					
4. Bridey Gardner	Dallas, Texas					
5. Nelson Jackson	Tulsa, Oklahoma					
6. Clarence LeBlanc	Okmulgee, Oklahoma					*Calf Roping Winner*
7. James Lightfoot	Ames, Texas					
8. Booker Blackmon	Muskogee, Oklahoma					
9. Kenneth LeBlanc	Okmulgee, Oklahoma					
10. Allen Cooksey	Stillwater, Oklahoma					*Bull Riding Winner*
11. Tim Franks	Chicago, Ill.					
12. Jerry Vaughn	Muskogee, Okla.					
13. Archie Wycott	Chicago, Ill.					
14. Gene Ray	Los Angeles, Calif.					
15. Chris Prophet	Houston, Texas					
16. Charlie Reno	Farmingdale, N. J.					*Bull Dogging winner*
17. Sidney Reagor	Tulsa, Oklahoma					
18. Rubin Hura	Tulsa, Oklahoma					
19. Eddie Adams	Tulsa, Oklahoma					
20. Cleo Hearn	Stillwater, Oklahoma					
21. Larry Jordan	Tulsa, Oklahoma					
22. Chester Jackson	Tulsa, Oklahoma					
23. Ron Gibson	Detroit, Michigan					
24. Rocky Wallace	Chicago, Ill.					
25. Casley Harris	Chicago, Ill.					
26. Albert Franks	Houston, Texas					
27. Vincent Jacobs	Crosby, Texas					
28. Calvin Greeley	Richmond, Texas					*Bareback and All Around*
29. Ray Rodriguis	Cliffwood, N. J.					
Jessica Rodriguis	Cliffwood, N. J.				Barrel	*Barrel Race winner*
ny Cook	Hockley, Texas					
as Hubert	Hockley, Texas					
le Cook	Hockley, Texas				Barrel	
a Cook	Hockley, Texas				Barrel	
oe Cook	Hockley, Texas				Barrel	
Wycott.	Houston, Texas					
y Sim	Houston, Texas					
rgan	Washington, D. C.					
Martin	Washington, D. C.					
er Johnson	Haskell, Oklahoma				Barrel	
es Evans	Tulsa, Oklahoma					
ckson	East Orange, N. J.					
k	Hockey, Texas					
Lewis	Irvington, N. J.					
ie Whitner	Newark, N. J.					
ed Chambers	Franklin township, N.J.					
onnie Wright	Newark, N. J.					
48. Tim Randoph	Newark, N. J.					
49. Robert Mitchell	Dallas, Texas					
50. A. J. Bailey	Houston, Texas					
Jerry Layjay	Houston, Texas					
harlie Amos	Houston, Texas					
hillip Andrews	Cameron, Louisiana					
ry Driver	Tulsa, Oklahoma				Barrel	
ssell Bolden	Haskell, Oklahoma					
bba Walton	Houston, Texas					
e Kelly	St. Louis, Mo.					
ie Walker	Cowtown, N.J.					
ie Walker	Cowtown, N.J.					
y Thomas	Cowtown, N.J.					
Jackson	Tulsa Okla	*Barrel Race*				
owell	" "					
Hickmon	" "					
Thomas	Chicago, Ill					
Reno	Tulsa, Okla	BARREL				
Scott	Muskogee, Okla					

22. Entry list for event at Freehold Raceway in 1973. Courtesy of Bud Bramwell.

PERISCOPE ASSOCIATES

455 ELIZABETH AVENUE
NEWARK, N. J. 07112
PHONE: (201) 242-1961

PARTIAL LIST OF MEDIA PUBLICITY

DURING OR AFTER THE BLACK RODEO AT FREEHOLD RACEWAY

Freehold, N.J.

This is a partial list of what we know has run, as of July 23, 1973, or is
scheduled to run about the BLACK RODEO at Freehold Raceway. Since we do not
have a clipping service, it is impossible for us to know about all the coverage
we had. This list, therefore, is composed only of those clippings in our
posession, those for which the local Urban Leagues have clips, which they have
promised to forward to us, and those stories which are still upcoming, but
which we helped the assigned reporters to gather.

TELEVISION

ABC-TV....used BLACK RODEO on 6 p.m., 11 p.m., News, on Friday, July 20,
as well as morning news show on Saturday, July 21, with full
full four-minute presentation.

NBC-TV....used BLACK RODEO on their 6 p.m. and 11 p.m. News show with action
films, as well as interview on horseback between reporter and
Bud Bramwell, president of American Black Cowboy Association

ABC-TV....shot all day Friday for their half-hour show "People, Places & Things",
scheduled tentatively for September airing

ABC-TV....showed film clips of BLACK RODEO and did half-hour interview, with
live demonstration, with Cleo Hearn, Vice-President of American
Black Cowboy Association, on their "A.M., NEW YORK" show.

RADIO

WNJR....did a half-hour interview with Cleo Hearn and Charles Lewis for their
"Fact and Opinion" show.

WTNJ....taped two half-hour interviews, both of which were aired during the
week before the BLACK RODEO

WNJR....did a 20-minute interview with Cleo Hearn and Mel Ford on Bernice Bass's
"News and View" Sunday evening show on July 15, 1973

WNJR....taped four 5-minute spots with Cleo Hearn which were aired at 8 a.m.,
11 a.m., 4 p.m. and 7 p.m. on Friday and Saturdy, July 20 and 21.

WTTM....had Cleo Hearn on for two hours on Prince Weeton's "Prince Of Soul" show
on July 13, 1973

PRINT MEDIA

NEWARK STAR LEDGER....June 21, 1973

JERSEY CITY JOURNAL...June 21, 1973

NEW YORK DAILY NEWS...Sunday, June 24

TRENTON EVENING TIMES....June 27, 1973

ELIZABETH DAILY JOURNAL....June 28, 1973

MORE

23. Media list for event at Freehold Raceway in 1973. Courtesy of Bud Bramwell.

24. Charlie Reno. Courtesy of Charlie Reno.

25. Charlie Reno bulldogging at a Sunday afternoon rodeo held in Putnam Valley, New York, at the Cimarron Dude Ranch. The late Barry Moore is hazing for Reno. Courtesy of Charlie Reno.

26. Lee McClain and his horse Wynonna. Courtesy of Sue Cermak.

27. Advertisement from 1983 for a rodeo produced by Charlie Reno. He has kept the flyer in one of several scrapbooks for nearly forty years. Courtesy of Charlie Reno.

28. Publicity photo of Charlie Reno. Courtesy of Charlie Reno.

29. Mike Latting. Photo by Tom Woodridge. Courtesy of Mike Latting.

R.F.K. WASHINGTON D.C. '75   HAROLD CASH
                                    ON BAR-9

30. Harold Cash at RFK Stadium in Washington DC in 1975. Courtesy of Harold Cash.

31. *Back row, left to right*: Freddie Gordon, John "Rev" Marshall, and Willie Thomas. *Front row, left to right*: Harold Cash, Bailey's Prairie Kid, and Myrtis Dightman. Courtesy of Harold Cash.

32. *Left to right*: Kenneth, Tim, Roy, Gary, and Clarence LeBlanc. Gary, the only one of the four brothers who did not rodeo, is wearing a buckle he borrowed from four-time world champion calf roper Kenneth "Dexter" Bailey Jr. Courtesy of Kenneth LeBlanc.

33. Kenneth LeBlanc at the practice pen working on his bulldogging skills. His brother Clarence is in the background, having pulled the gate open. Courtesy of Kenneth LeBlanc.

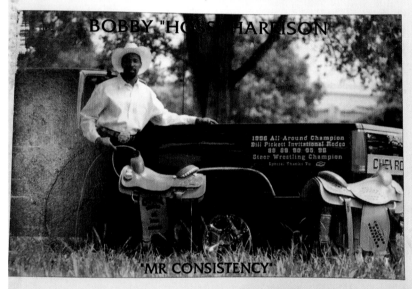

42nd ANNUAL OKMULGEE INVITATIONAL RODEO

FRIDAY, AUGUST 8
SATURDAY, AUGUST 9, 1997
OKMULGEE, OKLAHOMA

BOBBY "HOSS" HARRISON

"MR CONSISTENCY"

34. Forty-second annual Okmulgee Invitational Rodeo program from 1997. Courtesy of Kenneth LeBlanc.

35. Donald (*left*) and Ronald (*right*) Stephens in their firefighter outfits, with their horses. Courtesy of Donald Stephens.

MYRTIS DIGHTMAN
CHAMPION BULL RIDER

January 12, 1999

Rodeo Historical Society
National Cowboy Hall of Fame
1700 N.E. 63rd Street
Oklahoma City, Oklahoma 73111

Dear Sirs:

It is with the highest of honor that I submit this letter requesting the induction of Mr. Willie Thomas into the National Cowboy Hall of Fame.

I have had the privilege of knowing Willie Thomas since 1956. When I started my adventure into the rodeo circuit, Willie Thomas was my main foundation of support. He was a father to me in rodeo when I suffered despair. When I would get bucked off my bull, he was there to encourage me and to guide me and was there to praise me in my victories. He was always there to tell me what to do.

Willie Thomas was a dynamic cowboy. It is said that *"a tree is known by the fruit it bear"*. An apple tree bears apples. A Willie Thomas Tree bears a Myrtis Dightman and a Myrtis Dightman Tree, a Charles Sampson. It spreads from generation to generation. With the help of Willie Thomas, I went on to become on of the greatest Bull Rider's. Charles Sampson won the World. We are products of Willie Thomas. His unselfish spirit and his rodeo knowledge helped me to win a many, many victories. He was a great cowboy and an excellent bull rider. I always thought that he was much better than I could ever be. He is my Mentor.

Sometime I sit and I think that Willie did not get the recognition he deserved because he was to early. If he could start over again, no doubt, he would be the world's greatest but we know that it's impossible to do. That is why this induction into the Hall of Fame would be one of the greatest gifts Willie could ever receive. We are only promised three scores and ten of life expectancy, some live less, others more. Willie Thomas is 69. It would be a great honor to induct Willie into the Hall of Fame while he is still alive. He did not receive what he was entitled to while he was rodeoing but it is never to late. He would be proud to know that his hard work and paving the way for other black cowboys did not go in vain. This induction would establish another part of history.

It is the greatest of honor that I, Myrtis Dightman recommend one of the finest men I know to be inducted into the National Cowboy Hall of Fame.

Sincerely,

My Riis DiChTMAN

Myrtis Dightman
PRCA #7479

36. In 1999 Harold Cash lobbied to get his mentor and father figure Willie Thomas inducted into the Rodeo Hall of Fame in Oklahoma City. He sent a nomination form along with more than ten personal letters written by both white and Black legends among rodeo cowboys (such as Harry Tompkins) and promoters. Among those letters was this one from Myrtis Dightman Sr. His letter was typewritten with the help of his son Myrtis Jr. and then signed by Myrtis Sr. Courtesy of Harold Cash.

37. Robert Brown. Courtesy of Robert Brown.

38. Reginald T. Dorsey. Courtesy of Reginald T. Dorsey.

39. & 40. Reginald T. Dorsey (*left*) and fellow actors Blair Underwood (*middle*) and Glynn Turman (*right*) after a day spent riding horses. This particular photo was taken by Darrell Keith Harrison. Dorsey (*right in fig. 40*) and Turman (*middle*) often ride together. On this day, they are joined by actor Obba Babatundé (*left*). Courtesy of Reginald T. Dorsey.

41. Myrtis Dightman Sr. (*left*) with Dennis Davis (*right*) at a rodeo in Conway, Texas. Courtesy of Dennis Davis.

42. Clarence LeBlanc at his home on October 5, 2019. Courtesy of the author.

43. John Harp Jr. (*left*) and Mike Latting (*right*) at the 2019 NFR in Las Vegas. Courtesy of John Harp Jr.

44. Dwayne Jr. and Aaron Hargo. Courtesy of Nanette Hargo.

45. Ezekiel Mitchell during a 2019 PBR photoshoot in Nashville. Photos and clips from this shoot were used to promote the 2020 and 2021 seasons. Courtesy of the author.

By then he had sold his property in Malibu and married his current wife, Jo-Ann, whom he married in 1992, a full decade after separating from Aretha Franklin and finally divorcing in 1984.

In addition to a new home in Los Angeles, the couple bought a twenty-acre ranch in Lake Hughes, California. Together, they formed the IX Winds Ranch Foundation following a challenge from Coretta Scott King.

King thought Turman's idea to bring one hundred inner-city kids to his ranch for a weeklong summer camp was a wonderful idea. He challenged the Crips and Bloods to help identify some at-risk children ages nine to eighteen who would benefit from the experience. And so began the annual Camp Gid-D Up, which continues almost thirty years later.

Turman approached a trio of his *A Different World* co-stars—Kadeem Hardison, Sinbad, and Dawn Lewis—to ask for the initial donations he used to fund the camp.

"I thought I was going to do it that year and that would be that," said Turman, looking back on nearly three decades of camp experiences. "The look on the kids' faces—they had such a good time and I couldn't believe they were enjoying something we were able to provide, so we did it again and again. It just grew and grew and grew."

As an actor and a philanthropist, Turman's life could not have been much better for him and his family.

By the late nineties, he was a member of the U.S. Team Roping Championships, and in 1999 he and his partner, whom he has since lost touch with, won the region and qualified for the tenth annual USTRC National Finals in Oklahoma City.

Turman drove out early and stayed with Jesse "Slugger" Guillory.

Guillory won all-around rodeo titles in the Texas Rodeo Association, Southern Cowboy Association, and Bill Pickett Invitational Rodeo and was Vason's righthand man for two decades before going to work for Dodge. Charlie Sampson, who had already become the first African American to win a world championship in the PRCA, was there, too. Sampson was a pro rodeo bull rider and also pretty handy when it came to calf roping. More importantly, Sampson knew what it took to win.

Before the trio left for the finals, Sampson said, "Glynn, you're looking good. Horse is looking good. You're doing great."

Then he added, "But I hate your saddle."

Turman was not sure if Sampson was serious or kidding until the 1982 world champion bull rider said, "That saddle is not a champion saddle. If you're going to be a champion, you got to be a champion all the way."

That's when Sampson gave Turman one of his own saddles to use. In rodeo, for a world champion to give another competitor his personal saddle is the ultimate show of respect.

Turman finished the national finals event a career-best fifth in the world.

To this day, Turman, who won a Primetime Emmy for Outstanding Guest Actor in a Drama for his part in HBO's 2008 series *In Treatment*, still has Sampson's saddle at his ranch—the same ranch where he continues to introduce inner-city kids to horses, the outdoors, and Western culture. And he's been on screen more in the past two years than, perhaps, any other two years since arriving in Hollywood. He had eleven credits in 2019, including his Emmy-nominated arc on the television series *How to Get Away with Murder*, eight more in 2020, beginning with *The Way Back* with Ben Affleck, and eleven episodes from season four of *Fargo* alongside Chris Rock. In addition to these, Turman was named Best Supporting Actor by the LA Film Critics Association for his role in the critically heralded Netflix film *Ma Rainey's Black Bottom*. The film, which was produced by Denzel Washington, co-starred Viola Davis and Chadwick Boseman, who—despite never speaking publicly about his illness—died of colon cancer three months prior to the film's release in November 2020.

It's been a life well-lived. Turman has gone from being that kid sitting on the fire escape dreaming of owning a ranch to having former campers—and their parents—come up to him in public and thank him for changing their lives. Whether they took up the sport or not does not matter, so long as it kept them off the streets.

"It's a wonderful gift to be able to share with others," Turman said.

13

Tommy Cloud
(aka Tommy Cleoll Browning)

All kids need is a little help, a little hope, and somebody who believes in them.
—EARVIN "MAGIC" JOHNSON

GREENVILLE, TEXAS, AND LOS ANGELES, CALIFORNIA

Having just gotten home from school, fourteen-year-old Larry Taplet was sitting on the front porch of his Los Angeles home with a friend who mentioned a stable with lots of horses not far from where they lived.

"There ain't no horses around here," scoffed Taplet, as the other boy assured him that he had seen the horses. Together, they walked two miles from where Taplet lived—he was the youngest of three latchkey kids, whose single mother was working her second job—to the corner of El Segundo Boulevard and Figueroa Street.

And there they were.

Taplet was scared to death of the horses' size and the power they seemed to have, but discovering El Fig Stables was his "first exposure to people that didn't look like me."

He had moved to Los Angeles from New Orleans three years earlier, just ahead of the Watts Riots in August 1965.

"I'm just a boy from the South—ten years old—and people are running down the street with TVs and cash registers. I'm like, 'What?' I didn't understand none of it, but that was my exposure to California."

In Los Angeles, life was not much different than it was back in New Orleans. After splitting from his mother, Taplet's father spent time in the Louisiana State Penitentiary, historically known as Angola Prison or "the Alcatraz of the South."

No matter where he lived, Taplet was an inner-city kid from a broken home with no positive role models in his life.

"The only people that looked like they were doing any good [financially] were the dope dealers and the pimps," recalled Taplet. "They had tailormade clothes and Cadillacs, money and pretty girls around them. Naturally, I saw that and thought, 'That's what I want to do.' I didn't know any better. I'm going to be one of them. I wanted tailormade clothes with a pretty girl and a Harley Davidson chopper."

Then came the random afternoon in spring 1969, when he and his friend walked to El Fig Stables. That day, they met Bennie Moore and Edward Lee McClain, who managed the place for Tommy Cloud. They both took a liking to Taplet, but it was Moore who took the teen under his wing and taught him not only how to bulldog but also what it meant to be a man.

"That was it," said Taplet, who was in love with the idea of becoming a Black cowboy. "I just wanted to be around that. Whatever *that* meant."

There are so many stories and lessons like Taplet's—too many to be covered in a single chapter—that can be traced back to Tommy Cleoll Browning, who was born in 1913 and raised in Greenville, Texas. Browning was one of thirteen kids. He was raised to appreciate music and played trumpet. Before he was a teenager, he dropped out of school and joined a band that played around Texas and Louisiana. Instead of a car, the family—his mother, Nora, and father, Connie—had a horse and wagon, which proved to be his introduction to a life of horses.

He married his childhood sweetheart and came to Los Angeles in the mid-1940s after returning home from World War II. He worked several different jobs before owning and operating a gas station. After going to Central Casting, he became professionally known as Tommy Cloud and started getting calls to work as an extra in Hollywood movies, especially Westerns.

Cloud almost never appeared as a Black cowboy. Because of his lighter complexion, he was mostly cast to play the parts of Indians. His earliest credit, *Lady Godiva of Coventry*, was in 1955 and he last appeared onscreen alongside Burt Reynolds in the 1978 action-comedy *Hooper*, in which he was cast and credited as an "Indian." That was the same credit he received in *Quest*, *The Immortal*, *The Outcasts*, and *Hondo*.

He eventually sold the gas station and owned a small horse stable, Studio Stables, in the San Fernando Valley area of Los Angeles and, later, El Camino Stables. Around 1958—so many years have passed, said daughter Tomi Carroll Wright, it might have been 1962—he relocated to the now infamous corner of El Segundo and Figueroa in a sliver of LA that tightly parallels the Harbor Freeway.

The area was largely undeveloped with a few dirt roads, and by '68, the properties adjacent to El Fig Stables included a trio of horse stalls—leased by John Davis, Lucky, and Frenchy and owned by a man only remembered as Mr. Hicks—that lined the alley going south from El Segundo down to 132nd Street.

El Fig was up on 129th. Next door, at 130th Street, was AC Junkyard, and then Lucky and Frenchy had a pair of small places between 130th and 131st. The Hill was at the far end of the alley between 131st and 132nd Streets. The most visible of the properties, and certainly the most famous, was El Fig Stables. There was a north and south barn—both visible from Figueroa. The north barn had a front recreational room with a pool table, jukebox, and a bar that Cloud dreamed of transitioning into a café.

There was a small indoor arena where he kept all the rent horses. Once the studios learned of his horses, which were mostly used by casual riders who saddled up for guided trail rides underneath the powerlines that ran along the Harbor Freeway all the way down to Rosecrans Avenue, Cloud started getting hired to provide horses on movie sets. He used the connection to help get a lot of the Black cowboys, who were hanging out at his stable, work in the movies and on television.

Moore and McClain were two of them, so were Bill Terrell and Gene Smith.

Cloud befriended Iron Eyes Cody and Woody Strode. Around the same time that he was nominated for an Academy Award for Best Supporting

Actor as Sonny Corleone in *The Godfather*, James Caan spent time roping and doing some gambling with the boys.

There was plenty of work to keep everyone busy from before sunrise until well after sundown, but they always found time for poker and dice. And drinking. Lots of drinking. Although Nippy sounds like a nickname for a puppy, that was what they called Smith because he was known to nip at his flask all day long. It's not a coincidence that he lost his horse in a dice game with John Davis.

"One Friday night, my father and my uncle [Davis] came home and Saturday morning we had two horses," recalled Jimmy "Bernard" Bright, who started hanging out at El Fig in 1968 with his parents, uncles—Davis and Smith—and cousins, "and so that's how we got started there."

The whole damn cast were likable misfits—Genie Boy, Nard, Nippy, Chuck, Frenchy, Lucky, Mr. London, Foots, Pee Wee, L.T., Legs, Frog, Strawberry, Sugar, Handsome Harley and all the others—but do not mistake them for ne'er-do-wells or even do-gooders. They all learned how to cowboy, but the life lessons—those were learned the hard way.

Payday was Monday, and for some guys, it never went as planned.

Chuck earned his nickname because he came by every afternoon with a chuckwagon. He would extend guys credit and then collect on Mondays. Pee Wee was a hustler and won his share of money shooting dice, and Cloud usually won the rest of his payroll back playing poker.

Cloud used to tell them, "There's a sucker born every minute. Don't be a sucker." And then, recalled Taplet, "He'd try to run game on you and if you let him, he'd do it."

That was the old man's style. He didn't care if it was a new, inexperienced stable hand who made a few bucks shoveling shit or a well-dressed, well-paid pimp from the neighborhood, Tommy Cloud was going to collect. "It sticks with you forever," said Taplet of the lesson he learned a time or two before realizing, "I'm not going to be one of them suckers."

At night's end, everybody—even the suckers—still thought of one another as family.

Much like Taplet had Moore, many of them found something they never had at home. In McClain, Cloud saw the son he never had, and eventually, even McClain became a father figure of sorts for a kid named Kevin Ford.

Those relationships meant something to everyone who found their way to El Fig—C. B. Alexander, Will Dawson, Robert Brown, Fletcher Forte, Chauncey McClain Sr., Johnny Smith, R. C. Jennings, Leo Joseph Jr., Wayne Orme, Alfonso Eland, Johnny Kimbrough, Bright and so many others who made El Fig and The Hill what it once was.

There was also James Isabel, a popular Black rodeo cowboy-turned-country singer, and Hollywood stuntmen like Johnny Ashby, Tony Brubaker, and Bob Minor.

In stark contrast to Edward Vincent, the former mayor of nearby Inglewood who stabled his horses with Cloud for ten years, were the pimps and some local gang members who had an affinity for horses. At the stable, they were not Bloods, Crips, or Pirus. They were not even Black cowboys. They were just cowboys. Or as McClain told the *Los Angeles Times* in July 1989, "Plain cowboys. Regardless of where you come from, we are all cowboys at heart."

Once the horses were in their stalls and the tack was put up, they certainly knew how to get wild and Western once the sun went down. Or, as Bright recalled, "There was a lot going on in the sixties and seventies."

"I wish Lee [McClain] was here," said his longtime girlfriend, Sue Cermak. "Now, he could really tell you some stories."

There are still plenty of stories to be told. Some of them may or may not have happened as they're remembered and some of those have even made it into print. In 1994 a *Los Angeles Times* article included the line, "A motorist could pass that corner daily without knowing that more than two thousand head of horses call it home." There were never even two hundred horses at one time, let alone two thousand, and the neighbors definitely knew they were living and working next door to cowboys and horses.

Like paydays, Friday and Saturday nights were a party for those who were not at a rodeo. There were hayrides for the kids and barbecue for the families, and the men had a little room to their own where Cloud's daughter, Tomi Wright, recalls her father and the others would "be drinking and gambling." When the sun went down, the music got louder and the alley was lit with burn barrels.

Some of the older kids, especially the young cowboys, would stay around, but Cloud knew it was not a place for young girls like his daughter. Wright still remembers the sinking feeling whenever she saw the old Lincoln pull up. "I would hate it when I would see my stepmother come to pick to me up," she still recalls with a noticeable tone of disappointment in her voice, "and it was time for *me* to go."

At home Cloud loved to unwind at the piano with a short shot of Ancient Age whiskey. Then he'd lay back in his recliner and light up one last Marlboro. Some nights, that's where he slept until sunrise, which is probably why the armrest was littered with charred holes from when the cigarettes fell from his lips as he dozed off not long after Wright would pull the boots from her father's feet. As '83 turned to '84, he got sick, and for more than two years, he underwent dialysis treatment. Wright has never forgotten the last time she drove him from the home he built on 112th off Wadsworth in Watts to Daniel Freeman Hospital. He had pneumonia and they kept him.

Cloud died in 1986 and El Fig was never the same.

By the 1990s, the stables were still there, but as the *Times* described, the "horse shanties" were a "recycled collection of old wood" and sheets of tin.

Many of the original cowboys had either died—sadly but not surprisingly to those who knew and loved him, Lee McClain drank himself out of Hollywood before drinking his way to an early death—or fanned out across Los Angeles or moved back to their hometowns. Some had pursued more traditional careers and drifted away from the stables, while others spent their time working at local racetracks. A few were still working in the movie business. "Bennie kept going and he retired from it," said Cermak of Moore's successful career, "where Lee blew it."

Bennie Moore and McClain, who had gone to school with one another and came of age managing El Fig, had not seen each other in quite some time. Taplet, who recently retired from the Los Angeles County Fire Department, would visit McClain during his cancer treatments and during McClain's last days, Taplet called Moore, "You need to get over here and see Lee. He's checking out." They never saw one another in person, but Moore and McClain spoke on the phone one last time.

They had grown up into such different guys from the same neighborhood.

"As I grew older . . . that was a very weak person," said Kimbrough of McClain's inability to control his drinking. "Some of us survived and we made it through. It was God's will for us to make it—me and guys like Kevin

[Ford]. Lee's whole life was right there in front of him. He could have been living up there in Hollywood and gave it all up just to be on The Hill."

By 2000, what was left of the once vibrant collection of stables fell into complete disrepair. City officials hassled those who were still coming around, and in 2012, what was left of The Hill side of the property mysteriously burned to the ground. Three horses and a goat died in the June 17 blaze.

Bright drives by every now and again. So does Wright.

"I go to church out in Compton and sometimes we would drive through there," Wright said, "but it was not the same."

There's a nursey and what Bright describes as a "rubbish or storage yard." Where a few of the stables stood and later collapsed from all the rust, there are abandoned cars and trailers parked there now. The rent horses have been gone for years. So are the tent and the ponies, the goats, the chickens, and, yes, the circus monkeys that Cloud would "cast" in movies.

Today, in place of the tent is a nondescript bar with nude dancing—where the only comparison to the sixties and seventies are whiskey and women—underneath a marquee that reads Rio Gentlemen's Club.

Those day are a distant memory now, and fading.

"I don't call it The Hill no more," said Bright, laughing. "I call it The Sidewalk. There's nothing there."

"It's a sad story," concluded Kimbrough, who built a nice, five-bedroom house on sixty-three acres of land he bought in Texas twenty years ago, "but it's a true story and people need to know about it."

14

Eugene "Cowtown Gene," Jimmy Lee, and Willie Ed Walker with Abraham Morris and John Harp Jr.

Start where you are, with what you have. Make something of it and never be satisfied.

—GEORGE WASHINGTON CARVER

COWTOWN, NEW JERSEY

The Walker brothers grew up in rural New Jersey along Interstate 295 in the shadows of the nearby DuPont plant in Deepwater. There were four brothers and three of them—Eugene, Jimmy Lee, and Willie Ed—were cowboys.

Their family moved to Pilesgrove and lived on the grounds of the Cowtown Rodeo in 1955.

New Jersey was one of the original thirteen colonies and today is the most densely populated state in the country. In addition to mobsters and diners, New Jersey is famously home to the first Indian reservation, site of the first baseball game, first drive-in theater, and home to the oldest running weekly rodeo in the United States—right there in Cowtown.

Eugene was nine, Jimmy Lee was five, and Willie Ed was only two when their daddy, Willie Rogers Walker, started working as a ranch manager for Stoney Harris, but the Walker boys, including brother David, were fearless and tough for their age.

Growing up, all four Walker brothers rode ponies, but when Eugene and Jimmy Lee and then Willie Ed started riding and roping calves and then bulls, David, the second oldest, was the only one who never showed an interest.

"We always called him mama's baby," said Jimmy Lee, who is in his seventies and still lives on the same grounds where he grew up.

Their daily exploits—many of which took place with Howard's two sons: Grant, who currently manages the weekly rodeo, and his younger brother, Andy—were torn from the pages of the Mark Twain classics *The Adventures of Tom Sawyer* and its sequel *Adventures of Huckleberry Finn*, which had been written nearly one hundred years earlier.

They all went to school in nearby Woodstown.

The Walkers and Harrises learned how to rodeo together at Cowtown, which they had to themselves every day. If they weren't getting on calves and steers, they were horseback riding and poking around the fox caves.

Ten miles south, there was an artificial island in the middle of Salem River.

The U.S. Army Corps of Engineers built the island prior to World War I, and later, during World War II, the military used it to keep an eye on the bay in case the Germans tried to send in one of their U-boats. From the end of the war until construction began on the Salem Nuclear Power Plant in 1968, the elder Harris rented the island from the state of New Jersey. Harris planted cornfields and used the pastures for grazing sheep, goats, pigs, and cattle.

In the summertime he would send the boys down to help round up cattle and bring them back up on a barge to be sold at Cowtown's weekly livestock auction on Tuesday nights.

Even though there was no electricity on the island, the Harris family built a cabin. The boys spent many nights down there with lanterns. They cooked and warmed the room with a woodburning stove.

"You couldn't ask for a better childhood," said Jimmy Lee.

"Instead of playing Babe Ruth baseball and football, we were at Cowtown and we were riding ponies and calves. We had more fun growing up there than Huckleberry Finn and Tom Sawyer, and they're fictional characters."

Willie Rogers Walker and his wife were from Florida. He migrated north and found work picking tomatoes.

Eugene "Cowtown Gene" Walker was the oldest. He was born March 17, 1947, followed by David and then Jimmy Lee in 1950. Willie Ed was born in

1953, two years before the Walker family moved less than ten minutes from Sharptown, New Jersey, on the west side of Woodstown, to Pilesgrove on the northeast edge of town, when their father was hired by Stoney Harris as a ranch hand. Later, Stoney's son, Howard Harris, made the elder Walker manager of the ranch at Cowtown Rodeo.

For all the male bravado the Walker men were known for, there also were two sisters—Barbara and Christine—in the family.

The boys were fortunate to grow up in the country, and like their father, they worked for the elder Harris. Mostly, they bailed hay and did other farm chores. They did not grow up poor, but the $100 they earned for the summer was enough to pay for their own school clothes.

But it wasn't about money.

It was about being outside.

The Walkers and the Harris kids rode calves and steers and roped anything within ten feet.

"It was in their blood," said Eugene's widow, Carol Walker. "All the boys, it was in their blood."

Some of their classmates were farm kids and messed around with the 4H Club and Future Farmers of America (FFA), but other than Grant and Andy Harris, none of the other kids around town had an interest in rodeo—except for a pair of cousins, Abraham "Abe" Morris and John Harp Jr.

The first summer Morris begged his mother to let him stay with his older cousins at Cowtown, Jimmy Lee laughed at her response, "No. You ain't going up there with them bad ole Walker boys."

She knew how hard Gene and Jimmy Lee had leaned on Willie Ed, and more importantly, she knew Willie Ed would be just as hard on Abe. Even Jimmy Lee admitted, "Now, Willie Ed had somebody he could pick on." And he did.

All day long he could be heard: "Get on that pony. Get on that horse; it ain't going to hurt you. Come on, get up." When it came to Morris, who chronicled his story in his autobiography *My Cowboy Hat Still Fits*, Willie Ed was relentless.

In 1966, before Gene left for college, Morris was competing in the junior rodeo at Cowtown. He was only ten.

"It was so much fun," Jimmy Lee said. "We were kids and Abraham had three teachers—Gene, myself, and Willie Ed."

Harp was the youngest, but he was right there with them, and Willie Ed looked after him.

Their fathers—John Sr. and Willie Rogers—were half-brothers. Both of them worked for Stoney and Howard Harris and they lived across the street from one another right behind the rodeo arena.

Gene was older and on his way out of town, so that left Jimmy Lee and Willie Ed to pal around with Morris and John Jr. Just as Willie Ed and John Jr. would eventually rodeo together, Morris followed his older cousin out west. At one point, Morris traveled quite a bit with Gene.

Gene was the firstborn, the strongest and the most revered and accomplished. He became the most famous and remains the most talked about of the Walker brothers.

Almost as quickly as he started riding calves when he was eight, Gene rode junior bulls and then big bulls long before any of the boys his own age even dared to think about it. Howard Harris took him in like a son and personally taught Gene how to ride.

As a preteen, he would regularly enter the bull-riding event on Saturday nights and outscore the more experienced men. Gene was not only good, he was a tough son of a bitch. So tough, the elder Harris nicknamed him Cowtown Gene.

"For him to give Gene the name of his family business," said Jimmy Lee, "that tells you just how good he was."

Before he could drive, Gene had a pair of mules—Jack and Jenny—he used to get around until he left Jersey in 1966 for Casper (Wyoming) College on a rodeo scholarship.

Two days before leaving town, he shattered his cheekbone.

Doctors stuffed three yards of gauze up through the roof of his mouth and out his nostril. In describing the dried blood, Gene told NJ.com, "Talk about stink." Gene pulled the first yard of gauze out two inches at a time before asking a college teammate to yank the last two yards out his nostril with one long, continuous pull.

But he still wasn't sure if he was ready to compete.

Years later, Gene told NJ.com he would stand on the first step outside his dorm and jump down. When it didn't hurt, he would move to the second step and then third. When he was able to jump from the fourth step down to the ground without succumbing to the pain felt in his face, he knew he was ready to rejoin the team.

And what a team Casper College had assembled.

Joe Alexander, who went on to become a five-time world champion bareback rider, was on the team, so were Dave Brock and Chris LeDoux. Brock was the 1978 world champion tie-down roper, while LeDoux was the 1976 world champion bareback ride. (LeDoux is, perhaps, best remembered as being labelmates at Capitol Records with Garth Brooks.) Grant Harris was on the team and so was Ivan Danes, who won the saddle bronc title at the College National Finals Rodeo.

Walker became the first African American to qualify for the College National Finals Rodeo.

"Gene was definitely without comparison riding bulls," Jimmy Lee said. "He and Sandy Kirby were arguably the two best bull riders that ever came out of Cowtown."

Kirby was a fourteen-time qualifier at the NFR—nine times as a bull rider and another five times in bareback competition.

Gene's widow, Carol Walker, added, "It was a way of life for my husband. He was a cowboy all the way through."

As a professional rodeo cowboy, Gene rode bulls and bareback horses and worked as a bullfighter until 1975, when he was offered a job at Six Flags Great Adventure in Jackson, New Jersey. They paid him $250 a week to clean stalls and, before the end of the first season, offered him $650 a week to perform jousting stunts as part of a show.

As Gene often joked, after years of trying to ride bulls, they paid him to fall off a horse.

"Shit, that's easy," Jimmy Lee joked.

The stuntmen he was working with offered him a job in Hollywood. Gene turned them down and returned to Great Adventure where he met Carol, whose father worked at Cowtown Rodeo. They married in 1977. He was twenty-seven and she was eighteen.

"It wasn't like dating any of the eighteen-year-old boys," recalled Carol. "He was a man and he treated me like a woman. I fell in love with him and he was always there for me. He took care of me."

They were together for forty years—thirty of those spent in California.

In 1978 he took up the offer to get involved with movies, so he and Carol moved to Los Angeles. He was offered a choice between driving, being a wrangler, or stunt work. He chose to become a wrangler and joined the Screen Actors Guild and the Local No. 399. Originally, Gene was the only Black wrangler in the union.

"He had trouble along the way because he was Black," Carol said. "There were certain people that didn't want to work with him."

But he continued to get work because of his ability.

He amassed more than two hundred film and television credits as a wrangler, animal handler, and, later, as a stuntman.

He trained horses and camels, and director Ron Howard asked Gene if he would teach Tom Cruise and Nicole Kidman how to ride horses for the film *Far and Away*. He taught Michael J. Fox and Mary Steenburgen how to ride for *Back to the Future Part III*. He worked with Will Smith and Halle Berry.

Three-time Academy Award nominee Viggo Mortensen took such a liking to Gene during the filming of *Hidalgo* that he brought a tape recorder to the set. Carol recalled Mortensen telling Gene, "I want you to record all your stories for me. I'd love to write a book about you someday."

Gene's first credit was *Black Stallion* (1979). His last credit was the acclaimed series *Deadwood* in the early 2000s.

For a long time, Gene and Carol—who had two children, Jason and Deana—lived on a ranch forty-five miles north of LA in Agua Dulce. He named his ranch "Little Bit Acres" in honor of his youngest brother, Willie Ed, who was known as "Little Bit."

Unfortunately, illness—lupus and chronic obstructive pulmonary disease—damaged the nerve endings in Gene's fingers and the tips turned black.

Gene and Carol returned home to New Jersey. Son Jason moved back east about a year before his father passed, on May 3, 2014, and took a job at Cowtown, where he works alongside his uncle Jimmy Lee.

"I can't believe he's a cowboy," said Carol of her son, who previously worked as a stuntman. His most notable credit was *Scorpion King* starring Dwayne "The Rock" Johnson, but Carol noted three generations of Walker men are naturally drawn to the cowboy lifestyle. "It's something they've got."

Decades before Jason followed in his father's footsteps, so too did Jimmy Lee and Willie Ed, along with their cousins Abe Morris and John Harp Jr. "What Gene did, we did," said Jimmy Lee, but he admitted it was his younger brother who "was probably the most talented of us all."

But it did not start out that way.

Willie Ed had it rough. His two older brothers, especially Gene, picked on him and beat him up until, eventually, he outgrew them. By the time he reached his twenties, Willie Ed was five feet eleven, 190 pounds, and had become an ass-kicking steer wrestler.

For years, he held the arena record of 3.5 seconds at Cowtown.

"He could do it all," recalled Jimmy Lee, who said his brother competed in all three rough stock events—bareback, bull, and saddle bronc—in addition to steer wrestling. Hell, Willie Ed was a better team roper than most. He just didn't care for it.

That said, anyone who was around Cowtown in the 1960s, including Jimmy Lee, "copied Gene."

Jimmy Lee started riding full-size bulls in 1968—a year before he graduated from Woodstown High School—and, later, fell in love with bareback riding. He started his bullfighting career when Howard Harris offered him $50 to get in the barrel. Having made $100 as a ranch hand all summer, he did not hesitate.

And that is how he began his clowning career.

Jimmy Lee used an old metal barrel wrapped with worn-out car tires on the outside and just a pair of ropes inside to hold himself in place. There was no padding. He banged up his elbows and skinned up his knees and shins.

It was a crude way to make a living.

"I thought, 'This is not for me,'" recalled Jimmy Lee, who spent a year as a barrel man before stepping out and becoming a bullfighter until 1998. He loved the thrill of the Cowtown crowd whenever he made a good save. "That was real rewarding."

Unlike Gene and pro rodeo legends Sandy Kirby, Bobby DelVecchio, and, later, Abe Morris, who headed west, Willie Ed and Jimmy Lee stayed behind.

Jimmy Lee graduated on a Wednesday, and on Thursday morning, he started working at DuPont, which started as a gunpowder plant in the 1800s and, decades later, became the world's fourth-largest chemical plant.

At the end of his shift on Friday, they paid him $98 for his first two days.

"I was hooked," Jimmy Lee admitted. "Hook, line, and sinker."

He added, "In this area, working at DuPont was just like being a doctor or a lawyer—very prestigious job."

Perhaps, but after growing up outdoors, he felt as if he was "stuck inside." Jimmy Lee worked on the fifth floor, two hundred feet below the Delaware Memorial Bridge. He could look out the windows above him and watch the traffic go by. He rotated shifts and unless he was working from 4:00 p.m. to midnight, he could still rodeo locally.

He spent nine years there.

Unlike his brother David, who made a career at DuPont and retired from there, Jimmy Lee quit. He was only twenty-eight when they offered voluntary layoffs to anyone with five or more years of service.

"I hated that job," Jimmy Lee. "I just couldn't take it anymore."

He hit the rodeo trail. It was Jimmy Lee, his lifelong friend T. J. Hawkins, and, as Garth Brooks would one day sing, "an old worn-out tape of Chris LeDoux."

Even in 1978, it was not easy being Black.

"We had to win by ten to lose by two," said Jimmy Lee, who points the finger squarely at the judges. It only takes one bad judge to keep a man from winning. But on a Fourth of July trip to Oklahoma, things got a whole lot more serious than being cheated out of a few points.

Jimmy Lee and three others were stopped at a red light when another truck going in the opposite direction pulled up alongside theirs. A man they never met motioned for Jimmy Lee to roll his window down and casually said, "You niggers better get out of town before dark."

"Holy shit," Jimmy Lee thought.

That was the first time he had ever experienced such a blatant act of racism. None of them quit, much less left town before the rodeo. Instead, situations like that one only made Black cowboys like Jimmy Lee mentally stronger, which ultimately gave him a competitive advantage in the arena.

"We had to be a lot better than average," Jimmy Lee explained. "They made us that way. They made monsters out of us. If you use racism as a crutch, you can never excel. You can't be blaming them for everything that goes wrong. In the beginning, they wouldn't let us win, but before it was all said and done, we dominated. We put Cowtown on the map, and the Black community was proud of us. We were doing something other than being gangsters on the corner."

The Walker story started with Willie Rogers and his half-brother John Harp Sr. It continued with Gene, Jimmy Lee, Willie Ed, John Harp Jr., and Abe Morris. It endures with Gene's only son, Jason, but without Gene, their story might have never been told, and in some respects, the final chapter was Gene's death.

"He was my hero," Jimmy Lee said. "He was all of our heroes."

Gene was a proud man. He was a great husband and father and an even better grandfather. He was amazing, but not perfect. Whenever they argued, Carol would walk away.

"Come over here," Gene would call out.

Carol would be so mad she didn't want to talk with him, but she could never help herself and would always ask why. Gene, who liked to drink a little too much, a little too often, would walk up behind his wife, wrap his arms around her and just hold on until she could feel the love.

Ultimately, he was strong enough to quit drinking when he knew he had to and had not touched a drop of alcohol in more than ten years before he died.

"There were a lot of ups and downs, but believe me, I'd give anything to have him come back and fight with me," admitted Carol, and after a dramatic pause she concluded, "We had our moments. I love him."

15

Thyrl and Mike Latting

The whole world opened to me when I learned how to read.
—MARY MCLEOD BETHUNE

CHICAGO, ILLINOIS

A roughneck boomtown like Casper, Wyoming, whose economy ebbed and flowed with the demand for oil-and-gas drilling, could not have been any more different than a cosmopolitan cityscape like Chicago, Illinois, especially for an eighteen-year-old, first-year college student making the trip west on a rodeo scholarship.

Casper is the second-largest town in the state, and by Wyoming standards, it too is a metropolis of sorts with just over fifty-eight thousand people.

Back in August 1970, when Mike Latting drove to town in a road-worn pickup truck pulling a trailer with two horses, there were barely thirty-nine thousand people living there. Even locals described Casper as a remote, wind-blown town a hundred miles past the middle of nowhere.

Latting arrived a few weeks before classes started.

He thought he was the first Black cowboy to receive a rodeo scholarship from Casper College, but was surprised to learn he was the second. A long-legged, lanky young man named Gene Walker from Pilesgrove, New Jersey, had been recruited two years earlier. Cowtown Gene, as he was known from coast to coast, wore the biggest hat he could find and had a mustache just as big to go with it.

At the onset of the seventies, they might have been the only two Black kids in Casper—had it not been for a few African American roughnecks working in the oil fields that outlined the city limits.

Once you got past those cruddy oil and gas wells, the scenery stretched as far as the eye could see. The clear blue skies made Latting literally feel as though he was sitting on top of the world.

Picturesque mountains framed the wide-open spaces. The air was fresh. There were plenty of rodeos, cowboys, and cowgirls. It was also rugged. Winter months were unusually long and cold—even for a kid from the suburban Chicagoland area. The first word Latting used to describe his memory of Casper was *windy*, an ironic twist of fate for someone who moved there from a place famously known as the Windy City.

"I pull into this parking lot and there wasn't a lot of cars there," Latting recalled. "I stepped out of the pickup and my hat blew across the parking lot. I've never seen it since. I mean, wind blowing one hundred miles an hour. Snow forever. It was probably the best thing that could've happened to me."

Mike Latting was the oldest of three children and the only son born to Harriet (Brown) and Thyrl Latting.

The patriarch of the Latting family, Thyrl, was born June 10, 1932, on Chicago's west side and raised in nearby Robbins. He loved watching the early Westerns of the 1940s every Saturday afternoon. The more he saw, the more he wanted to be a cowboy.

Inspired by the Hollywood cowboys he saw up on the silver screen—Gary Cooper, Henry Fonda, Tex Ritter, Roy Rogers, Gene Autry, and John Wayne—or performing at the annual rodeo in downtown Chicago, Thyrl spent entire summers with his uncle, who taught him how to ride and care for horses. His grandmother gave him the $60 he needed to buy his first horse, Tappy. He took a job in the local onion fields for five cents an hour and rode bucking horses for $5 a head at small Wild West shows to pay for hay and feed.

"Nobody ever told me I couldn't be a cowboy," he told *American Cowboy* in 1996.

A shade under five feet eight inches, Thyrl was the perfect size and had the strength and grit to ride bulls and broncs. At seventeen he forged his mother's signature and entered his first rodeo. He was hooked.

And so began a thirteen-year professional career—mostly in the North and Midwest—as a bull rider and a steer wrestler.

"Being a Negro in rodeo can be an asset because people pay attention to you. But, *boy*, you better be good," he told *Ebony* magazine in 1964.

Oftentimes Thyrl was the only Black rodeo cowboy competing locally, but he was good. Real good. When asked about any racism he faced at rodeos, Thyrl told the *Chicago Tribune*, "The [white] cowboys were never a problem. The problem was getting a place to stay or buying a meal. Even in Illinois you'd run into that."

Thyrl and Harriet met at a horseshow held at the Boots and Saddle Ranch, in 1948, and married three years later, on September 29, 1951. They raised their family in Robbins, a suburban village in Cook County that fell on hard economic times. Mike was their oldest child. JoAnne, who was three years younger, died at thirty-three from sickle cell anemia. Tracy, a barrel racer, is twelve years younger than Mike.

"With family responsibilities, I no longer like to take chances," Thyrl told *Ebony*, "and a good cowboy has to take chances."

He gave up competing and often worked multiple jobs to support his family and *their* rodeo pursuits. The long hours the elder Latting worked to provide for the family did not go unnoticed. "I understood the sacrifices my dad made for us," Mike recalled.

Black cowboys might not have been common in the Chicago area, but that did not keep Thyrl from starting Latting's Rodeo School in 1961. He taught farmers, sales reps, teachers, mail carriers, and secretaries how to run barrels and wrestle steers. They were mostly white. Every now and again a few classmates from school would ask Mike and his sisters about coming over. Most of them were more curious than they were serious about rodeo.

In 1964 Thyrl started Latting Rodeo Company and produced his first event—a fundraiser for the Robbins Fire Department—right in the family's backyard. It was not an all-Black rodeo. It was for everybody. It wasn't until his father went to an all-Black rodeo in Oklahoma that Mike, who wasn't even a teenager at the time, became aware of Black rodeo cowboys.

He dreamed of one day becoming a professional rodeo cowboy.

"It's not that I couldn't have done anything else," said Mike. "The option was always there, but it just happened that I really enjoyed it and was relatively good at it."

He was also a good student with aspirations of attending college.

Mike ran track and played football his first couple of years in high school, before focusing on rodeo fulltime and caring for their livestock every day after school. When Thyrl got home from working as a shop teacher, he would make time to buck broncs and work as a ranch hand so his son could practice steer wrestling.

Unfortunately, where the Lattings lived, there were no high school rodeos.

In the 1960s the National Little Britches Association did not have any events nearby. So at twelve, Mike began riding full-size bulls, and by fourteen, he was riding broncs at semipro events against men in their twenties and thirties.

He was unfazed by the age of the men he was competing against, mostly because he won more often than not. Mike said, "In our family, if you're going to do it, you give it all you've got. That's just kind of the way we were raised."

Near the end of his senior year at Marist High School, he was competing at an open rodeo in Iowa. Mike had just gotten off a bareback horse when John Sloan, who was attending Casper College on a rodeo scholarship, walked up and introduced himself. Sloan asked Latting, "Are you interested in going to college?"

Truth be told, Mike was interested in talking to anyone who might offer him a scholarship—even if it was twelve hundred miles west of Chicago.

Dale Stiles was the legendary rodeo coach at Casper College. He led the Thunderbirds to four consecutive national titles—from 1963 to 1966. Based on Sloan's good word and the reputation Mike had made for himself. Stiles offered the Illinois native a two-year scholarship.

Mike headed west to rodeo and major in physical education.

He was replacing the poetic bareback rider Chris LeDoux, who won the PRCA world title in 1975. LeDoux is best remembered for his raucous rock 'n' roll–like energy as a country singer, whose live performances inspired the massive success of Garth Brooks.

In hindsight, Mike said he was unaffected by any racism that might have existed in Casper, where less than 1 percent of the population was Black. Mike and Gene Walker had their teammates and Coach Stiles to look out for them.

"You're always going to have some people that [say], 'Well, he's Black, he's this, he's that,'" Mike said. "The one thing that I took away from Wyoming is that a man was judged on his character, and that leaves it all up to you. You carry yourself a certain way. You be a certain type of individual, and then you will get the respect.

"You let your talent speak for itself."

After two years in Casper, his talent led him to Southern Colorado State College in Pueblo, which is located thirty miles south of Colorado Springs. In his final two years of college, Mike was the bareback champion in the Central Rocky Mountain region, as both a junior and senior. He was also the regional champion in bull riding as a senior.

Money wasn't always easy to come by on the rodeo trail, and Mike admits there were some lean miles logged on the road traveling from one rodeo to another.

"I'd be out on the road and not wining much," he remembered, "call home and say, 'Well Dad, I've been winning a lot, but I haven't got paid yet, and I need to buy a suitcase—so I can put all my money in it. Can you send me some cash for a suitcase?'"

Without fail, the elder Latting's answer was always, "You gotta talk to your mom." He said it every time.

Not one to let her son's wallet go empty, Harriet would always ask, "How much do you need?"

Mike followed Thyrl's dream of being a rodeo cowboy and then worked side by side with him at Latting Rodeo Company. Mike managed M&M Ranch—a one-hundred-acre spread fifty miles south of Chicago—since graduating from college and still manages the same ranch today. Together, the father-and-son team produced twenty to thirty weekend and summertime rodeos a year with each cash payout reaching $20,000.

Throughout much of that time, they were also both educators during the week.

Thyrl came to the profession as a second career, but Mike put in forty years as an educator. He primarily served schools in which the entire student body came from families living below the poverty limit. He sees himself as fortunate for having an opportunity to spend a lifetime doing two things he loves most—rodeo and turning kids around.

"In those two fields, I was able to be a very happy person," he said.

One particular student he impacted was a Chicago native named Mike Moore. After working for the Lattings for a couple of summers, Moore also went on to rodeo at Casper College and then the University of Wyoming. As a pro, he is one of the few Black rodeo cowboys to qualify for the NFR and one of only eight to have done so as a PRCA bull rider.

Moore understood that Mike and his father, Thyrl, were *real* cowboys. Never mind Black cowboys. Thyrl set out to change that. Or at least try.

After retiring as an educator, in 1990, the elder Latting started the Thyrl Latting Rodeo Spectacular, which included dramatic re-creations and rodeo events designed to preserve the legacy of Black cowboys.

Until then, for those who relied on history books and Hollywood, it seemed as if the Black race—as far as the American West was concerned—had all but disappeared after the Civil War. "You'd never see a Black in a Western movie then, or, if you did, it was only as a joke," Thyrl told *American Cowboy*.

The idea of producing Friday matinees for elementary-aged children appealed to the Lattings and the years they had spent advocating on behalf of getting a public education. Tributes to Bass Reeves, Bill Pickett and the impact of Black cowboys in the Old West provided attendees "near-forgotten history" lessons.

"They were heroes too," Thyrl told the *Chicago Tribune*.

Thyrl Latting was involved in rodeo for more than sixty years of his life.

He produced and supplied bucking horses—Big Enough, Phoenix, and Sunset—and bucking bulls for rodeos throughout the Midwest, including "The World's Toughest Rodeo," which was held in Chicago, Washington DC, Atlanta, Toronto, and Madison Square Garden in New York City.

He suffered a stroke a few years before his death in 2013. He was slower and physically limited, but he still had day-to-day operational duties on the ranch. When the books opened and rodeo contestants called to enter, it was

Thyrl who took the phone calls. Mike made sure it was his dad who still signed all the contracts and wrote his name on every check.

"That was his job," said Mike, pausing to collect his composure. "I owed that to him, and he did it up until a year before he passed."

For Mike, it was a sign of respect.

It was a son saying thank you to his father.

If Thyrl was anything, he was a family man, and by God, they bled together. They sweat together. They cried together. They worked together. They laughed together. It did not come as a surprise that family entertainment was the cornerstone of any Latting-produced rodeo, and that tradition continues.

Thyrl was eighty when he passed away. He died having never told his son he made a good ride or did a good job. That was for someone else. As the patriarch of the family, he believed it was his place to tell his children what they could improve upon in order to do better the next time. As a young hardworking man or an old proud man, Thyrl was not the back-slapping, high-fiving type.

But there was no doubt in anyone's mind that the elder Latting loved his family until his last breath.

16

Charlie Reno (aka Jesse C. R. Hall)

Either you deal with what is the reality, or you can be sure that the reality is going to deal with you.

—ALEX HALEY

VICKSBURG, MISSISSIPPI, AND NEW YORK, NEW YORK

Halfway between Memphis and New Orleans is Vicksburg, Mississippi. It was there that Jesse "Charlie Reno" Hall was born July 24, 1943—eighty years to the month after the Union Army seized control of the small town located along the east side of the Mississippi River.

Eight decades following what is widely chronicled as a key turning point in the American Civil War and the emergence of Maj. Gen. Ulysses S. Grant, life in Mississippi was no place for a Black family with aspirations, much less a single mother raising eight children.

Penola Hall did not hesitate in packing up her family and moving more than twelve hundred miles northeast to New York City after the death of her husband, who long before she left Mississippi had already established himself as an absent father.

She felt like there was no hope for her and, more importantly, no future for her children beyond sharecropping and tenant farming in the cotton fields had they stayed in Vicksburg.

"There was no way she could survive down there in the 1940s," said Hall, pausing before adding, "in that environment."

The *environment* he spoke of was racism.

The Halls were part of the second migration of African Americans from the South to the North, which took place between 1940 and 1970 because of a lack of economic opportunities afforded to Blacks. The Hall family was just one among the millions of Black people on the move who proved to be important precursors to the civil rights movement of the 1950s and '60s, when African Americans fought for racial equality nationwide.

When they arrived in New York City, Penola and her children lived with her sister. She quickly found employment and worked two, sometimes three, jobs to provide a better opportunity for the kids.

Charlie, the sixth of eight siblings, was five years old the first time he asked his mother about his father.

"You don't need to know nothing about your father," she replied.

And before he could even ask about why they left Mississippi, Penola added, "You don't need to know nothing about Vicksburg, Mississippi, so don't ask me no more."

Charlie never spoke of his father again. He did not even ask his older siblings what they remember about him. All he knows is that his father was a gas station attendant and not much else—not even his name.

"I don't know if my father died because he was hung"—whites in Clarke County, due east of Vicksburg, bragged in *Time* magazine about a bridge they kept in the 1940s "for stringing up niggers"—or if he died by some other means, because Charlie honored his mother's wishes.

Penola passed away in 1998 without ever saying another word on the subject.

"That lady was the toughest lady I ever known in my life—ever—because she sacrificed all the hurt and pain she endured by not letting us get involved with that," said Charlie, who after becoming a husband, father, and grandfather had gained the wisdom to realize, "she was trying to convince us to have a life without revenge."

Penola did not allow her children, especially her youngest, to be affected by negativity. She taught them to think positive and to be a force of change.

Having "eliminated the pressure" of living in Mississippi, all eight of Penola's children—Theresa, Johnny, Josielee, Catherine, Rose, Charlie, Geneva, and Nathan—grew up to experience success in their own ways. Some went to college. Others own businesses. All of them became homeowners—a simple right their mother never even dared to dream of.

Those cumulative successes, Charlie believes, were "because we did not have that mountain to climb over."

No, they never had to worry about life in Mississippi, but growing up in Manhattan had its own obstacles and issues.

There were five different gangs in Charlie's neighborhood. As long as he stayed between East 96th and East 103rd Streets, he was safe. Venture above or below those boundaries and Hall would risk getting his ass kicked by the Dragons, the Viceroys, the Red Wings, the Enchanters or the Untouchables.

And Brooklyn, well, it was off-limits.

At the time, kids his age from tough neighborhoods like Bedford-Stuyvesant and Fort Greene had an image of being *rank*. "We would not go into Brooklyn," Charlie recalled. "There were some bad-asses over there."

No one went anywhere alone after dark, and of course, Penola was tough on her children. "We didn't get involved with none of that nonsense," Charlie said.

On the eve of his high school graduation, Charlie began riding horses at New Kentucky Riding Academy. He and his high school classmates had spent the day boating and were driving home when they exited the Pelham Parkway in the Bronx and decided to go horseback riding.

Charlie went back every weekend. At the stable, no one cared where anyone else was from or what color his or her skin was. A person either enjoyed riding horses or they did not, and Charlie loved horses. He felt like he took to it naturally.

His friends thought differently, and so did his mother.

"Why are you doing that?" she asked. "That's a white man's sport."

Penola did not give her son a chance to explain himself.

"They're not going to give you a fair shake," he recalled his mother saying. "They may even kill you down there."

But Charlie had the last say in the matter.

"Well, we'll find out," he declared.

Charlie, who was now living in Harlem, would eventually meet other Black cowboys from the East Coast. Bud Bramwell and Steve Robinson were from Stamford, Connecticut, and in 1963, he started tagging along on Saturday nights when they drove down to the weekly Cowtown (New Jersey) Rodeo.

That's where Charlie met the Walker brothers—Jimmy Lee, Willie Ed, and Cowtown Gene—and their cousin Abraham Morris. Charlie would eventually start competing with them after he bought his pro rodeo permit.

He was nineteen and 130 pounds the first time Gene DiLorenzo, an accomplished steer wrestler from the 1950s, who was born and raised in the Bronx, coaxed him into jumping off a horse onto a steer. In 1965, the same year he entered his first rodeo, Charlie bought his first horse. He boarded him at Pelham Bay Park Academy for $100 a month, which he paid with the $33 a week he was making from bagging groceries. It seemed like a lot, but it was better use of his money than spending a $20 fee every time he rode someone else's horse for a couple of hours.

He befriended two other cowboys with the name Charlie, so each man took the name of his primary horse. That's when "Jesse Hall" became professionally known as "Charlie Reno." Nowadays, friends and family know him as everything from Charlie Reno to C. R. Hall to Jesse Hall—it just depends on when or how you met him. On social media, he's Jesse C.R. Hall.

"I've never met anyone who didn't like him," said Robinson of the friendship he's fostered with Charlie for more than fifty years, "or had anything bad to say about him."

In the early days of competing, Charlie was self-taught. He learned from watching others and became known from one Saturday to the next for his spectacular buck-offs.

Eventually, he cobbled together $300 and headed down to Austin, Texas, for a bareback-riding clinic. He started winning and, in 1967, became an accomplished bareback rider. He credits the late Fred Davies for being responsible "for my rodeo career." Davies was born in Connecticut, served his country in the U.S. Marines, and then moved to Texas, where he proved himself to be an all-around cowboy that rode bulls, steer wrestled, and roped calves. Charlie said Davies gave him the confidence and inspiration to reach his goals whenever he began to doubt himself or felt ignored because of the color of his skin.

Like so many other Black rodeo cowboys in the 1960s and '70s, Charlie was not always scored fairly. Despite his low marks, he stayed focused. His goal was to ride well enough that, years later, those who cheated him would be reminded of the time "that Black guy came out here and rode the shit out of that bareback horse."

Much like he dealt with growing up without a father, Charlie made the most of his situation, gathered himself up, and stayed out on the rodeo trail, even though it wasn't always a kind place to be.

"You're never going to get a win by quitting," Charlie said. "You can win if you can hang in there."

Right about the time he started winning, Charlie found himself in Boley, Oklahoma, where he discovered an all-Black rodeo for the first time. Boley is due east of Oklahoma City and not far from Okmulgee, where Roy LeBlanc and twenty-one other Black rodeo cowboys had been producing an all-Black rodeo since 1956. Charlie befriended Roy's sons, Clarence and Kenneth, and often competed with them. He also met and befriended Myrtis Dightman.

However, Charlie encountered an entirely different experience at an event two hours south of Boley, in Durant, Oklahoma, where he was one of only a couple of Black cowboys entered. The others knew better than to compete in Durant.

During the opening ceremonies, a local priest blessed the cowboys, wished them good luck and health, and then ended his prayer with, "God bless everybody, even some people we don't want here." Naturally, he was referring to Charlie and the other Black cowboys. Years later, Charlie recalled the experience in a 1999 interview with the *Asbury Park (NJ) Press*.

"It made me feel kind of uneasy," he told them. "You could see the hatred there. You could almost reach out and touch the ignorance."

Like so many others—before and since—Charlie overcame the bigotry and racism. Unfortunately, injuries continued to set him back, and eventually, a broken neck prematurely ended his career.

It was June 1, 1968, and Charlie, twenty-five, was back in New Jersey. It was a Saturday night. He was at Cowtown competing among his friends when he drew a horse named Dark Moments—a bareback horse "that was just too much for me."

It was yet another spectacular buck-off for Charlie, only this time, he never stood up. He never waved to the crowd. Instead, he laid motionless on the arena dirt.

They transported him to Salem County Memorial Hospital. Charlie had survived the accident, but the outlook was grim. Doctors feared he could be paralyzed. A specialist was flown in and Charlie spent five hours in surgery, eight months in traction with a halo screwed into his skull and two years rehabbing from having three cervical vertebrae—3, 4, and 5—fused together.

During his recovery, he started mentoring Barry Moore, whose father, Arthur, a longshoreman from nearby Newark, New Jersey, had unsuccessfully pursued the dream of bringing all-Black rodeos to the East Coast. Together, they went through rigorous weight training and miles of jogging through the neighborhood in anticipation of Charlie's fulltime return to rodeo in 1972.

Less than a year later, in 1973, at a rodeo in Fort Worth, Texas, Charlie broke his wrist in three places and gave up rodeo for good—or so he thought.

He married his first wife, traded his horses for a motorcycle, and went back to working in a grocery store. The fact that he kept his memberships current with the RCA, IRA, and the American Rodeo Association (ARA)—all three of which eventually added Pro to their names in front of Rodeo—should have been an indication that it was only a matter of time before Charlie would be back on the rodeo trail.

Six years later, in 1978, at thirty-five years of age—which is *old* for a bareback rider—Charlie made another return. In 1979 he was within five events of claiming the bareback title when a bull fell on him and broke his foot.

At his age and with the impact of all the mounting injuries over the years, another return seemed improbable. Yet he and Moore traveled 100,000 miles to as many as sixty rodeos—primarily ARA events on the East Coast—in '78 and '79 and again in 1980.

While other cowboys in Charlie's same boots might have focused on steer wrestling—"an old-timer's event" because they rarely got hurt—Charlie carried on. If he earned $25,000 in competitions, he spent $27,000 in expenses, and that still meant spending a majority of the nights sleeping in the back of his Chevy pickup.

But the sacrifice paid off. In 1980 Charlie not only returned to bareback riding, but he also became the first Black cowboy to win the ARA bareback title and an all-around championship.

Finally, he could retire on his own terms and feel satisfied with the outcome of his career.

By 1981 he was the night manager at a supermarket, and within two years, he was working with the Urban Western Riding Program, a nonprofit in the South Bronx that used horseback riding to keep city kids—ages eight to eighteen—off the streets and out of trouble.

Charlie was part of an event celebrating Black History Month at Public School 144 and played a significant role in the Urban Western Riding Program's first rodeo at the Kingsbridge Armory in July of that same year. *Ascent* magazine estimated twenty thousand were in attendance (a figure that seems to have been exaggerated by the writer of the article), but it led to three more events—Coney Island, a return to the Bronx, and Bridgeport, Connecticut—in 1984.

Dr. George Blair, then chair of the board of directors for *Ascent*, reached out to Charlie, and Blair's own dream of forming Black World Championship Rodeo became a reality.

And so began Jesse "Charlie Reno" Hall's career as a rodeo producer and a lifelong ambassador of the sport.

17

Steve Robinson

Black people don't have an accurate idea of their history, which has been either suppressed or distorted.

—KAREEM ABDUL-JABBAR

NEW HAVEN, CONNECTICUT, AND BECKET, MASSACHUSETTS

Steve Robinson was born to be a cowboy.

His mother, Catherine, gave birth to him on July 7, 1956, but Steve's journey to becoming a rodeo cowboy and horse trainer was made possible fifty years earlier.

That's when his paternal great-grandfather, William Foster Robinson, purchased 160 acres of land just outside of Becket, Massachusetts, for $900 in cash (less than $26,000 by today's standards).

The elder Robinson had been diagnosed with black lung disease, which was common among coal miners. William had cleaned coal-burning furnaces in Naugatuck, Connecticut. He bought the land in search of a place to live where he could breathe fresh air. As kids, his cousin worked as a cook at a YMCA summer camp in the Berkshire County, so he was familiar with the area.

When they arrived in 1906, the Robinsons became the first African American family to own their own home in the county.

Two years later, William became the first man in town—regardless of color—to own a Model T, America's first full-size economy car. Although it only featured a twenty horse-power engine with a top speed of barely forty miles per hour, it was a lot of car for the old man to handle.

One afternoon, while driving through town, a man stepped out in front of him. William's first instinct was to holler, "Whoa," as if he were bringing a horse-drawn wagon to a stop. The earliest Model Ts did not have a modern braking system. The right foot pedal was connected to the transmission, which stopped the back wheels from turning.

William never even got his foot on the brake, until it was too late. The man was dead.

Though it was unrelated, not long after his first and only car accident, William died.

His widow was left to raise their nine children, so the state of Connecticut paid her to take in several orphans to supplement her otherwise meager income. Upon his great-grandmother's death, it was discovered that she did not leave a will, which meant her nine biological children were all equal heirs to the farmland and the family logging business.

Prior to his death, William had owned teams of horses that he used to help clear timber for the roads that were being built back in Connecticut. He made more money from the state for supplying the horses than he did from the manpower it took to lead them in and out of the forest. William had always felt he bred, raised, and trained harder-working horses than anyone else. It's a pride his great-grandson, Steve Robinson, feels today.

Steve's grandfather, Franklin Foster Robinson, worked as a logger and, like his father, William, raised a team of logging horses, so he assumed the responsibility of looking after the day-to-day operations of the farm and the business.

After reconnecting with his estranged wife, Marie, Franklin was able to buy out his siblings' shares of the farmland in Becket.

A short time later, Franklin died, followed by Marie, who left the land to their son Bill and his wife, Catherine. The couple were living in New Haven, Connecticut, and would take their two sons, Steve and his brother, to Massachusetts for the summers. They did not have a horse of their own, so Steve, who was twelve at the time, and his brother would rent one from a local horse trainer.

The next summer, in June 1968, a month shy of his thirteenth birthday, Steve rented another horse and paid for a subscription to *Western Horseman* magazine. He would read every single word from cover to cover and then lay the magazine atop a fifty-five-gallon drum with two rocks to keep the pages from blowing closed.

He would read the columns detailing how to train a horse and was surprised to learn "it kind of worked." A month later, when the owner came to check on his horse, he was amazed at how well the young kid had done with the animal and asked Steve to come work with him at a nearby camp to "help with these horses that are getting sour."

Locals knew Steve as "that kid from Connecticut" who was "crazy enough" to get on hard-to-handle horses. "And that's how I got started in the horse deal," Steve recalled.

Steve was born and raised in New Haven.

His mother was a licensed nurse and also started a Tiny Tots program, which years later inspired Steve to mentor troubled kids. Catherine was known as a feminist and happened to be friends with former vice-presidential candidate Joe Lieberman. Steve remembers Lieberman visiting their house when his mother ran for alderman. She eventually was the first person of color to serve on the board of the New Haven Community Foundation, and later President Lyndon B. Johnson invited her to Washington for a civil rights event.

Steve's father was a policeman on the midnight shift. Despite his father and grandfather having each taken pride in raising the strongest team of logging horses, Bill had absolutely no interest in horses. None whatsoever. Growing up, Bill's father, Franklin, owned a small dairy farm and Bill was expected to work with the cows before and after school. He hated the experience. Steve, on the other hand, was less like his father and more like his grandfather and great-father before that.

From an early age, Steve was fascinated with horses.

"The first time I saw somebody rope, I knew that was what I wanted to do," Steve said. "I thought that was just poetry."

His passion for horses was fostered during the summers he spent in Becket with his grandfather. Franklin shared stories about his own father, along with some experiences he had growing up and a few when he got older.

One, which may or may not be a tall tale, involved a horse named John who "could pull any log out of the woods." One day, Franklin got a call from a friend whose team of horses was stuck down in some swampy land. Franklin took John into the woods and they pulled the entire team of horses—and the load of timber it was pulling—out of the mud.

His grandfather always told Steve, "If you're going to have a horse, have a good one."

Franklin was beloved by nearly everyone and what little racism he encountered in the Northeast, "he fought with humor, because he could get you to laugh at how stupid you were."

"I thought, this works better than screaming and yelling. I saw it firsthand," said Steve, and it became a lesson that has served him well throughout his life.

Though Franklin tried to introduce his son to horses, he never really did the same with his grandson. In an article published March 22, 2012, Steve told the *Berkshire (MA) Eagle* that his mother really was the facilitator of his dreams.

She would drive Steve and his brother across town to the Yale Armory—a short distance from Yale University—where the polo team used to practice. The two boys would clean stalls, and in return they could ride with the team after practice if they would help brush down the horses afterward.

"We'd hobnob with the Yale guys," Steve said, "and they realized, 'Hey, these kids can ride.'"

That's when Catherine knew her sons, especially Steve, were serious about becoming great horsemen. She put a pair of Texas Tan saddles on layaway, and by Christmastime, she had them paid for, even though neither boy had a horse of his own.

Near the end of the summer of 1972, sixteen-year-old Steve reached out on his own to Morton Builders for an estimate on what it would cost to build a relatively small, thirty-by-thirty-foot barn behind their house in Massachusetts. On the day the contractor showed up to give the Robinsons an estimate, Bill answered the door and had no idea what the guy was talking about.

When the contractor explained to the elder Robinson why he was at his home, Bill turned away and yelled for his son, "*Steeeeeeven.*"

"I knew I was in trouble," Steve recalled.

He was embarrassed by his father's reaction. He understood that his father thought his so-called passion for horses might be just a phase—even though it had been four years—but Steve had saved his own money. He had worked all summer washing dishes and training horses and had $1,850 in the bank.

The next day, Steve went to the public library and found a book detailing how to build a pole barn. He read it from cover to cover in one sitting.

Steve met an old logger friend of his grandfather, who was running a lumber mill. He charged the teen $1,800 for materials, but that did not include a roof. Steve's mother told him not to worry about it. She talked with Bill and they ordered a roof from the *Sears 1972 Suburban, Farm and Ranch Catalog*.

In one of the last great memories he has with his aging grandfather, Steve and Franklin built the barn together. All the local old-timers would come by, and the moment they saw it was built without a foundation, each one of them said it would not hold up a full year.

Almost fifty years later, it is still standing.

It's another reason Steve sees the family's property in Massachusetts as "a magical place." Back in Connecticut, Steve was sixteen when he met Bud Bramwell, Billy Wilds, and Charlie Reno.

Bramwell and Wilds had gone west to rodeo for Oklahoma State University before returning home. Bramwell, an all-around cowboy who could rope and ride, had a roping arena in his backyard, despite living in suburban Norwalk.

Steve modeled himself after Bramwell.

He calf- and team-roped and did some steer wrestling, but never rode bulls. "I didn't have that in me," said Steve, whose knees are torn up enough from steer wrestling. "I didn't have no desire to go to the hospital when the rodeo was over."

A couple of years later, it was Wilds who took Steve under his wing. They started with ARA events in the Northeast. When he wasn't at a rodeo, Wilds made a handsome living shoeing horses and was known for always having cash in his pocket. He fronted the money Steve needed to rodeo in the PRCA—"a lot of it"—and together they headed west.

Steve had never crossed the mighty Mississippi River until he and Wilds went to Oklahoma and Texas. He met Cleo Hearn, another Black rodeo cowboy who attended OSU, and a Native American roper named Sonny Victor, who once missed qualifying for the NFR by one spot in the world standings.

One issue with competing in the PRCA, especially for a young Black cowboy from the East Coast with a lack of funds, was the PRCA did not allow its members to compete in any non-PRCA-sanctioned rodeos. In order to progress from having a permit to becoming a full card member, a cowboy—Black or white—had to earn $3,000 in a single season. That was a rich amount of money for the 1970s.

Steve filled his permit and became a PRCA member, and later, he was surprised to learn he would have to write a letter to the PRCA competition department asking for permission to compete in his hometown rodeo.

Back east, he met a rodeo and stock producer from the Catskills area in New York. His name was Andy Camp and every weekend Camp produced IPRA events that offered rodeo cowboys from up and down the Eastern Seaboard a chance to make more money with less travel.

"Listen here, you want to judge?" Camp asked Steve. "Because I can use you at the rodeos."

The deal was, Steve could steer wrestle and team rope on Friday nights and then work the rodeo all day on Saturdays and Sundays. He could win money and be assured of leaving with his paycheck. That was the end of his career in the PRCA and, more importantly, the beginning of a transition to a post-competitive career.

Together, the men headed to Bartlett, New Hampshire.

On the drive up, Steve told Camp he always wanted to work as a pickup man—"I thought it was an art picking up guys off a [bucking] horse"—and as grateful as he was to judge the rodeo, if there was ever an opportunity to work as a pickup man, he sure would like the opportunity.

That night, the pickup man was knocked unconscious when his horse ran into the front of the bucking chutes. Two things played into Steve's favor. The man was seriously injured and during the week, Steve worked as a paramedic for the New Haven Fire Department, a job he held for twenty years until he retired. So, everyone asked, "Steve, what should we do?" He and the others helped the man from the dirt and carried him back to the sports medicine tent.

Then Steve ran back out and hopped on the guy's horse and went to work.

After the rodeo, country singer Willie Nelson was leaving the beer tent with his bodyguard when he spotted Steve. Nelson tipped his hat and asked, "Hey, cowboy, can I ride your horse?"

"Absolutely," replied Steve, who led Nelson on horseback in a circle around the empty arena. They made two laps. Nelson jumped off and said, "Thanks, cowboy."

Based on that night's events, Camp hired Steve to work the Northeast Circuit Finals.

Though he was through competing at the PRCA, Steve made his way back to Oklahoma, where he competed in all the Black rodeos from Boley to Grayson, Drumright, and others. This time, he was traveling by himself.

"I went to a Black rodeo in Okmulgee and I thought I was going to get killed because that night they were fighting and carrying on," Steve said.

He knew the LeBlanc brothers—Clarence and Kenneth—but not many other Black cowboys from Oklahoma and Texas. He could sense some dissension among the cowboys. Steve was chatting with a woman when he was approached by a man who told him he needed to stop talking with her. She was married and her jealous husband did not like that Steve was carrying on with his wife—even if it was only a conversation.

"I didn't know enough people to really feel comfortable being there," Steve recalled, "so it was interesting."

In subsequent years, while working with the fire department, Steve would judge rodeos from time to time and help produce others. He trained horses and—inspired by his mother—began giving back to the Western culture by mentoring young Black kids from the inner city. He continues this work today down in Williston, Florida, where he has been training horses.

A lot of the young cowboys have a chip on their shoulder but have no idea what Black cowboys before them endured, and that's where Steve comes into their lives. He talks with them about the past and emphasizes the importance of hard work over complaining, even as he realizes life isn't always fair.

He recalled mentoring a fourteen-year-old named Lonnie Love. The boy had no father in his life and his mother was a drug addict.

According to Steve, "She didn't give a shit about where [Love] was, which is why he'd be hanging out with rodeo cowboys until early morning hours," whenever the Black World Championship Rodeos were held in Harlem or especially Queens and Brooklyn.

Steve took an interest in Love. The kid could really ride bulls. He was not good for being a kid from the projects. He was good—period.

In fact, Steve is convinced Love could have been New York's answer to Charlie Sampson, who came from Watts, California, and was the first Black rodeo cowboy to win the PRCA gold buckle when he won the bull-riding world title in 1982.

That's how good this kid *was*.

Love was too young to enter a pro rodeo, but Steve packed him up anyway and hauled the kid along to an event. When the rodeo secretary wouldn't let the teenager enter, the kid challenged Ronnie Martin—a stock contractor—$100 that he didn't have a bull in his trailer that could buck him off. Martin asked Steve if the kid was for real. Steve nodded in approval and Martin accepted the challenge.

Martin loaded his best bull in the chute, and Love climbed in the bucking chute, put his hand in the bull rope, nodded for the gate, and eight seconds later he fanned the bull with his cowboy hat. He might have been cocky, but there was no denying the kid had as much charisma as he did talent.

And he had $100 in his wallet.

On the drive home, Love was beaming with pride. He felt good about himself. He felt good about being a cowboy and, more specifically, about being a bull rider.

As they approached New York City, Love took off his cowboy hat. He pulled his dreadlocks back and fashioned a backward ballcap on his head. He even took his favorite cowboy boots off and put them behind the seat of Steve's truck.

Steve asked why.

"I can't wear that in my neighborhood," replied Love, who gave Steve a look as if to say, "Don't you get it, old man?"

Steve offered to have Love come stay with him on his farm in Connecticut.

"Nah," Love said.

He went home that night and, like his mother, ended up getting mixed up in drugs. He wound up arrested and sent to Rikers Island, where ten of New

York City's most infamous correctional facilities are located. Love never did compete in a rodeo—pro or otherwise.

"That's what makes it sad," said Steve, holding back tears as his voice cracks. "He had all the talent. It just blows my mind."

Steve knows it was not easy for Love. It was not easy for him either. Just as it was not easy for Sampson, who was only eight years old when he lived through the Watts Riots in August 1965. It was not easy for Charlie Reno, whose family moved from Vicksburg, Mississippi, to New York City as part of the second Great Migration. It was not easy for Willie Thomas, who had a stock contractor in Lake Charles, Louisiana, threaten to shoot him off the back of a bull if he did not jump. It was not easy for Myrtis Dightman or any number of Black cowboys, but color barriers and urban upbringings never stopped any of them from becoming pioneers and trailblazers.

"I've worked on one system in life and it's called WIT—whatever it takes," Steve concluded. "Some people are only willing to give half of that, and you can't."

18

Barry Moore

We all have dreams. In order to make dreams come into reality, it takes an awful lot of determination, dedication, self-discipline, and effort.
—JESSE OWENS

NEWARK, HOWELL TOWNSHIP, AND ASBURY PARK, NEW JERSEY

The last time Barry Moore ever saw Mike Latting was at an IRA event in the winter of 1981—two years before it was rebranded the International Pro Rodeo Association.

Truth be told, that's one of the last times Moore saw a lot of his old rodeo friends.

The legendary John Wayne had died eighteen months earlier and the Lattings—Mike and his father, Thyrl—were hauling Wayne's horse Dollar to a series of indoor rodeos and using him as part of a tribute to the late Academy Award–winning actor. They would saddle up the big chestnut-colored quarter horse with boots in his stirrups and lead him around the arena while the rodeo announcer honored the man known to many as "The Duke."

They were at the convention center in Buffalo, New York, and afterward Mike was moving the steers and calves from the catch pen down to the chutes at the opposite end of the arena to be loaded onto one of the cattle trailers for the trip home to Illinois.

"You want to give me a hand?" Mike asked Moore.

"Yeah," he replied.

Mike asked if he had anything to ride. Moore shook his head no. Mike pointed and said, "Jump up on old Dollar."

Moore thought he had to be kidding—"You can't just jump up on John Wayne's horse"—and when he realized Mike was serious, the otherwise brash Moore got a little nervous.

Wayne had ridden Dollar in *Chisum* (1970), *Big Jake* (1971), and *The Cowboys* (1972), and was so fond of the horse, he signed an exclusive deal with his owner, Dick Webb Movie Productions, to allow only Wayne to ride the horse. Wayne and Dollar also teamed up for *Train Robbers* (1973), *Rooster Cogburn* (1975), and *The Shootist* (1976), their last film together.

In the latter, a dying Wayne famously gives Dollar to a young Ron Howard—who, by that point in his career, had played Opie Taylor on *The Andy Griffith Show* but had not yet taken the role of Richie Cunningham on *Happy Days*—so that he can "get him a double helpin' of oats." Three years later, in July 1979, Wayne died of cancer at age seventy-two.

Dollar was eleven years old.

A year later, Dollar was sold to the IRA, and the Lattings used the horse that winter at a series of events, including in Washington DC, their hometown of Chicago, and Buffalo. Fans would pose for photos with the stoic horse before and after the rodeo.

Back in Buffalo, Moore was hesitant to get on the legendary horse.

"That was my fifteen minutes of fame. I got to ride John Wayne's horse," joked Moore, who laughed and then added, "I hope he didn't get mad about that. . . . Now, Mike Latting, he's a good man. That's the last time that I saw Mike—yeah, yeah—so I'm going back a minute."

The life and the oh-so-good times of Barry Moore—a rodeo cowboy who lived more like a pot-smoking, skirt-chasing playboy—makes for a cautionary tale of a bulldogger with the raw, natural talent to win a world title, yet a fast and loose lifestyle that never ever allowed him to reach his full potential in the arena.

Going all the way back to the beginning, Moore was born September 21, 1950, and is the oldest of three siblings.

His father, Arthur, was a longshoreman down at the docks, where he worked as a crane operator loading shipping containers onto large cargo vessels.

Unlike his father, who would watch old Westerns and daydream about another life as a cowboy, Barry was drawn to horses. Despite living in the heart of Newark—known more for drug and gang violence than anything having to do with Western culture—Barry was determined to become a rodeo cowboy.

Prior to his seventh birthday, his father sold their house in Newark and moved the family forty-five miles south to Howell Township. Barry was nine when his father bought a horse for him and his middle sister, Sheila. Both loved horses and enjoyed having thirteen acres of land on which they could ride at their leisure.

Weather permitting, Barry rode every day.

As a youngster, he was singularly focused on horseback riding and unfazed by changing schools. In Newark twenty-eight of the kids in his class were African American. There also was an Italian boy and a Puerto Rican girl. In Howell Township, he was the only Black student in his classroom.

"We were kids," Barry recalled. "We got in trouble together. . . . It was a clash of two societies, but it worked itself out. It never proved to be a problem and, I'd say, it paid off."

Arthur was never a horseman, but the elder Moore paid the feed bill and bought a saddle and a used truck and trailer. Barry recalled that his parents were the catalyst for everything and "loved taking me to [horse] shows."

Barry's first mentor was an older man named Jimmy Jeburke, an African American horse trainer who taught the boy everything he knew about horses.

Barry and his best friends, Steve Dubrosky and Sue Dollinger, all learned under Jeburke, who was a legend and a sought-after mentor. The inseparable trio were the envy of other kids their age. Barry had the talent to become his most successful protégé.

In September 1965 Barry was a freshman in high school when he met Charlie Reno.

Reno was merely two years older than Barry but had already been competing at amateur and open rodeos and was on the verge of turning pro. Because of his experience and maturity, Reno, who lived a mile away from the Moores, became a father figure the first time he and Barry met.

It was Reno who entered the two of them in rodeos that featured pros and amateurs alike.

Arthur, who was jealous of Jeburke and especially Reno, dreamed of staging an all-Black rodeo in New York City. He saw it as an opportunity for him to make his son proud and share in his newfound rodeo career, not for the seminal moment it would eventually become in 1971.

In 1967 Arthur and his wife, Evelyn, traveled to Oklahoma. Reno told the couple they needed to meet Bud Bramwell, who introduced them to his best friend and former OSU teammate Cleo Hearn. Bramwell and Hearn took the Moores to see a pair of all-Black rodeos in Drumright, Oklahoma, and nearby Okmulgee.

Arthur was busy asking questions of everyone he met, while Evelyn captured scenes from both rodeos with her Super 8 camera.

In an unpublished autobiography by Ingrid Frank, she wrote about a man known only as Big Apple, who made the trip to Oklahoma with Arthur and Evelyn. Bramwell has no recollection of anyone traveling with the couple, and prior to his death in October 2019, Barry said his parents made the trip alone. He also said he had no memory of his father working on the docks with anyone by the name of Big Apple, who Frank described as a "vocal leader of the Black longshoremen's union."

Inspired by what they saw, Arthur was excited to return home. However, he was unable to get anyone, much less the executives at Madison Square Garden or potential corporate sponsors, to take his proposal seriously.

According to Frank, it was Big Apple who knew her husband, George Richardson—a New Jersey politician who became a civil rights activist and owner of a marketing firm, Periscope Associates. Whoever made the introduction—the more than fifty years that have passed have taken their toll on everyone's memory—Richardson and Frank were enamored with Evelyn's footage.

They would eventually go on to market the first all-Black rodeo in Harlem and four other all-Black rodeos that the American Black Cowboy Association—cofounded by Bramwell, Hearn, Marvel Rogers, and Charlie Moore—and Periscope Associates teamed up to produce in a three-year span from spring 1970 to June 1973. Despite his best efforts, Arthur played no role in any of the events.

Out of love and loyalty, the younger Moore could not bear to compete in the steer-wrestling event in Harlem.

"My father, God rest his soul, was my biggest fan," said Barry, who did not like how Arthur was treated, even though he knew damn well his father had no experience producing, managing, marketing, or publicizing a rodeo, nor did he have the political gravitas in a tri-state area often ruled by politicians and union heads.

"I didn't realize it at the time," Barry said, "but I saw it stolen away from him, out from underneath his nose. Not that they had great success with it, but just the fact that they pulled it off at all because prior to my dad trying do it, it was unheard of in this part of the country."

Barry may have passed on the Harlem event, but Reno convinced him to compete in the subsequent rodeos produced by the American Black Cowboy Association in 1972 and '73.

Whenever he did compete, Barry was good—as a teenager, he was beating more experienced men—but without Reno, he didn't have the motivation or responsibility to advance his career.

He was doing day work on construction sites to help pay for entry fees.

Two months removed from his high school graduation, one of Barry's first jobs was working as a carpenter—"basically banging nails and carrying lumber"—helping to build stage platforms for Woodstock. He and a classmate, who knew how to weld and "had an in with the iron workers," arrived at the Upstate New York concert site three days early.

"I never made it to the concert," said Barry, who can be seen in the opening sequence to the documentary that was filmed. "I never saw any of the groups until a year later when the movie came out. I was too busy partying. I'm not going to lie to you, I was too busy over at the lake helping the girls swim around on the logs."

He inadvertently made the final cut of the movie when a camera crew randomly came by one of the nights he was working on the stage. It was a plywood circle that spun like a lazy Susan. "In the opening minutes of the movie," Barry recalled, "all you see is the silhouette of me. I'm down on one knee nailing the sheathing on the deck."

Unfortunately, what Barry jokingly referred to as "part of my misspent youth" sadly became the norm for the unfulfilled promise of a steer-wrestling career that could have been so much more.

As good as he was, he was undersized for a steer wrestler. Had he gained some muscle and strength, he would have become that much better. Instead, he spent too much time smoking marijuana and hanging out with the wrong crowd, which led to speed, cocaine, pills, and other illicit drug use.

Too many times, he was more focused on chasing women than he was on winning gold buckles. He did not care about what others thought of his reputation.

"He just cared about himself and he was the prize," Reno said. "Barry had so much talent, but he wasted it. He really wasted it."

Like his father, Barry was stubborn and hated advice—even if it would have led to a world title. Instead, he carried a chip on his shoulder.

Had it not been for Reno's miraculous return to rodeo following a broken neck that nearly took his life, Barry may well have drifted away from competition a decade before his best season in 1979.

Early that year, Barry and Reno were in Chicago.

Barry weighed all of 155 pounds soaking wet. The top-ranked steer wrestlers who had him by twenty-five to thirty pounds were surprised when the scrawny twenty-nine-year-old—he preferred "wiry"—managed to finish the first round in the top five of the average, despite having an inferior horse.

Barry and Reno had driven together. Reno used another bulldogger's horse and when Barry asked if he could do the same, the owner told him no. It's unfortunate, because Barry was a good guy, but once he got away from the East Coast, all people knew of him was that he liked to party.

"I wasn't offended; I was miffed," Barry said. "I didn't go there to make a fool of myself and if that horse was good enough for Charlie Reno to get on, then that's the one I want to get on, right?"

Thankfully, Thyrl Latting was close enough to home to get another horse for Barry to use.

It was an impressive run for Barry, and with a better horse in round two, he would be in a position to possibly win the event. But when the owner of the superior horse Reno was riding complimented Barry and offered to let him use his horse after all, Barry told him no thanks.

He let his pride get the best of him and sacrificed the opportunity for a payday.

He won two rodeos that year, but Chicago could have been his first.

"Before I left [Chicago], they knew I could steer wrestle," Barry said. "I would have liked to have made some money, but I ended up getting back at him when they had the Black rodeo in Washington DC. I took my own horse there."

Just before the finals for the ARA, Barry's pride intervened yet again when he told Reno if he couldn't find a new horse to compete with, he was not planning on attending the finals, much less competing, even though he was in the top five of the ARA standings.

Naturally, Barry blamed his lack of success on others.

He never took into consideration his own actions. It was not his fault. It never was.

He felt like he was being undermined by Ralph Gale, a fellow steer wrestler who also happened to be a member of the ARA board of directors, so Barry found a horse, Leaping Lenus, in South Jersey that he could use. However, Reno found a better one for sale and, knowing Barry did not have enough money on his own, agreed to buy half interest.

When they arrived to buy the horse, Barry ran four steers with him. He did not even bother to throw down the steers. He simply wanted to know what the horse, Boley, felt like standing in the box and how fast the horse was.

"He was a real prick to ride," said Barry, who never rode Boley for pleasure.

Reno paid half the money, so the owner agreed to haul the horse to the finals and help haze for Barry. Unfortunately, at the finals, Barry left the box early in the first two rounds in what he said would have otherwise been a pair of round wins to open the finals. He ended up dropping one spot in the final standings and was not able to pay for his share of the horse until he won an event in Washington the next season.

Reno looked after Barry when no one else would.

"When we were together, they couldn't beat us," Barry said.

That was only half true.

Healthy and at his best, no one could beat Reno.

"With too much partying and drugs, Barry blew it. He blew it," said Reno, who wavered between disappointment and sadness and is easily brought to tears recounting Barry's lost opportunities. "It didn't bother him. It bothered me."

They did not see one another again until the final days of Barry's life. He was staying with his youngest sister, Andrea, in Greensboro, North Carolina.

Reno flew down to be with his friend, who had laid on a couch dying of cancer for more than a month with no medical treatment.

Reno made the trip alone, but he had a message from Barry's childhood friend Sue Dollinger, who asked if he would make sure Barry knew that she had forgiven him for everything that had happened in the past. Barry was unable to talk, but his eyes lit up when Reno mentioned her name.

Two days later, on October 22, 2019, his eyes closed forever, and at sixty-nine, he peacefully passed away.

"And that's Barry Moore," concluded Reno.

19

Tex Williams and Larry Callies

Color is not a human or a personal reality; it is a political reality.
—JAMES BALDWIN

EL CAMPO AND ROSENBERG, TEXAS

Tex Williams is a third-generation cowboy from Texas.

His granddaddy, Morgan Williams, was a working cowboy and is believed to have been among the original Black cowboys who pushed cattle up the Chisholm Trail from South Texas all the way to railroad in Kansas. His daddy, Collie "Big Preacher" Williams, was also a working cowboy, who saddled up at 4:00 a.m. every morning. Tex started riding in the saddle with his daddy at three years old, learned to ride on his own at four, and in high school, he became the first Black cowboy to win a Texas high school rodeo title. Williams won the bareback title, in 1967, as a junior and then won two more championship buckles—bareback and bull riding—a year later, as a senior.

However, he never once competed in his hometown of El Campo because even though public schools were integrated in 1964, that never happened in Wharton County, Texas, until almost a decade later. There simply was no accountability.

Black teens in all sports, including rodeo, which is an individual sport and actually not affiliated with the school system, were told they could not compete, and there was nothing those kids, including Williams, could do about it. Laws merely govern, and in El Campo and the rest of Wharton County, those laws were not enforced until local officials were made to enforce them in the early 1970s.

It was eerily similar to one hundred years earlier, when slaves were not emancipated in Texas until two years after every other state in the South. That defiant nature was still evident in the 1960s.

As disappointed as Williams was with the idea of having never been given a chance to compete in his hometown and having never been locally honored for his accomplishments in the fifty-plus years since, Williams remains more upset about a local weekly rodeo that took place 254 miles away, in Leesville, Louisiana, in 1970.

He had been drafted by the U.S. Army and was halfway through boot camp when a fellow enlistee from Texas arranged for himself, Williams, and one other soldier to compete on a Saturday night in Leesville. After being told by the rodeo secretary he had been assigned the sixth bareback horse out, Williams was quickly told by another fellow contestant he would not be able to compete.

"What are you doing?" asked the man, as he watched Williams putting his rigging on the horse.

"I'm rigging my horse down."

"No," said man, motioning for Williams to stop.

Williams was initially confused and then quickly realized he was being told it was not the wrong horse, so much as he was being told he would not be riding at all that night.

"What's your name?" the man asked.

Realizing this was a racial confrontation, Williams pushed the brim of his hat up above his eyes, so he could clearly see. He then wiped the sweat from his brow and proudly said, "Tex Williams."

"Well, you didn't draw no horse."

The two continued back and forth.

Eventually the man, whose name Williams never knew, said, "We've had problems with Blacks, and we don't want you all riding in this rodeo."

"All I want to do is ride a horse and then I'm on my way to Vietnam," said Williams, who fifty years later still grows bitter with the retelling of the story.

That night in Leesville ended with Williams being told, "I don't give a *damn* where you ready to go."

All these years later, Williams's calm, laidback demeanor is offset by his anger, which, ironically, is the only thing keeping him from shedding tears of sadness.

"I was going to Vietnam to fight for them," Williams explained, "and they would not let me ride a fucking horse. Not good enough to ride a horse and not good enough to be in the same arena with him.

"The only thing I wanted to do was compete," concluded Williams, who is convinced racism will still exist another hundred years from now. "Just let me ride my horse, rope my steers and we all can get along. Yeah, that would be perfect."

But that is not how the rest of his life story played out in South Texas in the shadows of the civil rights era.

Tex Williams was born September 26, 1948, in Markham, Texas, and raised twenty-five miles away in nearby El Campo.

He's pretty sure his mama was thirty years old when she had him; and his daddy, who was born in 1899, was twenty years older than her. Williams thinks his daddy lived to be eighty-something and—*again*—is pretty sure his mama was eighty-four when she passed, but admitted, "Dates and times just never really registered with me."

"All I know is rodeos, ranching, cows, and trucks," Williams said. "That's it. That's pretty much all I ever done."

Williams grew up on horseback. If he wasn't in school, he was on a horse. Every weekday and every weekend, he was out in the pasture working cattle right alongside his daddy, Big Preacher. No one ever taught him how to ride. And he was only four when Big Preacher found a horse gentle enough for his son to ride by himself.

"I don't know that I ever said I wanted to be a cowboy," Williams said. "I was born into it and I've been riding ever since."

Williams and his brother would work out in the pasture. Most afternoons, Big Preacher would take a nap along the edge of the Colorado River. While he laid out on a sandbar or leaned up against a tree, the two boys would take turns riding their horse back and forth across the river with the other one trying to rope the other. Williams can remember roping his brother off the back of his horse "like the cowboys and Indians would do."

"I'd rope him and jerk him off the back of his horse," he said, "and I dragged him back across the river."

From the time they were five to ten years old, they would grab ahold of a big milk cow "and they would beat us up and down the fence until we got them caught."

His younger cousin Larry Callies joked that Williams and his brothers "almost made me not want to be a cowboy. They were so tough."

For years, Williams wanted nothing more than to be like his daddy—work cattle and train horses—at thirteen, he started riding saddle broncs, much like the younger version of the Big Preacher he had heard so much about. In 1963, at fourteen, he won the saddle bronc riding at the Southwestern National Cowboys Association—an association his daddy co-founded and served as the first president of back in the 1940s—and did it again a year later in 1964.

Although the RCA never officially barred Blacks from competing when it was formed in 1936, Jim Crow laws prevented them doing so in many states, so the SNCA was a minor league of sorts for Black rodeo cowboys.

Those events attracted the best Black rodeo cowboys along the Gulf Coast of Texas, and at thirteen, fourteen, fifteen, and sixteen years old, Williams was not only competing against more experienced men, he was winning against the likes of Bailey's Prairie Kid, Freddie Gordon (who was competing under the alias of Skeet Richardson), Calvin Greely Jr., Clinton Wyche, and other greats of the sport.

"I couldn't rodeo with the white kids," said Williams, who was finally allowed to rodeo as a high school junior and senior, but they still did not let him compete in Wharton County. After winning a state title in 1967, Williams became the first African American to compete at the National High School Rodeo Finals, in Elko, Nevada. He rode bulls, bareback, steer wrestled, and was the runner-up for the all-around title even though "they kicked me out of the bull riding because, in Nevada, only seniors could ride bulls."

He didn't win the steer wrestling, but he "threw one down" in a record time of 3.1 seconds.

As a high school senior, in 1968, the National High School Finals were held in Topeka, Kansas. Rodeo legend Jim Shoulders, known as a "Babe Ruth of

Rodeo," hauled livestock that year and Williams, who was nineteen at the time, drew Mighty Mouse in the bull riding.

Larry Callies came along in 1970 and '71, and like Williams, he was not allowed to rodeo in Wharton County either. In South Texas, racism still ran deep.

In the summer of '68—a few months after Williams had won his second and third state titles—Callies, who was not even eighteen, at the time, went to see a local Charlie Pride concert. Pride was a Black country singer who had a national recording contract. Callies was a guitar player who fancied himself as the next Charlie Pride—"I could sing just like him."

That summer night, he was the only Black in Wharton County to buy a concert ticket. Everyone else was scared. Callies should have been scared, too, but he wasn't. Then a group of white men chased him away from the concert.

Callies is certain they wanted to hang him just like they did seven years later, "when they hung a Black man for dating a white girl." They hung that man from the rafters of a barn outside of nearby East Bernard. Authorities claimed he hung himself, but Callies said the man was found with his hands tied behind his back.

"That was in '75," said Callies, who was also the first cousin of Calvin Greely Jr. "I was [at the concert] in '68. Man, you know, they wanted to kill me."

Decades later, on a quiet Sunday afternoon, in July 2017, in the back of a modest 1,600-square-foot storefront that Callies has transformed into a small but historic Black Cowboys Museum, he and Williams recalled one disturbing story of racism after another.

Callies's mother once told him a story about her sister sitting in the colored section so she could watch her son, Tex Williams, compete at a high school rodeo. Williams would often pull his hat so far down that the brim would cover his face. He was spurring his horse so good one time, Callies said, the crowd stood up and cheered. As soon as his hat blew off they went from cheering to booing.

"That's what my mama told me," recalled Callies, as Williams rummaged through a box of his rodeo buckles.

Intent on finding the three buckles he won as a high school state champion, Williams seemed unbothered by the story. Without looking up, he replied, "I don't remember that."

"You don't remember that because your mom didn't tell you," Callies explained, "but she told my mama that because I was listening to it and she said, 'Tex don't even know they booed him when he got off his horse.'"

A half-century later, Williams was still unfazed by the booing. Go ahead boo him, he reasoned, just don't bar him from competing because of the color of his skin—especially if you are going to draft him to defend our country.

In the short time he competed as a pro, his highlight came in Bay City, Texas, when he outscored all-around champion Larry Mahan. Williams remembered being marked seventy-nine points. Mahan was seventy-eight in the saddle bronc competition that night. But those who remember Williams can only recall his two years of high school rodeo. Not long after high school, he went off to Vietnam.

When he came back from the war, Williams passed on returning to rodeo. Instead, he made a career as a long-haul truck driver.

Horses and trucks, he likes to say.

"That's it," said Williams. "That's all I ever done.

"The only thing I regret is that I didn't keep going once I got back from Nam. There [are] two things that I always wanted. I wanted a nice truck and a nice trailer, and the only way I could get it was work for it, so I had to go work."

For twenty years, he hauled cattle from Texas to California and Oregon or clear across the other direction to New York and the rest of the Eastern Seaboard. He'd drive from Texas up to North Dakota and back down. And to the best of his recollection, the only state Williams never drove out to was Washington State.

He bought a brand-new Peterbilt, a pickup truck, and a horse trailer.

There was one time he even built a brand-new, brick, ranch-style home— four bedrooms and two full baths—that he lived in for five years, but he "couldn't find a woman to get married to" and sold it in favor of a travel trailer. And then kept his horses with his uncle.

Some would say Williams was and still is a simple man.

Others would say he's quiet and certainly unassuming.

As a matter of fact, a lot of rodeo cowboys who would have ridden with him don't even remember the name Tex Williams because "you'd probably never see me until I got ready to crawl up on my horse."

That's just the way he was.

He wasn't loud, and even though he was a bull-riding son-of-a-gun, Williams never was a showboat. It's why so many people never heard of him and—fifty years later—the few who did, forgot about him.

"Do I regret it?" Williams asked himself. "Nah."

20

Obba Babatundé

I think it's really important to be conscious of yourself and the world around you.
—TA-NEHISI COATES

QUEENS, NEW YORK, AND HOLLYWOOD, CALIFORNIA

He is a quintessential, multihyphenated entertainer: an Emmy-winning actor, director, producer, writer, poet, and a Tony-nominated song-and-dance man. In all, he's been in nearly twenty stage productions, starred in nearly forty movies and appeared in more than sixty television shows. Obba Babatundé is also a rodeo cowboy and world-renowned horse whisperer who has appeared at every performance of the Bill Pickett Invitational Rodeo held annually in Los Angeles since 1987.

A nationally touring all-Black rodeo series founded by Lu Vason, the BPIR attracts fellow celebrities like James Pickens Jr. and Jamie Foxx, along with Glynn Turman and Reginald T. Dorsey. All of them, including Babatundé, have ridden in the ceremonial grand entry and some of them—Pickens, Turman, and Dorsey—have competed in the team roping and team penning and have been on horseback working livestock during the event.

"I absolutely love it," Babatundé said. "I love it because people that know me from my career are always pleasantly surprised and shocked when they see me around horses and the way I ride. I had a signature move that I did for years."

Babatundé was a featured performer during the grand entry in which he would ride into the rodeo arena with both hands extended out to the side parallel to the ground. He would hold the reins between his teeth and ride in at a full gallop. Using only his legs and knees, he would command the horse to turn left or right, slow down or stop.

Audiences and spectators would be in awe of his horsemanship skills.

Afterward Babatundé often would make his way up into the stands, where he would receive a similar reaction from one year to the next. He would ask, "Have you been here before?"

The response was almost always, "It's my first time."

"At the Bill Pickett Rodeo—generally every year—over 80 percent of the audience are first-timers," said Babatundé, who enjoys the smiles, shrieks, and shrills of excitement that come with introducing urban audiences to a lifelong passion that has provided his extraordinary life with balance.

Donald Cohen was born in Upstate New York on December 1, 1951.

He grew up in a strong, two-parent household and described his father as a man's man with a formidable work ethic. Cohen's mother shared the same sentiment. Something of a progressive family, the Cohens would often sit together and discuss issues of importance. It was during those conversations that his parents encouraged him and his brother to develop their own identities.

As such, Donald (and later Obba) never thought of himself as a native New Yorker.

"Where I was born just happened to be where my mother gave birth to me and there's no superior ethic to that geographical location," he explained. "I was raised to function on the basis of natural law over man's law."

That philosophy would prove influential throughout his life.

He's long been recognized for wearing a necklace with a lone domino hanging from it.

No, he does not play dominoes. Nor does he gamble.

"It's in reference to the domino effect," he explained, "which years ago was called the golden rule: Do unto others as you [would] have them do unto you."

It is the philosophy of putting in what you want to get back in return. Again, it circles back to the work ethic he was exposed to as a young child.

He was four when he was introduced to a friend of his father's who had horses. There he learned the difference between a houlihan loop, which is used to rope a horse, as opposed to a slipknot, which is used to rope a steer. A year later, the family moved to the Jamaica neighborhood of Queens. Located on Long Island across the East River from Manhattan, it's the largest of New York's boroughs in size but has a slightly smaller population than Brooklyn.

Influenced by his mother and uncles, who were musicians, he started performing for his family at age six. He began singing, dancing, and eventually acting professionally at fourteen, although he and his siblings were exposed to horses on the weekends.

"My career—sort of my formal career—was sprung out of writing poetry in my last year of high school," said Babatundé, who attended Brooklyn College after graduating from Jamaica High in 1969 and taking the name Obba Babatundé (pronounced Oh-ba Bah-bah-toon-day), "and my first year of college expanding that poetry into one-act plays that I would direct and cast and hire other people to be in."

He is a self-taught multi-instrumentalist—trumpet and West African percussion—and learned just about every style of dance. Incidentally, he also taught himself American Sign Language.

His career began off-off-Broadway and quickly moved off-Broadway. After finishing a tour of *Guys and Dolls* alongside Leslie Uggams and Richard Roundtree, he made his Broadway debut in 1978, playing four different roles in *Timbuktu!* That year, he also toured with Liza Minnelli and met the man whose career he most wanted to emulate, Sammy Davis Jr.

The tour opened at Harrah's in Lake Tahoe, Nevada.

Afterward, Babatundé was in his dressing room when there was a knock on the door and a familiar voice, "Ob, it's me, Sam." Babatundé recalled the moment in a September 20, 2017, interview with www.inquisitr.com, telling them that when he opened the door, Davis looked him in the eyes and said, "You, my man, are a bitch on wheels." They exchanged pleasantries, hugged, and before Davis left, Babatundé told the website that he said to Davis, "Sir, I want to thank you for coming in through the kitchen, so I could come in through the front door."

Later, he was a dancer in *Baryshnikov on Broadway*, which led to him originating the role of C. C. White in the Broadway production of *Dreamgirls*, for which he was nominated for a Tony Award in 1982.

In a story that ran on January 25, 1987, the *New York Times* described him as "a graceful dancer with a mellow pop baritone, a pleasant personality, and the good looks of a contemporary matinee idol." They went on to characterize him as an all-around entertainer with well-honed talents.

While acting in New York, Babatundé would go out to Pelham Bay and rent horses a couple times a month. It provided a sense of levity at a time when he was hyper-focused on his career and establishing himself among the Broadway community.

After a successful career back east, he arrived in Los Angeles in 1990 and found himself sleeping on couches "for at least about a year and a half."

He heard about a horse stable, Sunset Ranch, that had horses for rent. Babatundé hit it off with the manager. Whenever he was not auditioning, working on a film or television project, in the gym training, or at a dojo working on martial arts, he was working with horses at Sunset Ranch.

In 1993 it became more than a hobby when he bought his first horse, Alamo. The horse was well-known for his bad habits and being nearly impossible to ride. Through the discipline of time and consistency, the next year Babatundé rode Alamo in the grand entry at the BPIR in Los Angeles.

Several cowboys recognized the horse and asked, "Is that Alamo?"

Babatundé proudly told them, "Yeah," and that was the moment he realized he had a special talent with horses. "I have an ability to communicate with them and they kind of trust me," he said. "I'm learning the language, and so that's when the study of it became something which I engrossed myself to."

He started to read everything he could get his hands on. He studied the anatomy of a horse and the way in which it functions. Much like a seven-foot center in the NBA would not make a good horse jockey trying to compete in the Kentucky Derby, you cannot make a plow horse out of a thoroughbred. "I can never train the nature out of that creature," Babatundé said. "I can pretty much bring out the best of what's in [it]."

He quickly discovered that most issues people have with horses are caused by riders who don't understand the animal they are sitting on.

The more he read, the more interested he became in the science of breeding and caring for farm animals, so he enrolled in an animal husbandry class at Los Angeles Pierce College. He met an old farrier—a craftsman who trims and shoes horses' hooves—who had worked with Trigger on some of the classic Westerns with Roy Rogers and gleaned more knowledge.

Ultimately, Babatundé became more practical with his training methods.

"I have learned so much about a better way to communicate with humans by dealing with horses," he admitted. "It's simple: Horses don't have ego. They do not feel—I have not found that they deal with love or hate. They deal with trust or mistrust because their nature is fight or flight."

His process brings about trust between himself and the horse. And equally important for him, it offers a balance between the pressures of Hollywood and a life away from the industry.

He recalled a time when two men pulled up to the barn with a wild, untrained horse in their trailer. They could not untie him to let him out because anytime someone got near the trailer, the horse would kick the back gate uncontrollably with its hind legs.

Babatundé stood back and watched.

Clearly, no one knew what to do.

The driver, who was exasperated, told the owner of the horse he needed to get that horse out of his trailer. Neither of them wanted anything to do with the animal. And that horse wanted nothing to do with them. Finally, Babatundé walked over and asked if they needed his help. They nodded. He told them to back the trailer right up to the gate leading into the arena.

Rather than trying to untie the lead rope, he reached through the trailer and cut it with a knife.

Once free, the horse spun around in the trailer and blew out of the back gate into the arena. He was jumping and kicking and bucking. Babatundé told them to leave the horse alone for twenty minutes. He ran hard and jumped some more until he was tired out. He slowed down and then stood there looking at everyone.

Eventually, the horse ran into the only stall that was open.

For the next couple of days, Babatundé stopped by the stall and the horse would pop and kick and snort. Babatundé would just smile and walk away, only to return a day later. He did this every day until the horse finally stopped snorting at him.

Babatundé would take fresh manure and rub it on his pants.

When the horse would smell him, he was smelling himself and he became less afraid of Babatundé. By the next week, Babatundé had a halter on the horse and could lead him into the arena. In a matter of three weeks, he had him saddled, "and that's when the training started."

At the same time he was finding success as a horse whisperer, Babatundé also was staying busy acting.

On the big screen, he appeared in one blockbuster after another. There was *The Silence of the Lambs*, *Philadelphia*, and *That Thing You Do!* followed by *The Notebook* and *The Manchurian Candidate*. But perhaps it was his popularity on television that made him one of the most recognizable character actors in Hollywood. Able to move between sitcoms and dramas, Babatundé's résumé is a greatest-hits list of the past thirty years: *The Fresh Prince of Bel-Air*, *Chicago Hope*, *Dawson's Creek*, *Boston Legal*, *Friends*, *Madam Secretary*, and *NCIS*. He also guested on *Grey's Anatomy*, which stars his friend and fellow cowboy James Pickens Jr.

In 1997 he received a Primetime Emmy nomination for Best Supporting Actor in the HBO movie *Miss Evers' Boys*, and twice he's played Kerry Washington's father, most recently in the Hulu series *Little Fires Everywhere*.

His career keeps him quite busy these days: He's simultaneously appearing on the long-running soap *The Bold and the Beautiful*, for which he won a Daytime Emmy, the Netflix series *Dear White People*, and the CBS drama *S.W.A.T.*

When he is working in Los Angeles, he never misses a day at the stables, and you can bet he will be at the Bill Pickett event in LA every year in mid-July. Babatundé, whose grandson Tarik "The Human Joystick" Cohen is a running back for the Chicago Bears, sees the rodeo as an opportunity to "break the false narrative" that has led many to think the Old West was void of Black cowboys.

Much like other professional rodeos, Babatundé said the Bill Pickett event reinforces two characteristics that have long represented his own life—family values and a commitment to hard work.

"It really represents the best of the best," said Babatundé. "I'm so honored to be a part of that tradition. I'm so proud to be a member in good standing and I'm honored that they allow me to be identified as one of their grand marshals."

21

James Pickens Jr.

In the racial picture things will never be as they once were. History has reached a turning point, here and over the world.

—MEDGAR EVERS

CLEVELAND, OHIO, AND HOLLYWOOD, CALIFORNIA

Ten years prior to becoming a household name playing Dr. Richard Webber on the long-running television series *Grey's Anatomy*, James Pickens Jr. was a recognizable working actor in Hollywood. Not all viewers might have known his name, but he had guest-starred in everything from *Blossom* and *Beverly Hills, 90210* to *L.A. Law*, *Doogie Howser, M.D.*, *Murder She Wrote*, and *Touched by an Angel*. Pickens also had been cast in small roles in feature films *Menace II Society* and *Nixon*.

In 1995 he was in San Diego filming a made-for-television movie, *Bloodhounds*, with Corbin Bernsen.

One day between takes, Pickens sat back and watched as the driver of a camera truck pulled out a roping dummy to practice roping steer horns while the crew set up the lighting for the next scene.

Pickens had done a little bit of trail riding in Central Park while doing theater work in New York and, more recently, had taken up team penning on

Wednesday nights at the Equestrian Center in Los Angeles. Unlike roping, the recreational sport of team penning did not require a lot of skill.

The driver, a team roper from Oklahoma named Pete—twenty-five years later, Pickens said he is doing good to even recall a first name—noticed him and handed the actor a rope. By his own admission, Pickens fiddled with it and "halfway by accident," he roped the horns of the dummy.

"I didn't know what I was doing, but I could catch it," said Pickens, who then sought roping lessons from a team and tie-down roper named Scott Perez, "and I got hooked. There was an adrenaline rush. It was a lot faster than team penning, that's for sure. It was a lot of fun for me."

James Pickens Sr. and Ruby were married in Buffalo, New York, and shortly thereafter moved to Cleveland, where James Jr. and his two younger siblings were born and raised. James Sr. worked as a steel worker for Republic Steel, the third-largest steel manufacturer in the United States.

Ruby was a stay-at-home mother, and according to James Jr., "She was amazing . . . and did pretty much everything."

His parents were "somewhat older" and settled by the time they started a family. James Jr. was born October 26, 1952, and likened his upbringing to "a Black version of 'Leave it to Beaver.'" His mother cooked breakfast *and* dinner every day—without fail—and even though the family lived right across the street from the elementary school, she also packed daily lunches for all three kids to take with them.

Their father was "very involved" in the lives of his children.

James Sr. introduced his kids to the outdoors and a love of hunting and fishing, which was something he developed growing up in Mississippi. James Sr. especially enjoyed taking the kids out to hunt for rabbits. He had only a sixth or seventh grade education, but that did not mean he was not interested or curious in new experiences.

They would take family trips to visit national parks, and once a week back home, the entire family would get dressed up and James Sr. would take them to a nice restaurant downtown. One time, he stopped off at the fish market on his way home to buy an octopus that he made into a salad.

"He was that kind of guy," said James Jr. of his father. "And I was a child of the fifties and sixties—back when there were only three channels [on the television]."

Even though Zenith popularized the television remote in 1956, the Pickens family did without. That's what the kids were for. Well, mostly James Jr., who, like his father, was a fan of Westerns. Together, they watched *The Lone Ranger*, *The Rifleman*, and *Gunsmoke*.

"My interest in the Western lifestyle was really germinated right there and it's kind of carried over through my adulthood," recalled James Jr., even though he never saw an African American in a starring role until Otis Young co-starred in the short-lived Western series *The Outcasts*, from September 1968 to May 1969.

James Jr. was in college by the time *Buck and the Preacher*, the first serious big-screen Western starring African Americans (Sidney Poitier and Harry Belafonte) in the lead roles, was released in movie theaters. The film also starred Cleveland native Ruby Dee.

"They had a very strong presence in that film," James Jr. said. "They were not just there to serve as a foil for a white star or whatever. They did have a real story to tell. I remember that very well."

He may have been a fan of film and television, but James Jr. was not yet acting and had not even given it a thought. In fact, in high school, he played football and tried his hand at track and field. He thought of himself as a hurdler, but that did not work out when he "found out how slow I was" at the first track meet. In college, he was unsuccessful in his attempt to walk on the football team at Bowling Green State University.

Pickens was pursuing a fine arts degree at Bowling Green, located fifteen miles south of Toledo in the northeast corner of Ohio. He wanted to be an illustrator or a cartoonist.

"That was my first love," he said. "I would draw every chance I got. *That* was my passion."

A turn toward acting came about as a fluke.

Pickens was a senior when he met a doctoral candidate trying to earn a PhD in directing. The would-be director was lamenting the dilemma of needing to cast one more actor for his student film when their mutual friend saw Pickens from across the crowded student union. She introduced the two. Pickens was not very interested in auditioning, but the two film students were persistent, and at the time, Pickens was dating a young lady who had done some acting, so he thought it might impress her if he said yes.

He got the role.

Then again, he was the only person who read for the part.

It ran one, maybe two weekends at the campus theater and Pickens thought it would be his one and only film, but then he was asked to audition for *No Place to Be Somebody* for which Charles Gordone became the first African American playwright to win a Pulitzer Prize.

Asked of his plans after graduation, in spring 1976, Pickens said he thought he would return home to Cleveland and, perhaps, teach. Told he had a gift for acting, Pickens auditioned for Karamu House—the country's oldest continuing multicultural community theater, founded in 1915. A mainstay in Cleveland, the Karamu House had been a proving ground for Ruby Dee, Robert Guillaume, and Ivan Dixon.

"I started as a stage manager," said Pickens, who took classes and studied theater, "and from there, they put me in plays. I was there for a couple of years and then they said, 'You need to go to New York.' They kind of shoved me out the door, so I went to New York and kind of started this journey."

Upon his arrival in New York, he found his way to the Roundabout Theater, where he starred in the Negro Ensemble Company's production of *A Soldier's Play* alongside a pair of then unknown actors named Denzel Washington and Samuel L. Jackson.

In Cleveland, the closest Pickens ever came to riding horseback was the merry-go-round, but in Manhattan, of all places, his apartment was just down the street from the Claiborne Stables—a New York institution on Eighty-Ninth Street between Central Park West and Columbus, which has since closed. It was an old firehouse that had been converted. The horses were kept down on the basement level, where the fire engines had been for years before that.

They were all English-saddled horses—no Western saddles—but Pickens could rent a horse, walk him down Eighty-Ninth Street, and then cross over into Central Park, where they had horse trails to ride.

"I would do that as often as I had money," said Pickens, who was still a struggling actor, "and from there I would go up to the Bronx to City Island and they had a horse stable there, and they did have Western saddles."

He developed a passion for horses and, at the same time, met his future wife, Gina. They married in 1985, and two years later, he began a four-year stint on the daytime soap opera *Another World*, which led the couple to Los Angeles.

As his career took off, horseback riding was an opportunity to decompress from the mounting pressures of Hollywood. He met some stuntmen who rode horses and picked up work as wranglers; he even went in halves on leasing a horse with a fellow actor. In due time, Pickens, who was in his forties by then, began spending more time on horseback and it became his first real experience with owning a horse and caring for it.

"Looking back on it, I got started pretty late," said Pickens, who had always been focused on his career; riding horses was merely recreational. "I guess there's really no age barrier."

After arriving in LA, he spent the next fifteen years appearing in everything from *Roseanne* to *Seinfeld*, JAG, NYPD *Blue*, *The District*, *The Practice*, and *Crossing Jordan*, but the most personal role came in 1996, the same year as *Bloodhounds*, when Pickens was cast as Medgar Evers in *Ghosts of Mississippi*.

Evers, a World War II veteran and Mississippi's first field secretary for the National Association for the Advancement of Colored People, was gunned down in his driveway.

He died almost an hour later at the hospital.

Evers was thirty-seven.

It was not until February 1994—nearly thirty-one years after the fact— that Byron De La Beckwith was finally tried and convicted of murder. That trial became the basis for the film *Ghosts of Mississippi* starring Alec Baldwin, Whoopi Goldberg, James Woods, and Pickens.

Pickens called his participation cathartic and pivotal.

Shortly after *Ghosts* was released, Pickens received a phone call from a cousin living in Mississippi. It was the youngest son of his father's only sister.

"Do you know where Medgar Evers was coming from the night he was killed?" asked his cousin.

Pickens had no idea.

In fact, like so many others, he never thought to question exactly where Evers had been.

"He had come from our home," Pickens was told.

His uncle was a prominent pastor and regularly entertained civil rights activists, local community leaders, and politicians. He was doing exactly that on the evening of June 11 when Evers and others discussed recent actions taken by Alabama governor George Wallace to prevent African American students from enrolling at the University of Alabama.

Evers joined the Pickens family for dinner, led the meeting, and then watched President John F. Kennedy address the American people on national television before declining an offer to spend the night. There had been previous threats on Evers's life, but he was determined to return home to be with his family.

He arrived at 2332 Margaret Walker Alexander Drive—just a few blocks from the intersection of what is now Martin Luther King Jr. Drive and Medgar Evers Boulevard—shortly after midnight.

"And that was the last evening of his life," Pickens recalled. "I was floored when I heard that."

Pickens had filmed that fateful scene in the driveway of the actual house Evers shared with his wife, Myrlie, and their three children. The home, which is now a national monument, was preserved just as it was the night Evers was assassinated. He was shot in the back and the bullet pierced his heart as it passed through him, broke a kitchen window, caromed off the refrigerator—"You can still see the dent"—and hit the toaster.

More than thirty years later, Pickens met the same neighbors who had lived next door to the Evers family and also had a brief conversation with Evers's older brother Charles.

"We were talking about that night and he kept looking at the car we were using in the driveway," Pickens said. "It was an old '56 Chevy—beautiful car—and he kept looking at this car. He obviously knew it wasn't the real car, but he said, 'That was the car I gave my sister-in-law.' He had given that car to Medgar's wife, and it was just compelling."

Pickens added, "It's something that has always lived with me, just the circumstances of being part of that."

Years later, he attended an event celebrating Black women in history. Myrlie was among the honorees.

Pickens, who was there with Blair Underwood, among other African American celebrities, had an opportunity to speak with Myrlie. She did mention the film, *Ghosts of Mississippi*, but Pickens elected not to mention his own family's connection to her slain husband.

"I can't tell you why I didn't," said Pickens, who stammered while he thought about that evening and then added, "I was not going to change her perspective of that evening."

Back in Los Angeles, as his career continued to pick up momentum, Pickens learned to rope calves on an old gray mare that he described as a "very forgiving horse" when he made mistakes. He began roping more often and the sport became his recreation of choice. The experience quickly led to him buying his first team-roping horse, named Smokey.

Pickens eventually became a regular at the annual BPIR in Los Angeles, where he would be featured in the grand entry alongside fellow actors Glynn Turman, Reginald T. Dorsey, and Obba Babatundé.

However, his true passion has always been less about roping, more about riding. Pickens won't pass up an opportunity to rope calves at the practice pen if it means he and Gina, who understands and appreciates the peace and joy her husband feels on horseback, can trail ride together along a dried-out river bottom and enjoy the beauty of being outdoors.

A week before the premiere of *Ghosts of Mississippi*, Pickens made a trip to Las Vegas with Gene Blank, who at the time was vice president of casting for ABC Television—this was almost ten years before Pickens was cast for *Grey's Anatomy*—and was introduced to the NFR for the first time. The two were team penning and Blank was talking about the NFR when he invited Pickens to come along with him. The first year he went, in December 1994, Pickens stayed at a small place off the strip called Hotel San Remo.

"I was hooked," Pickens said. "It was packed every night. Over those ten days, it's the hardest ticket in town to get. Vegas is a cowboy town for ten days. That's all you see are cowboy hats and boots. It's really something."

He's gone every year since.

Pickens had already become a regular during the second weekend of the NFR by the time *Grey's Anatomy* became a top-rated television series. He has been continually surprised by how many rodeo cowboys—well, mostly their wives and girlfriends—"were huge fans of the show," but ultimately, they embraced Pickens because of his passion for the Western lifestyle.

As the years continued and the popularity of the show increased—*Grey's Anatomy* premiered in 2005 and is the longest-running dramatic medical series in television history—Pickens befriended more cowboys, especially tie-down and team ropers. He became friends with then PRCA commissioner Karl Stressman and was even asked to provide some guest commentary as part of the ESPN telecast.

Pickens, one of the only actors to have appeared on *Grey's Anatomy* throughout its entirety, and his wife started the James Pickens Jr. Foundation in 2008. Two years later, in 2010, they organized their first annual charity team roping. The event now takes place every April and is strategically held midweek prior to a PRCA rodeo in Lakeside, California, and comes on the heels of a trio of other California rodeos—Red Bluff, Oakdale, and Clovis.

Among the charities his foundation has helped support is Turman's week-long summer camp that introduces inner-city kids to the Western lifestyle.

The event was originally held at the historical Tejon Ranch, located an hour north of Los Angeles—"They were great and very gracious and let us have the arena free of charge"—before becoming part of a bigger celebration surrounding the annual Clovis Rodeo, which has been in existence for more than one hundred years.

Held the last week of April, it has become one of the top jackpot team-roping events of the spring.

Pickens is still part of the cast of *Grey's Anatomy*, but his passion for the history of Black cowboys finally intersected with his career when he was cast as "an old cowboy" in the first season of Kevin Costner's acclaimed television series *Yellowstone*.

His own production company also optioned a biography, *Black Gun, Silver Star: The Life and Legend of Frontier Marshal Bass Reeves*, which was researched and written by Art Burton, and his foundation sponsors up-and-coming tie-down roper John Douch, who was the 2017 college reserve champion before turning pro in 2018.

Grey's might have changed the course of his career, but ultimately, Pickens pines for those quiet days he can spend on horseback.

"That's where I do my praying and seeing how much beauty God has put around us and try not to take him for granted," Pickens concluded. "There's something about doing that on horseback. I don't have anything else that can compare to that. Maybe there's something, but I haven't run across it yet. There's just something about that—the peace of it all—and knowing there's something bigger than yourself out there, and sharing it with this animal that puts 100 percent of its trust in you to take care of it, is pretty awesome."

22

Reginald T. Dorsey

When *12 Years a Slave* got that much attention, everyone started to copy that.
That story has to be told, but there are a lot more stories to be told than slavery.
—LOUIS GOSSETT JR.

DALLAS, TEXAS, AND HOLLYWOOD, CALIFORNIA

Reginald T. Dorsey is used to receiving glances that turn into double takes
and outright stares when he's out in Hollywood sporting *his* cowboy hat and
boots. But on this particular afternoon in May 1992, he was dressed in full
cowboy regalia—in addition to his customary hat and boots, Dorsey was
wearing chaps, spurs, vest, and even a wild rag tied around his neck.

He made the nine-block walk from his apartment near the corner of Sunset
Boulevard and Wilcox Avenue south to an office building on Melrose Avenue
near Seward Street.

For months, he had been pressing his agent to get him an audition for
Return to Lonesome Dove.

His peers—none of whom were authentic Black cowboys, much less rode
a horse—had all read for various parts. Dorsey had grown up riding horses
in Texas, and yet his agent could never get so much as a callback from the
casting department.

Luckily, Dorsey knew the producer—Suzanne de Passe—who had brought Westerns back to the forefront in 1989 with *Lonesome Dove*, based on the Pulitzer Prize–winning novel of the same name. The five-part miniseries was nominated for eighteen Emmys, winning seven.

They had met at a Bill Pickett Invitational Rodeo in Los Angeles, and now de Passe was recasting the four-part follow-up, so Dorsey called her office. It's a damn good thing he called when he did. Her assistant said it was the very last day of casting.

She told him, "If you want to come in, you need to get over here now."

"Everything that I'd ever thought about doing came down to that moment," Dorsey said. "I wasn't letting anything get in the way of me getting this job."

Even if his car was not running.

He got dressed for the audition, walked a block down Sunset, took a left on Seward, and made his way down to Melrose. Along the route, he had to cross a section of Santa Monica Boulevard where male prostitutes were known to congregate.

"Let's just say, it was not a good look," Dorsey recalled, "but I was determined to get this job."

Once he got there, it was less of an audition so much as it was a casual conversation with de Passe and the director, Mike Robe. Actually, de Passe did not say much. It was Dorsey and Robe who did most of the talking.

Once Dorsey got up to leave, de Passe walked over and said the only thing he needed to hear, "Oh, by the way, you got the job."

"Man, let me tell you," said Dorsey, "I literally glided home. I didn't feel like I was walking. I was just simply gliding."

Reginald Todd Dorsey did not decide to become a cowboy—he was destined to be a cowboy from the time he was born at Parkland Hospital in Grand Prairie, Texas. He lived with his parents in Dallas, until they divorced when he was seven.

He was only three when his uncle, Wardell Young, held Dorsey in his lap on a horse for the first time.

Young had a small place south of downtown Dallas, in Lancaster, where he looked after twenty or more horses. In those early days, Dorsey's older cousins would put him in a saddle when he was four and five—"It was instant love." Beginning in kindergarten, every piece of art he did was a drawing of horses and cowboys.

He helped his family feed the horses every weekend.

When he was six, Dorsey's father surprised him with a pony.

Roy Rogers was his favorite cowboy and he loved seeing him sitting atop his equally famous palomino stallion named Trigger. When his dad backed up the family station wagon and unloaded a palomino pony from the trailer behind it, you could have knocked the young boy over with a feather.

"I don't think I'll ever replace that joy of just what a surprise actually means," he said, "and the enthusiasm."

That pony is one of only three "good memories" he has of his father, who also gave him a Super 8 camera and instilled in him a love and appreciation for nature.

Beyond that, Reginald, his mother, Tenora, and his sister, Shari, had it pretty rough. His mother remarried and they moved to the projects in Fort Worth.

Reginald "tolerated" his stepfather, which was only made easier by his Aunt Bea, who took him to rodeos and let him chase calves in the Fort Worth Stockyards.

He also discovered a horse stable five miles from his house. He would walk there through the Texas heat and shovel horseshit all day for fifty cents. Dorsey used that pocket change to buy lunch—a can of potted meat, crackers, and a pickle—to hold him over until he got home sometime after the nightly calf roping.

"There was one Black cowboy that used to rope there, and I couldn't remember his name if my life depended on it," Dorsey said, "but at that point in my life, this dude was like John Wayne to me."

Other than his Uncle Wardell and photos of his grandfather, Henry Young, who died months before Dorsey was born, this man in Fort Worth was the only other Black cowboy he had ever seen.

"He had a big impression on me," Dorsey said.

The family moved to San Jose, California, when Dorsey was ten.

"Coming from Texas, believe it or not, I hadn't faced racism," said Dorsey, but that changed when the family got to San Jose. "That was the first time I was ever called 'nigger.'"

Dorsey was becoming quite an athlete—he excelled in football and track—but that didn't stop the fistfights. Nothing stopped those until he dropped out of high school at sixteen and moved to Hollywood to pursue an acting career. He could never have known it beforehand, but Dorsey had a whole new fight on his hands—establishing himself as an actor and surviving in Hollywood.

He made guest appearances on *Good Times* and *White Shadow*, along with a recurring role on *Hill Street Blues*. Around the same time, in 1983, Louis Gossett Jr. became the first African American to win an Oscar for best supporting actor as drill sergeant Emil Foley in *An Officer and a Gentleman*.

Dorsey was watching the preshow of the Academy Awards with his girl-friend when he turned to her and said he was going to the show. He did not have a ticket, but that didn't stop him. With no time to spare, he went home and put together a makeshift tuxedo. He pulled out a coat and black bowtie, put on a white shirt and leather pants, and then drove down to the Dorothy Chandler Pavilion.

An officer from the Los Angeles Police Department was the only thing standing between him and getting into the awards show. The first time the unsuspecting officer turned his back, the athletic twenty-four-year-old Dorsey ducked under the waist-high wooden barricade and found himself standing on the red carpet next to Raquel Welch, who had won a Golden Globe ten years earlier.

She knew damn well Dorsey did not belong there.

"She looked at me," he recalled. "I looked at her and we continued to proceed. No one questioned me. I didn't touch her or anything, but when she moved, I moved, because one thing I knew for sure is they weren't going to tackle me while on camera with Raquel Welch."

Somewhere in the ABC archives is footage of the two walking down the red carpet.

When they reached the opposite end, a woman asked Dorsey for his ticket. He told her that he had gotten a beep on his pager notifying him that his car alarm had gone off and that his date for the evening was inside with both tickets.

"I told her my name and when she turned her back on me—bam—I was in," he said.

He was so nervous about being thrown out, he ordered a rum and Coke to calm his nerves, only to spill some of it on his jacket sleeve. Inside the lower portion of the auditorium, all the seats were labeled with names of invited guests and celebrities, so he headed for the escalator and watched from the balcony.

Gossett won, making him the first African American to win an Academy Award for acting since Sidney Poitier had become the first to win back in 1964.

A decade later, in August 1992, Reginald was sitting next to Gossett on the set of *Return to Lonesome Dove*. It was the first day of filming in Montana. The two played brothers—Isom and Isaac Pickett. Dorsey leaned over and said, "You have no idea what this moment means to me."

"What are you talking about?" replied Gossett, who was confused.

Before shooting the next scene, Dorsey told him the whole story about how he had snuck into the Oscars so he could be there to see him win. Gossett was flattered and humbled.

"You just never know the impact you're going to have on somebody's life and so that's why I'm always really careful about the way I carry myself," Dorsey said, "and the things that I say to a younger generation of not only cowboys but actors and filmmakers."

It was a lesson that also played out earlier that day.

Two-time Academy Award winner Jon Voight introduced himself to Dorsey, but before walking away, he took a step back and eyed Dorsey from head to toe. He looked him over a second time before asking if he was happy with his outfit.

"To be honest with you," Dorsey said, "not exactly."

Voight insisted the young, unknown actor from Texas follow him.

Dorsey had not yet filmed a single scene. Voight walked right up to the director, Mike Robe, and proclaimed, "He doesn't like his outfit."

It was not that Voight was trying to cause trouble. Quite to the contrary, he wanted to make sure his fellow cast member was comfortable and used his clout to get Dorsey into something that made him better connect with his character.

"The thing about Jon is that he cares about the production," Dorsey explained. "He cares about every aspect. . . . It wasn't just about him doing his job. He wanted to make sure that everybody rose to a certain level of expectation. That's why he has two Oscars. That's why Lou had an Oscar himself. They had no problem getting their hands dirty. They had no problem putting the work in, and I absorbed all of that."

By casting Dorsey as Isaac Pickett, producers got two for one—an actor who could ride a horse and do all his own stunts.

Dorsey had gotten away from his cowboy roots for the first ten years he was in Hollywood. But when he was twenty-seven, he guest-starred on *Magnum P.I.* and met stunt coordinator John Sherrod.

While the two enjoyed a rare day off at the beach, Sherrod told Dorsey that he, too, was a cowboy and invited him to ride with him once they got back home.

When neither was working, they were riding horseback together. Sherrod taught Dorsey how to rope and compete. More importantly, Sherrod became a father figure.

One Sunday afternoon after the annual BPIR, the two said their goodbyes and Dorsey told Sherrod he would be out to his ranch the next week.

Tuesday morning, Dorsey received a call from Glynn Turman.

"John is dead," he said.

Dorsey was confused. Turman explained their friend had finished work on the set of *The Five Heartbeats* and was involved in a head-on collision with an eighteen-wheel tractor-trailer.

"That turned my world upside down," said Dorsey.

But their time together served as a turning point.

"I needed somebody to touch my life like that," Dorsey said of Sherrod's influence and lifelong impact. "He was a cowboy and it reminded me of my uncle [Wardell Young] when I was a kid. It got me back to what my passion was, and it was a turning point in my life, for sure."

In the wake of Sherrod's death, Dorsey and Turman became inseparable.

Dorsey describes himself as Turman's little brother, and together, they were competing in team penning and later team roping events at rodeos in California.

"We started practicing and we started going down the road," Dorsey said. "We started off doing a lot of backyard rodeos and jackpots. And then we actually started competing."

In 1991 they won a team-penning championship.

Later, they tried to get Lu Vason to add team penning to the Bill Pickett Invitational Rodeo, but he would never agree to it, because he thought the event would take too long.

Dorsey pressed forward.

Yes, he would like to have a career that mirrors the likes of Samuel L. Jackson or Danny Glover. But if he's honest with himself, life has been a blessing. In addition to acting—he most recently was seen in the second season of *5th Ward*—Dorsey produced the film *Kings of the Evening*, which won several awards on the festival circuit, and the UMC series *Monogamy*.

But more importantly, he's become more involved in working with children.

In addition to raising and training horses at a stable less than thirty minutes north of Hollywood, he offers riding lessons, mostly to young kids, and cultivates a passion for the great outdoors.

"I accomplished what I set out to do as a filmmaker," Dorsey said, "but just the sheer joy of being able to do what I love to do and still be a cowboy ... I've never worked a day in my life as far as that's concerned."

He paused and surmised, "I still pinch myself. The fact that I was able to make a living at two of the things that I love the most. That's not to say that I haven't had challenges and really heavy moments. I've been injured riding horses and the whole nine yards, and I've had a lot of setbacks as an actor and filmmaker and what have you, but I've never shied away from the challenge, and I'd rather be doing those two things than doing anything else in the world. And everybody around me knows that."

23

Donald and Ronald Stephens with Cleatus Stephens

You must be bold, brave, and courageous and find a way to get in the way.
—JOHN LEWIS

TULSA, OKLAHOMA

Cleatus Stephens saw rodeo as nothing more than gambling.

He respected the athleticism and skills it took to rope calves and ride bulls or compete in any of the other rodeo events. He was even supportive of his twin sons—Donald and Ronald—despite the uncertainty of whether or not, as Black cowboys, they would be marked or scored high enough to win any money. Or, for that matter, whether they would even be paid if they did earn it.

But it seemed too risky for the patriarch of the Stephens family. The old man would have much rather his sons focus on becoming working cowboys instead of rodeo cowboys. That said, according to Ronald, their father helped them any way he could and "never really discouraged us."

In their younger years, Cleatus gave his boys a horse and four calves to practice roping.

The old, worn-out ranch horse wasn't much of a roping horse, but the boys made do.

Rodeo was a family event. Cleatus and his wife, Marie, were members of the Tulsa Round-Up Club and they hauled the kids—the twins, Cecelia, who is four years older than Donald and Ronald, and Regina, who is four years younger than the brothers—to everything from picnics and barbecues to the all-Black rodeos around Oklahoma. The family rode in parades and grand entries. Cecelia was a rodeo queen. Marie later took her boys to junior rodeos, and Regina always rode along wherever they went on a pony named Shorty.

But they were *city* kids, who lived along a paved street surrounded by dirt roads on the north side of Tulsa. They made the most of their weekends in the country.

"My dream was one day to walk out of my back door and be able to ride my horse in my own arena," said Ronald, who accomplished that dream in 1976—three years after graduating from high school—when he and Donald bought five acres together.

Cleatus Stephens was one of ten kids—five boys and five girls. He married the love of his life, Marie, ten days before Valentine's Day in 1950. The couple had five children together: Cleatus Jr., who died as a baby, Cecelia, Donald, Ronald, and Regina.

In March 1956 Cleatus was one of the first six African American firefighters hired by the Tulsa Fire Department, along with Clifford Harn, Merle Stripling, Robert Shanks, Milton Goodwin, and Henry Collier. All six were assigned to Station 19, which was on the corner of Mohawk Boulevard and Peoria Avenue, with two Black firefighters assigned to each of the three platoons.

In a story published in February 2020, KJRH reporter Dane Hawkins wrote, "They fought fires and racial injustice at the same time."

While their hiring may have desegregated the department, it did little in the way of impacting the racism they faced in an era of Jim Crow laws. The white firefighters lived on one side of the station, while the Black men shared open barracks and lockers on the other side with the truck bay separating the two. They even used separate bathrooms.

They did, however, share a kitchen and oftentimes would eat together.

Ronald told KJRH that his father, who never talked much about being a fireman, much less the racism he faced, once admitted, "I slept with my gun up under my bed to make sure no one bothered me at the fire station."

One rare story Cleatus shared with his family had to do with a house fire in which four children died. It was hard on him that he was unable to save them. On another occasion, Cleatus fought a blaze across the street from where the boys' aunt lived. The brothers stood in awe as their father—a mountain of muscle who stood six feet two and would hold his arms out to either side and walk nearly half a block with the twins hanging from his forearms—emerged from the flames with the homeowner in his arms as he crossed over the threshold of the front door.

She survived.

"He was Superman to me," said Ronald, who along with his brother joined the department in 1976 and '77, respectively. Cleatus worked twenty-three years as a fireman and retired in 1981—making the father and sons the first multigenerational family of Black firefighters in Tulsa.

More than sixty years later, Stripling, Harn, Shanks, Goodwin, Collier, and Cleatus—commonly remembered as "The Six"—were collectively inducted into the Tulsa Fire Department Hall of Fame.

Donald Stephens was born April 4, 1955, at Morton Hospital. His twin, Ronald, was born thirteen minutes later. The boys and their mother were quickly transferred to Hillcrest Hospital.

"They didn't even know my mother was having twins because you just couldn't go to the regular hospital back then," Ronald said. "You had to go to what they called the Black hospital."

The Stephenses grew up in a close-knit, urban, middle-class family. The twins still consider each other best friends.

They were a two-car family; both parents worked hard and managed their money so that once a year they could take a family vacation. The one time Ronald thought they might have been poor was when he and his brother asked for five-speed bikes for Christmas and their mother had to explain she could not afford two of those, plus two more for their sisters.

They got single-speed bikes instead.

All four kids made good grades in school—their mother would not have had it any other way—and the boys were athletic. They played football from the time they were in elementary school through their freshmen year in high school when junior rodeo became a priority.

Like their father, the boys grew up with a fascination for horses. They had a horse their father kept down the street from their house in a small development for Black families. Later their father rented a stall in a barn behind Booker T. Washington High School until he moved the family to a predominantly white neighborhood—at which point, the horse stayed with Donald and Ronald's aunt, who lived on seven acres.

The twins and their two sisters went wherever the horses were being kept and rode every weekend.

"They had an arena there we used to go to as kids," said Donald, who has fond memories of his parents joining one of two Tulsa Round-Up Clubs. It was a social gathering more so than a serious entry into rodeos. They brought their kids with them to monthly meetings and the whole family attended the now historic, all-Black rodeos in Drumright, Boley, Okmulgee, Muskogee, and nearby Grayson, which locals know as Wildcat Junction.

They looked up to the cowboys who were older than them, especially Reuben Hura, as mentors who taught them how to rope and ride bulls and bareback horses. But like their father, they were big, strong boys better suited for steer wrestling.

The first junior rodeo they entered was on the south side of Tulsa in Jenks.

Donald won the calf roping, but, Ronald said, "most everyone left" before his brother had a chance to collect the prize money, and those who stayed "came up with some rule and didn't pay us." Before leaving, Ronald made it a point to tell them, "My name is Ronald Stephens. I'm from the D&R Ranch and I'll be back."

Quitting was not an option for either of them.

They had too much pride in themselves and their family.

"You can't quit," said Ronald, a fourth-generation cowboy from Oklahoma. "If our great-grandparents would have gave up, we would have died out and we would have never been born. They had to take that punishment, so the next group would take less of it to keep going."

In spite of the racism and the uncertainty of whether or not they would be treated or marked fairly, they followed their passion and ultimately gravitated to bulldogging.

The twins were at a small jackpot rodeo in Kellyville, Oklahoma, where they met Stan Williamson. They were roping. He was bulldogging. After a short conversation, he invited the boys over to his place and said he would work with them. The more they learned and practiced, the more apparent it became to both brothers that steer wrestling was their passion. Donald loved the fact that, like football, it was a physically demanding sport, and both took it seriously once they reached high school.

Williamson proved to be a hell of a mentor.

He won the PRCA world title in 1979 and again in '82.

By their senior year in high school, the brothers were entering rodeos every weekend and, more importantly, winning money. In 1973, a few months before graduation, they bought a fully loaded Silverado pickup truck and had it delivered to the school. One of the first days they had it, Ronald was in the driver's seat when he was pulled over by the local police department.

The officer's first question was, "Who are you working for?"

"I'm working for Mr. Ronald Stephens," Ronald replied.

When the officer asked for his driver's license, he read the name and said, "Oh, you're Mr. Stephens."

"That's right," said Ronald, who was then asked whose truck he was driving, and again he said, "Mr. Ronald Stephens."

It might have been the first time the boys were hassled for having a brand-new truck, but it certainly would not be the last. "That's the way it was because of the color of our skin," Ronald said.

Once they were done with school, both turned pro. While they entered many PRCA and IPRA events, neither was on the road seven days a week. When they were out of state, they preferred the rodeos produced by Thyrl and Mike Latting—both encouraged the Stephens brothers to consider becoming certified IPRA judges—and in the mid-1980s, they became regulars at the Bill Pickett Invitational Rodeo.

"I couldn't stay on the road much," Donald said, "but I was a weekend warrior. That was what I designated myself as, and weekends I'll go pound."

In 1976 Ronald followed in his father's footsteps and became a firefighter. Donald did the same a year later.

Growing up, other kids played cowboys and Indians, while Donald and Ronald pretended to be firemen. "I thought these guys are giants," Donald recalled. "They were my heroes."

As men, both were now reflections of their father.

Things within the fire department were better than they had been back in 1956, when their father joined, but Donald said it was still "a good ol' boys club" and "when I came on the job, they didn't put two Blacks together at the same station."

Neither of them put up with any horseplay—racial remarks that white firefighters would later say were only made in fun—and on more than one occasion, Donald would pull aside a fellow firefighter and let him know that he didn't need to be liked, but he damn sure was going to be respected.

"I grew up having to fight and I've had my ass kicked before," Donald said, "but I told them, 'I guarantee you hadn't had your ass kicked by Donnie Stephens and you won't like it. I'm a guarantee you, you won't like it.' And I left it like that. I wasn't a little guy, so I guess they looked at you twice and say, 'Okay, do I really want some of this or not?' I'm not threatening. I'm just telling you the truth. It was going to happen."

The schedule was perfect for the brothers. They were one day on, two days off, and they would use those days to travel to and from pro rodeos until they both got tired of getting home and having to go right to the station. The moment Donald lost his motivation for competing he decided to quit while riding in the backseat of a pickup.

They may not have been competing, but neither of them had been forgotten. In 1988 Lu Vason gave their names to a Hollywood producer.

That year the twins used their vacation days "to go play in the movies," recalled Ronald, who performed stunts on horseback for both *Young Guns* and *Return of Desperado*. Both films were made in Santa Fe, New Mexico.

When they were going to rodeos as kids, it was a great opportunity to meet other Black families involved in rodeo. They knew everyone from in and around Oklahoma. And it seemed as though everyone liked them. Those relationships—built on the foundation of cookouts and trail rides—proved valuable when they began producing jackpot rodeos at their own arena.

They went to the Lattings and Cleo Hearn for advice, and over a ten-year period, beginning in the early eighties and continuing on into the nineties, the brothers produced jackpots the first and third Sundays of every month. Over the years, just about every rodeo cowboy from Oklahoma—Clarence and Kenneth LeBlanc, Ervin Williams, and others—came at least once, and they even hosted PRCA and IPRA world champions.

That's where Marcous Friday, who learned to bulldog from Donald, got his start as a rodeo announcer and "honed his craft" with the help of Charlie Evans, who had already become known as the "Voice of Black Rodeo."

"I wanted to have something to fall back on," explained Donald, who sold his house and his share of the land to his brother when he bought 260 acres in Bristow. He still operates a successful cow-calf breeding operation on his ranch.

"I saw a lot of old guys—old cowboys—and lot of them didn't have anything to fall back on," Donald continued. "I didn't want to be like that—broken up and nothing at the end of my days."

24

Marcous Friday and Charles Evans

There's only one way to break the color line. Be good. I mean, play good. Play so good they can't remember what color you were before the season started.

—HANK AARON

TULSA, OKLAHOMA

Marcous Friday's professional mentor and the man he came to see as a father figure was Charles Evans, but had it not been for Donald Stephens, that pivotal relationship might never have developed between the two Tulsa, Oklahoma, natives.

As the calendar turned from the seventies to the eighties, it was Stephens who approached Friday. "You're a little too big to be trying to ride bulls, but I admire your try," he said.

Friday had pursued bull riding growing up but admitted, "I wasn't worth a quarter. . . . I'd start one, but very seldom made the whistle."

Stephens explained that with his size and strength, if Friday tried as hard as he had at bull riding, he could become a mighty fine steer wrestler. Stephens began coaching the youngster on proper technique. Friday already could ride horses well enough to get up on a steer, but he needed to learn how to jump from his horse and throw down a steer.

Eventually, the two of them—along with Stephens's twin brother Ronald—would compete at BPIR events, as well as weekly rodeos produced by Thyrl and Mike Latting up in Illinois and other parts of the Midwest.

It was at one of Latting's rodeos that Friday got hurt for the last time. He hit the dirt so hard he blacked out and had to be carried from the arena and taken to a nearby hospital. On the way home, he had to lie down flat the entire drive because of the back and groin muscles he pulled.

Friday had had enough and told his travel partners that he was going to give up competing and spend more time producing his own rodeos, but no one took him seriously. Injuries often have a way of making rodeo cowboys question their confidence. But Friday wasn't looking for encouragement. The Langston University graduate had already begun conceiving Another Friday Productions—but that was before a whole other career presented itself.

A few weeks later, back in Tulsa, Donald and his brother were hosting a small jackpot rodeo. They asked Friday if he would be interested in announcing. He had never done anything like it, but the two brothers told him just to call the names of each competitor. So that's what Friday did. Instead of sitting up in the announcer's box, he stood down on the ground level and read off names. That's when a rather familiar man walked up to him.

It was Charles Evans.

Evans had already become nationally known as the "Voice of Black Rodeos." Friday had been just a boy the first time he heard Evans announcing at a rodeo he attended with his maternal grandfather, Clifton Morgan, who was an old-school farmer with some cattle and calves on his land.

Years later, Evans was announcing a lot of the rodeos Friday competed in, but the bull rider–turned–steer wrestler never fared well enough to impress Evans. The announcer had already befriended some of the legendary, all-time, great Black rodeo cowboys, from Cleo Hearn and Bud Bramwell to Marvel Rogers, Nelson Jackson, and Charlie Sampson.

Friday had grown up pretending to be Evans whenever he and his brother played rodeo together in their living room, so it meant the world to him when his hero approached him.

"You sure sound good behind that mic," Evans said.

Afterward, they talked some more, and Evans made Friday an offer, "I'm not going to be doing this very long—probably another three or four years—would you like to work with me?"

Marcous Friday never met his father.

While growing up, he said, "I never ran into a room yelling, 'Daddy, Daddy, Daddy.'"

Hell, Friday does not even know the man's name.

His mother, Beadie—friends and family call her Bea—was married prior to meeting her son's biological father. Friday was her first married name, so when Marcous was born, on March 25, 1958, she went ahead and wrote Friday as his last name on the birth certificate.

Bea's maiden name was Morgan. She had thirteen brothers and sisters. Her father, Clifton, had just as many siblings, which meant the annual Morgan family reunion brought together as many as one hundred relatives. Those memorable gatherings were loud, cheerful, and often lasted entire weekends.

Everyone would gather at Clifton and Nancy's farm and they all pitched in to pick tomatoes and okra. There were hundreds of chickens running around. The men would grab forty or fifty of them and wring their necks, then the ladies would dip them in hot water to more easily pluck the feathers. The freshly butchered chickens were grilled for everyone to enjoy.

Clifton and Nancy always made certain there was enough food for everyone. That's who they were as people—hard workers who were not shy about opening their home to others. They knew how to make people feel welcome. It's a characteristic Marcous inherited from his grandparents, and it served him well when he picked up a microphone.

Throughout the 1960s, Friday, his siblings, and most of his cousins spent their summers living with their grandparents. In those days, the farmhouse had no running water, which meant they used an outhouse and drank from a well.

The kids worked in the orchards doing what Marcous described as "slavery-type things," which actually meant they were mostly out in the fields in the dry, hot sun picking okra, tomatoes, and other vegetables and fruits. No one ever earned any money so much as they "got paid by having a meal to eat."

Clifton would butcher a hog, and on Sundays after church, he would barbecue it in a big, open pit behind the house.

Much like the family reunions, Clifton and Nancy would invite anyone who attended church to stop over at their place. The kids and adults would compete in horse and sack races, while others would fish down by the pond. It felt like the ultimate carnival, according to Friday, who remembers everyone eating pork lathered in sauce from wood-skewer sticks like you might find at a rural town's street festival.

"Everything I learned in life was through my uncles and my grandfather," Friday said.

And there was nothing about farming in rural Oklahoma and coming of age in Tulsa that left Marcous believing he was destined to one day become a Black cowboy.

As a seventh grader, he was attending George Washington Carver Junior High—a predominately Black school—when the school district was desegregated and kids from Black neighborhoods were bused to what had previously been white schools. That was a monumental moment for Friday and his classmates, especially considering Carver is within walking distance of the Greenwood District and just fifty years removed from the Tulsa race riots of 1921.

Friday, who graduated from Will Rogers High School, grew up attending rodeos with his grandfather, especially Black rodeos in nearby Drumright, Boley, and Okmulgee.

The LeBlanc family—Charles, Roy, and later Clarence and Kenneth—has been producing an annual all-Black rodeo in Okmulgee since 1956. That's where Friday remembers hearing Evans for the first time.

The Rockford rodeos on Sunday afternoons in Tulsa were another popular destination for Black cowboys and where Friday would listen in awe of Evans.

Charles Evans was born in 1930 in Oktaha, Oklahoma, a tiny town of less than four hundred located just north of I-40 between Okmulgee and Muskogee. Evans and his family eventually moved to the northern edge of Tulsa, where he graduated from Booker T. Washington High School—a school that may have turned out more Black rodeo cowboys than any other in the country. He promptly joined the U.S. Army and served in the Korean War as a paratrooper and military police officer.

After being discharged, he went to work as a mechanic for American Airlines and worked for them for thirty-eight years without ever missing a single day of work.

He grew up learning how to team rope and competed throughout much of his life—mostly at open amateur events—until he was nearly eighty years old. But he made a name for himself nationally as a rodeo announcer.

In the late sixties, Evans and fellow Oklahoma natives Cleo Hearn and Marvel Rogers and Oklahoma transplant Bud Bramwell teamed up and formed the American Black Cowboy Association with the intent of one day producing an all-Black rodeo at Madison Square Garden.

They never managed to host an event at the world's most famous arena, but on September 4, 1971, they did hold a seminal event in New York City at Downing Stadium on Randall's Island in the middle of the Harlem River.

An obituary—Evans died in March of 2018 at age eighty-eight—included a quote from *Tulsa World* about the event. "A lot of folks in the East thought we were joking when we told them what we wanted to do," he said. "We wanted to prove we had enough Black cowboys to put on a show."

They did.

Muhammad Ali was there and so was actor Woody Strode, and the entire event was chronicled in the documentary film *Black Rodeo*. Five years later, he was still being quoted in the *New York Times*, and in 1981 he was the subject of a profile that appeared in the *Washington Post* as a preview to the National Invitational Black Rodeo in Washington DC.

The *Post* was enamored with his good-ol'-boy phrases like, "Here's a fellow hotter than a two-dollar stove at bean-cookin' time," or, "You can always tell a bull rider because one arm is longer than the other." Even those who were familiar with the corny one-liners loved his southern charm and less-than-proper English.

He was loved. He was revered. He was one of them. He also was a man of *the* word.

Cowboys, cowgirls, and rodeo fans alike looked forward to his recital of the cowboy prayer as much as they anticipated the rodeo.

His son, Charles Jr., was quoted in his father's obit explaining the senior Evans loved seeing people enjoying themselves. "He was somewhat of an entertainer," said Charles Jr., who saw his father as a storyteller.

That is also how Friday saw him.

To him, his mentor was a raconteur as much as the legendary announcer who spoke with authority and charisma—whether he was at a backyard rodeo that drew fifty people or in front of a sold-out arena. It was a trait Evans passed down to his protégé.

Evans treated Friday like a son. In fact, Evans was the only man Friday ever gave a Father's Day card to. Evans and his wife, Ada, had four children— Charles Jr., Candy Williams, Sherri Reed, and Tamra Johnson—but he knew his relationship with Friday meant a lot to the younger man.

"He's the only person that ever even took the time to show me anything about life or being a man," Friday said. "He has his own kids and he did that just because of the type of person he is."

They spent so much time together that folks who didn't know any better often mistook them as father and son. That was all right with Friday.

He is forever grateful for the chance meeting that brought them together.

Along with the legendary Clem McSpadden, Evans was one of the first cowboys to announce a rodeo on horseback. Evans would be down in the arena on his horse, while Friday was in the booth playing music and, more importantly, listening and learning from one of the greats.

Evans is not simply the best Black announcer there ever was. He's in the pantheon of all-time greats—regardless of ethnicity—that includes Phil Gardenhire, Bob Tallman, Hadley Barrett, Boyd Polhamus, and, of course, McSpadden.

Knowing Friday had been a bulldogger, Evans would let him announce the steer wrestling. Eventually, the two developed a rapport and would announce the whole rodeo together—the two-man approach is rather common today. Before long, Evans made the decision to stay in Oklahoma and travel less.

Evans convinced various committees who had hired him to hire Friday as their rodeo announcer. Those events were not just handed over to Friday; he was a relentless worker who spent hours prepping before he ever left home. He not only knew the names and hometowns of the cowboys who were competing and where they were in the world rankings, but he also collected anecdotes, human interest stories, and memories from bygone rodeos. He made it a point to highlight two or three cowboys and cowgirls in each event and share those stories as they readied themselves for a run or ride.

Like Evans, Friday was as much a storyteller as the reporter covering the rodeo for the local newspaper. The more people heard him, the more phone calls he started getting from other producers, contractors, and committees.

"I've been to over forty states announcing rodeos," said Friday, who is not sure what would have become of him professionally had it not been for Evans's mentorship.

He would drive or fly out on Friday mornings twenty-five to thirty times a year and always be back home late Sunday night in time to get a few hours of sleep before going to work in the maintenance and engineering department for the Tulsa City–County Library.

Friday, who announces the Bill Pickett Invitational Rodeo Finals every September in Washington DC, jokes that oftentimes he can leave and get back to town without anyone other than his wife, Robin, knowing he was gone. The year his daughter turned sixteen, she traveled with him to the nation's capital and Friday arranged for the two of them to visit the U.S. Capitol and the White House.

Later in his life, an aging Evans would use a walker to make his way up to the booth in Okmulgee, or Friday would move down to ground level and sit next to Evans's wheelchair with a wireless microphone so the two could talk.

"Charlie, what are you doing over here?" Friday would ask.

"I'm just listening to you," he would reply. "I'm really enjoying this."

Friday took pleasure in making Evans feel special, because, for so many years, that was how Evans made him feel. "And that's how we did it," Friday remembered.

Like Evans once was, Friday is ready to travel less and finally spend more time producing and promoting his own events.

Just as Evans took Friday under his tutelage, Friday extended a helping hand to Steve Reagor, an accomplished tie-down roper eager to produce rodeos, timed events, and stand-alone roping events.

Together, they produce the Saddle and Buckle Series, which is a series of eleven events held within a couple of hours' drive of Tulsa—Bristol, Kellyville,

Mounds, and Okmulgee, among them. Cowboys have to compete in at least seven of the eleven events to qualify for the series-ending awards.

Friday and Reagor have also been asked if they would sanction events for the IPRA but chose not to because many of their local competitors would be forced to buy IPRA membership cards and entry fees would increase. Their decision to produce open rodeos makes it affordable for entire families to enter and compete.

As a producer, Friday is perhaps best known for the annual Juneteenth Rodeo held the second weekend in June right there in Tulsa. For its first decade in existence, Juneteenth was an all-Black rodeo. But because of a lack of sponsorship opportunities—"most of the people we would go to were white businesses and they had kids that rodeoed and they wanted to know why their kids couldn't get in the rodeo"—Friday eventually opened it up to rodeo cowboys and cowgirls of all ethnicities.

"Rodeo is rodeo," Friday explained. "The fastest time wins. That's how I see it."

Whether it was bull riding or steer wrestling, announcing or producing, Black or white events, open, pros, or amateur events, Friday has had a life-long love affair with the sport of rodeo. His maternal grandfather instilled a passion that still burns today. Donald Stephens and, later, Charles Evans mentored him and taught him how to be a consummate professional.

But ultimately, Marcous Friday was born with the heart of a rodeo cowboy.

"It's the best sport that anybody could get in because with football there's eleven people," Friday said. "That running back is nothing without that line. In basketball, LeBron James is nothing without those other four people. But when that calf roper backs in the box, you don't have [any] help. That bull rider [doesn't] have any help when he nods his head. It's him against the animal that he draws and that's what made rodeo so much better to me than the other sports—you have to go out there and make that accomplishment by yourself.

"I love rodeo. Man, I love everything about it."

25

Bud Bramwell and Cleo Hearn with Charles Evans and Marvel Rogers Sr.

You can't start changing things in your past. Everyone has challenges and lessons to learn—we wouldn't be who we are without them.

—SEAN COMBS

HARLEM, NEW YORK

The afternoon of Friday, September 3, 1971, was beautiful and sunny in Harlem as residents lined the streets and hung their heads out of second- and third-story windows to watch a three-mile parade of cowboys make their way through the city on horseback.

These were not the cowboys New Yorkers were accustomed to seeing on television or the silver screen, though. They were Black cowboys, and a day later, more than ten thousand people—many of whom had never seen a rodeo, much less an all-Black rodeo—made the short walk across the Triborough Bridge to Randall's Island for the Black Western Cultural Show and Wild West Rodeo, or what became known as a "rodeo with soul." Outside of Downing Stadium (since demolished), they bought programs for a dollar and cheap straw cowboy hats for children along with other Western-themed novelty items. Inside, many of the cowboys from out West were competing on grass instead of dirt for the first time and finding it a rather slick surface for calf and team ropers to stop their horses.

United Press International reported that the purpose of the event was "to show ghetto-bred youngsters that there are Black cowboys" from Texas, Oklahoma, California, Illinois, and Michigan, along with Connecticut, New Jersey, and even New York. The *Raleigh (wv) Register* ran the story under a headline that read "I Thought They Were All White." More accustomed to running rodeo stories, the *Dallas Morning News* headline simply read "Black Cowboys."

Muhammad Ali was there, and the Associated Press wrote that seeing the legendary fighter who turned war protester and civil rights activist "excited even the hard-bitten youngsters of the Harlem ghetto."

The history of Black cowboys intersects with America's struggle for racial equality, human rights, and social justice. New York's first Black rodeo brought out more than fifty of the best Black cowboys, who otherwise would have been competing in smaller, less publicized, and often overlooked events. The whole weekend was chronicled in a documentary titled *Black Rodeo* that has since defined the legacy of this historic event.

"With friends telling friends, America will again remember the heroes it has forgotten," Bud Bramwell, president of the American Black Cowboy Association, wrote in a letter published at the front of the event program. Bramwell went on to explain that cowboys had long symbolized strength and courage but that Black children had not been able to identify with them because they had never seen a cowboy who represented the Black community until now.

"From now on we want you, and your children, to know the proud role our people played in the Western history of yesterday and today," he wrote before proclaiming, "Let our pride in our past help us to build a prouder future."

The idea of staging an all-Black rodeo in Harlem began in earnest in 1969, when Bramwell, Cleo Hearn, Charles Evans, and Marvel Rogers formed the American Black Cowboy Association. A coin flip determined Bramwell would be president, while Hearn was vice president. The group quickly partnered with the plugged-in George Richardson, co-founder of the New Jersey–based marketing firm Periscope Associates.

Richardson had led Martin Luther King Jr. through Newark, New Jersey, after the 1967 riots there. "He was our contact man with everybody," said Bramwell.

The cowboys planned the rodeo events, while Richardson, the only African American elected to the New Jersey State Assembly in the Kennedy administration, raised money through corporate sponsorships. His wife, Ingrid Frank, who had escaped Nazi Germany in the late 1930s via the *Kindertransport* rescue efforts that brought Jewish children to Britain, handled publicity.

"When we found out there were Black cowboys—a friend of ours [Arthur Moore] went down West, up West or whatever you do—anyway, they came back from the West and they saw Black cowboys and they took some video and showed us," said Frank, in a videotaped interview for a 2017 award she received from Labor Arts, a nonprofit dedicated to understanding the lives of working people. "We were blown away by them. We said Black kids— American kids—have to know this, that they share the legacy of the cowboy."

Bramwell, who was raised in Connecticut before attending college in Oklahoma, didn't realize how often American history books had cheated Black students from knowing the truth about their Western roots until he returned to the East Coast. That knowledge gap was one reason that many of New York's movers and shakers thought Bramwell and Richardson were joking when they shared their plans for staging an all-Black rodeo.

"Two and a half years ago, we asked the Madison Square Garden people and others for space," Bramwell told the Associated Press at the time. "They said they didn't know if we were competent enough and whether we would draw people. Everywhere we went, we got the door shut in our face."

Bramwell, now eighty-two, recently clarified his comments from forty-eight years ago: "We had two or three meetings with Madison Square Garden. We just couldn't get the terms that we felt we could work with to get in, but we were close."

One issue Bramwell noted was that Madison Square Garden executives underestimated the willingness of Black cowboys to travel East. "They didn't think we would have enough guys to have a rodeo," he said.

Instead, the group settled on Harlem.

Underwritten by Rheingold Beer and Pepsi-Cola Metropolitan Bottling Company, the cowboy association and Periscope offered cowboys $500 for every truck that drove east from Texas, Oklahoma, or elsewhere.

The inducement worked: Mike Latting, who would become only the second African American to compete at the College National Finals Rodeo in

1973, entered the competition along with a pair of Hollywood stuntmen, Gene Smith and "Cowtown Gene" Walker. Bailey's Prairie Kid (aka Taylor Hall Jr.) and Billy the Kid were there, too, as was Alfred Peet, Rocky Watson, Archie Wycott, and Seneca Charles.

"As long as they had three or four guys in the truck and a couple of horses, it paid their trip up from Texas," Bramwell recalled.

Nelson Jackson made the trip from Oklahoma with Chris Prophet and Reuben Hura. The trio showed up two days early and used part of their $500 to stay at the Park Central Hotel across the street from Carnegie Hall.

"It's a five-star hotel," said Jackson, now seventy-eight, of the property that hosted the NFL draft from 1980 to 1985. "I wish I could stay there now."

It was Jackson's first time in New York City. He grew up in Bixby, Oklahoma, a town of fewer than four thousand people, guiding a horse-pulled plow and milking cows by hand. But the then thirty-year-old was not intimidated by what could have been an overwhelming environment. He won the steer-wrestling event and was third or fourth in the calf-roping competition that was ultimately won by Bramwell.

A year later, when documentary filmmaker Jeff Kanew released *Black Rodeo*, Jackson could be seen riding horseback alongside Ali, who arrived in Harlem in a white convertible Rolls-Royce before sitting horseback in front of the famed Apollo Theater. Later, Ali let a pair of Oklahoma cowboys—Clarence LeBlanc and Gerald Vaughn—"drive his car around the running ring" that circled the football field at the stadium.

Ali even rode on a tame, aging bull hauled east by Moses Fields Jr., who was a plumber by trade.

"Just slide down, Mo," a cowboy is heard in the documentary encouraging Ali, who was cautious because of the size of the bull's horns.

"If this bull bucks, sucker, you better run like hell," Ali said. "I'll whip you worse than I whipped Joe Frazier."

Actually, six months earlier, on March 8, Ali had lost a brutal fifteen-round decision to Frazier at Madison Square Garden, in a heavyweight bout that has come to be known as the "Fight of the Century."

Ali's appearance had been arranged by Kanew, who previously made a living editing movie trailers. Ali and Kanew shared the same lawyer, Bob Arum, who would form Top Rank two years later and go on to establish himself as a major force in boxing. Arum had been working with Ali since 1966, a year before he was banned from the sport for three years when he refused to be drafted.

According to Leigh Montville's biography, *Sting Like a Bee*, Ali suffered financial ruin in his years away from boxing. Bills went unpaid and he borrowed money from friends and acquaintances, including his heavyweight nemesis, Frazier, that also went unpaid. To make ends meet, he began making paid public appearances for a few thousand dollars each. Even after Ali returned to boxing in 1970, Arum continued negotiating a full schedule of appearances, including the all-Black rodeo in Harlem.

"I arranged it," Kanew said of Ali's visit the afternoon before the competition. "And paid it. It was $5,000 plus some net profit points [from the release of the documentary], but there were no profits."

Earlier that week, Jim Gibbons, a member of the documentary crew and, years later, an executive vice president of marketing at Paramount Pictures, was tasked with carrying an envelope containing Ali's cash payment to Arum's Manhattan office. In 2020, Arum, now eighty-eight years old, said he was intrigued by the idea of a Black rodeo, but no longer can recall making a deal that sent Ali to Harlem for an afternoon.

Ali was at the event for no more than two hours. Yet his appearance, which was featured as the climactic third act of Kanew's documentary, established the rodeo as a pivotal moment for all Black cowboys—past and present.

"He recognized that this was part of his culture," Gibbons said. "Once he was there, he totally understood what it was about, and I think he was as mesmerized by them as they were by him.

"He was a champ for more than just boxing. . . . They love that he took the time to be there."

Longtime New York councilman Bill Perkins described the combination of Friday's parade and Saturday's rodeo as a romantic and attractive moment in the city's history. He saw the competitors as "authentic cowboys" and tremendous athletes. More importantly, as Harlem natives, Perkins and Jacob Morris, president of the Harlem Historical Society, saw these never-before-seen newcomers to urban America as "real-life heroes."

The dream of bringing an all-Black rodeo to the East Coast actually began several years earlier after Arthur Moore, a longshoreman from Newark, New Jersey, and his wife, Evelyn, traveled to Oklahoma in the fall of 1967. Moore had been fascinated by cowboys for years and introduced his son, Barry, to horseback riding. Barry eventually met and was mentored by a Black rodeo cowboy named Jesse "Charlie Reno" Hall and went on to become a well-regarded steer wrestler.

On their trip, Arthur and Evelyn Moore met Bramwell and Hearn, both of whom attended Oklahoma State University and had been members of the OSU Cowboys rodeo team. Hearn had originally gone to Oklahoma State on a football scholarship, but within a year of his arrival he turned in his shoulder pads for a piggin' string and joined the rodeo team full time. Upon hearing their stories and attending Black rodeos in Drumright, Oklahoma, and nearby Okmulgee, Moore was inspired to showcase their talents.

But Moore was unable to get people to take his proposal seriously when he returned to the East Coast. Aside from introducing Richardson to Bramwell and Hearn, Moore ultimately played no role in the Harlem event or any of the five other all-Black rodeos that the American Black Cowboy Association and Periscope Associates teamed up to produce in a three-year span from spring 1970 to June 1973.

Barry Moore, who died in October at sixty-eight, understood his father couldn't pull off such a big event. But out of love and loyalty, the younger Moore could not bear to compete in the steer-wrestling event in Harlem. He chose to spend the weekend with Charlie Reno, who was recovering from a broken neck.

The first of the American Black Cowboy Association's events took place in 1970 in Newark, where Periscope was based. A year later, they organized a trio of events. The first was held in Baltimore, where newly elected mayor William Schaefer presented Bramwell with a key to the city. That was followed by an event at the National Guard Armory in Jersey City and then, on September 4, the far more memorable event in Harlem.

At the time, Bramwell, who was thirty-four, and Hearn, who was thirty-two, told various media outlets they planned to produce a twelve-city tour in 1972. The tour never happened. Instead, they produced one event the next year, in Philadelphia, and their final event, a year later, in 1973, at the Freehold Raceway, in Freehold, New Jersey.

Newspaper accounts claim twenty-five thousand people attended the Freehold event on Saturday, and ten thousand youngsters attended a performance on Friday. Bramwell and Richardson reached out to antipoverty organizations to offer a reduced rate of $2 per student for the Friday show.

In her 2017 interview, Frank recalled, "Friday afternoon we always gave a . . . performance for schools in the neighborhood, social service agencies. That was sold out. It was butt-to-butt on the benches."

In an interview at his home in Stillwater, Oklahoma, Bramwell said that despite their success, the American Black Cowboy Association ceased operation because its ultimate goal was to host an event at Madison Square Garden. With little chance of making that a reality, Bramwell and Hearn focused on their respective rodeo careers. There was not another Black rodeo in New York until George Blair organized a series of smaller rodeos in Harlem, Brooklyn, and Coney Island from 1984 to 1997 with the help of two East Coast–raised Black cowboys, Charlie Reno and Steve Robinson.

As for the documentary, unfortunately, *Black Rodeo*, which held a premiere screening in Tulsa, Oklahoma, failed to find an audience following its release in May 1972.

Kanew, now seventy-four, who later directed *Revenge of the Nerds* (1984) and episodes of the television series *Touched by an Angel*, did not go into the rodeo project with the idea of making money. He wanted to make a film that, according to Gibbons, was "different and original."

Cinerama was initially enthusiastic about the response to a test screening and acquired the rights to distribute the film. However, according to Kanew, some executives grew weary and were not sure a "clean, wholesome, positive Black movie" would find an audience at a time when blaxploitation films were popular.

Still, a film executive in Los Angeles saw the movie poster showing a Black cowboy on a horse set against the New York skyline and summoned Kanew to a meeting.

In Kanew's telling, the meeting was short-lived: "Tell me this is about a Black stud that comes into Harlem and f— everybody," Kanew recalled the executive saying.

"No," he replied. "It's a documentary about a Black rodeo."

"Then forget it," the exec said.

When he returned to New York, Kanew grew more frustrated when he learned that Cinerama had not budgeted any money for marketing his film. Despite receiving mostly positive reviews and national coverage, the documentary and the rodeo it chronicled both largely faded from memory.

"At the end of the day," LeBlanc shrugged, "it was probably just another rodeo."

"We were just putting on a rodeo," Bramwell concluded, "and that was it."

But maybe, with the benefit of hindsight, it was something more. The film's narrator was veteran actor Woody Strode, who appeared in the classic Western *The Man Who Shot Liberty Valence* and also helped break the color barrier in the NFL. "It's quite a thing for all of America to know all of its history and not have it edited out," Strode said before the closing credits of *Black Rodeo*. "[It's] the start of something new for Black people. I'm glad I lived to see it. . . . I am proud to see what it means for a man to live under the sun and make a place for him under the sun equal to all men."

26

Charlie "Pee Wee" Sampson

There is in this world no such force as the force of a person determined to rise. The human soul cannot be permanently chained.

—W. E. B. DU BOIS

WATTS, CALIFORNIA

The eleventh of thirteen children, Charlie Sampson was born July 2, 1957, in what he calls "a little town you might have heard of—Watts."

He was eight years old during the riots in August 1965. He was nearly eleven when he took part in a field trip with his Cub Scout pack to see monkeys, snakes, and ponies at a horse stable located at the corner of El Segundo Boulevard and Figueroa Street.

Black cowboys had gathered there since the mid-1950s. Some had horses of their own to ride, while Tommy Cloud—owner and de facto grandfather figure to all of those who found their way to El Fig Stables—had horses for adults to rent and ponies for kids to ride.

The scouts were inside a tent along Figueroa, while Sampson stayed outside because he was enamored with the ponies.

They cost twenty-five cents to ride.

He had two quarters.

He spent them both.

It was the first time he had ever ridden a pony, and afterward, Sampson told the man who collected his quarters, "I'm coming back tomorrow."

His parents had moved the family out of Watts to the far side of Athens Park, which was catty-corner from the stables, so he was within walking distance. He was back again the next day and the day after that, too. In fact, Sampson, who the older boys nicknamed Pee Wee, came back pretty much every day until he did not have any quarters left to spend. That's when stable managers Bennie Moore and Lee McClain taught him how to be a stable hand.

His reward, of course, was riding ponies.

Sampson would clean stalls and shovel horseshit. Anything to get on those ponies.

Until then, he had never imagined he would become a Black cowboy, much less a professional bull rider. No one could have known that just fourteen years later, in December 1982, Sampson would become the first African American to win a PRCA world title.

Watts was originally established by Spanish Mexican settlers as part of the Rancho La Tajuata, which received a land grant in 1820 and then sold off into small farms in the 1870s. It was incorporated as Watts in 1907 and did not become a predominantly Black neighborhood until the 1940s as the second Great Migration brought more than five hundred thousand migrants West from Louisiana, Mississippi and Texas. Tens of thousands settled in California, according to the Watts Neighborhood Council.

Cloud came west from Texas in the 1950s and Sampson found him and a cast of older and more experienced cowboys—Johnny Ashby, John Davis, James Isabel, Gene and Johnny Smith, C. B. Alexander, Will Dawson, Moore, and McClain among them—at the stables a decade later.

In a 1981 interview with the *Washington Post*, Sampson said, "I used to watch the guys at the stable break out into a gallop and just disappear into the hills. It looked like so much fun. I would say, 'Please, sir, will you give me a ride?'"

When he got a little older, Sampson would team rope with them down in Long Beach. That's where everyone from the stables would go on Wednesday nights.

Eventually, at thirteen, Sampson started riding steers on a trip to Oklahoma. Davis went back home with the Smith brothers, who had taken a liking to the young kid. McClain was on the trip and so was Alexander. Sampson's parents let their son ride along for the experience of watching the others competing at a pro rodeo in Tishomingo.

Afterward, there was a junior event. Gene Smith and McClain entered Sampson in the steer riding competition. He resisted, so they wanted to know, "Then why even come along?"

In a television interview with Washington DC-based broadcaster George Michael, whose *Sports Machine* program was nationally syndicated on Sunday nights, Sampson talked about that first experience. He did not want to compete, but was told by Smith, "You either get on one of these steers or walk home."

Sampson was nervous, so it's no surprise that he fell off and cried.

Back in California, McClain had Sampson sit on a bale of hay and then moved him to a practice barrel and explained to him that riding steers was no different than riding ponies. By the time he was in high school, Sampson moved on from steers to bulls.

He had befriended Myrtis Dightman, who became the first Black cowboy to compete at the NFR in 1964 and the first to qualify in 1966. Dightman would travel from Texas to California in the springtime for rodeos in Red Bluff, Lakeside, Clovis, and Redding and then come back in the summer for Folsom and Salinas.

Sampson idolized him.

In 1972 Dightman offered to work with the teenager and teach him everything he knew about bull riding, how to enter rodeos, how to travel, and how to handle any racism Sampson might face—but only after he graduated from high school. Dightman wanted Sampson to have the one thing he never received: an education.

"I wasn't the best student," Sampson said, "but I was good enough to pass."

His senior year, he signed up for a co-op credit and listed El Fig Stables as his place of employment. His English teacher, who was also his adviser, was not keen on accepting the stables as a credit. She thought he went there to ride horses and waste time. Without the co-op credits, Sampson was going to be one class short of graduation, so he asked Fletcher Forte and Alfonso Eland—a pair of Black cowboys he respected—to meet with his adviser and help change her mind.

"She was upset because he wouldn't put in the effort she thought he should put into his books," Forte said. "She didn't think [there] was no work involved, so I told her, 'Shoot, there's more work than you think training a horse.'"

Eventually, she agreed.

Sampson graduated from Locke High School—the same school steer wrestler Larry Taplet had graduated from two years earlier and Lee McClain before that—and earned a scholarship to rodeo at Central Arizona College, a two-year community college in Coolidge. When the coach asked if he would be interested in joining the rodeo team, Sampson replied, "You mean I get to go to college free? Sure."

Once he turned eighteen, in 1975, Sampson competed in a combination of college and other events from open and semipro rodeos to Black rodeos and even some pro rodeos; and then in 1977, he got serious about his career and joined the PRCA.

In his first PRCA event, he finished second in Fort Worth.

Afterward, while Butch Kirby, who won the bull-riding title a year earlier, was taking a shower, Sampson held Kirby's gold buckle up to his waist and envisioned having a world title of his own. It seemed unimaginable, especially a few months later when a bull stepped on the middle of Sampson's chest. His season ended with a broken sternum, two broken ribs, and a punctured lung.

It was the beginning of a career filled with devastating injuries. Sampson's season was again cut short in 1980, when he suffered a broken leg that required seventeen pins and two metal plates.

In 1981 he finally made it through an entire season and put together four PRCA event wins—Houston; Monroe, Louisiana; Cody, Wyoming; and Ellensburg, Washington—and then, at the NFR, he became the first African American cowboy to win a round when he was the top-scoring bull rider in the fourth of ten rounds.

In 1982 Sampson partnered with fellow bull rider Ted Nuce, who took care of entering both of them in competitions and handling the business side of rodeo. They would take turns driving from one event to the next in Sampson's four-door Oldsmobile Ninety-Eight. There was enough room for one of them to lay back in the passenger seat and get some sleep on an overnight drive.

Bill Putnam, a bull rider who would later found The Bull Riding Hall of Fame, met Sampson at a rodeo in Austin.

"He was really starting to make his push toward a world championship and really riding just lights out," recalled Putnam, who described Sampson as a showman with charisma that was contagious. For a little guy—he is five feet four and never weighed more than 135 pounds during his career—Putnam remembers Sampson as having an oversized personality with an air of positivity, which is exactly why Nuce wanted to travel with him.

They separately attended Gary Leffew's bull-riding school and learned the importance of travel partners encouraging one another. Nuce said, "Charlie wanted to do something and be somebody and not be like everybody else."

They were inseparable.

Neither one had a credit card in his name, which meant it was nearly impossible to rent a car on the occasions when they flew to an event. Although they might have enjoyed a beer or two, they certainly were not heavy drinkers, which meant they had a lot of free time on the road.

In Canada they would go downhill snow skiing, and in Del Rio, Texas, they would waterski. Once in Montgomery, Alabama, they headed to a local mall and as they were leaving, a man approached them in the parking lot and offered to sell them two brand-new televisions still in the box. Nuce was not interested. Neither was Sampson, until the man said he could have them both for $300.

Sampson changed his mind.

He backed his car up to the unmarked van and loaded the boxes in the oversized trunk of his Oldsmobile. The next day, Nuce flew back to California. Sampson "drove slow and easy" to Dallas because he didn't want to "wreck his new televisions."

Nuce called on Monday and asked about his purchase.

Sampson groaned.

"What?" asked Nuce.

Turns out, the televisions were empty shells.

Sampson replied, "I can't believe it. He took me."

They both laughed.

They still laugh.

Mostly, they were able to laugh it off because in the arena, Sampson was having a phenomenal season. He won nearly all the big rodeos in the winter and those he did not win, he placed high in the average and always left town with prize money.

"He was just on fire as far as drawing good bulls and making the whistle," said Nuce, who described Sampson's entire season in two words: "total domination."

Sampson, who held off second-place Bronx-born Bobby DelVecchio for the title, led the top of the PRCA standings for the entire season and amassed a huge lead by the time they got to Oklahoma City for the NFR. Once it became apparent that Sampson was going to be a world champion, he wanted to share the moment with Dightman.

In an interview with *American Cowboy*, Sampson told the writer, "I want Myrtis Dightman to pull my rope, so he can be part of this festivity. He meant so much to me . . . it was an honor to have him there."

With Dightman on hand for the final round, Sampson became the first Black cowboy to win a PRCA world title. His best friend, Nuce, qualified for his first NFR and said the reality of seeing Sampson holding up his own gold buckle was overwhelming.

They were goal oriented and both reached the pinnacle of professional bull riding. Three years later, in 1985, Nuce became the first Native American to win a PRCA world title.

"For twenty years, that's the way I made my living," Sampson told a group of inner-city kids he met prior to a PBR event at the Staples Center in downtown Los Angeles. The current home arena for the NBA's Los Angeles Lakers and the former stables are separated by only a ten-mile drive along Figueroa, the longest street in the city. "I was the only Black bull rider out there. Not that I felt different, but I felt that I had to fit in. The way I fit in, I got along with everybody . . . and they didn't care that I was a little Black guy.

"All they cared about was that I enjoyed my bull riding."

Sampson was a ten-time NFR qualifier, and in addition to his world title in 1982, he was the California Circuit Champion in 1984 and a three-time Turquoise Circuit Champion in 1985, 1986, and 1993. He was two-time winner of the Pendleton Round Up, Grand National Rodeo, California Rodeo in Salinas, and won the George Paul Memorial in Del Rio a record-tying three times. He also managed to win the Calgary Stampede.

It was easy to enjoy his successes until the injuries proved to be too much.

The most serious injury happened in 1983, when the defending world champion was competing at the Presidential Command Performance Rodeo in Washington DC. Sampson was matched up with a bull named Kiss Me when he broke damn near every bone in his face.

Somehow, miraculously, his nose remained in one piece.

Had President Ronald Reagan's personal physician not been at the rodeo, Sampson might not have survived. Thankfully, the doctor was watching from a suite with the president. He helped to stabilize Sampson on site before he was transferred to a local hospital.

Following his recovery, Sampson was among the first bull riders to trade his traditional cowboy hat for a lacrosse helmet but eventually went back to wearing his customary cowboy hat that he bought from a vendor out in front of a horse auction. Had he not, things might have worked out differently in 1988 when a bull's razor-sharp hoof caught the brim of his hat and sliced his entire earlobe from the side of his head.

These were serious injuries, but Sampson played along with an advertising campaign he was hired for by Timex in which he was featured in a commercial with the slogan, "Takes a licking and keeps on ticking."

He retired in 1994 and was inducted into the Pro Rodeo Hall of Fame (1996).

It was another few years before he emerged as an ambassador for the sport of rodeo.

And then came a series of inductions into the National Multicultural Western Heritage Hall of Fame (2003), PBR Ring of Honor (2004), Rodeo Hall of Fame at the National Cowboy and Western Heritage Museum in Oklahoma City (2008) and the Bull Riding Hall of Fame (2019).

"It's not where you come from. It's not who you are, but it's about your passion," said Nuce. "Knowing Charlie developed a passion very early, as I did, we were able to take advantage of our God-given ability to stay on and ride. Our passion and our ability collided."

Sampson agreed.

"My heart and my desire; I wanted to be a bull rider just like guys from Texas and Oklahoma," concluded Sampson, who offers this advice: "Find *your* passion."

27

Ervin Williams Jr.

There are some things so dear, some things so precious, some things so true, that they are worth dying for. And I submit to you that if a man has not discovered something that he will die for, he isn't fit to live.

—DR. MARTIN LUTHER KING JR.

WILDCAT JUNCTION AND TULSA, OKLAHOMA

Ervin Williams Jr. was the youngest of six siblings. He had three sisters and two brothers. They didn't grow up poor, but it was one hell of a tough household to live in. There were strict rules and consequences when those rules were broken, especially for the youngest of the Williams boys.

"Today, it would probably be abuse," said the soft-spoken Williams, who winced after admitting those words aloud for the first time. "It's probably why I took up bull riding, so I didn't have to listen to all that negative stuff."

Williams would not only hear it when his father, Ervin Sr., was angry, but he also would feel his father's rage more than any of his older siblings. In fact, their father was not nearly as violent with the older boys the way that he was with Ervin Jr., who proved to be little more than an easy target. The oldest of his two brothers is still bothered by the beatings—more so than Ervin Jr. ever was—and harbors guilt for not doing more to protect his youngest sibling.

The physical and emotional abuse was a daily occurrence.

"Shoot, he called me 'nigger' so much I thought that was my name for a long time," said Ervin Jr., who wonders if his father might have been abused by his father. "But I think that helped me. I was determined and focused on riding bulls."

The better he got at bull riding, the more money he won. And the more money he won, the less time he had to spend at home in Wildcat Junction, a small Black community located between Grayson and Morris, Oklahoma.

Even though bull riding is widely considered the most dangerous game on dirt, Ervin Jr. liked his odds of staying on the back of a bull more than he did facing another beating at the hands of his father.

"It's sad," he admitted, "but I forgave him."

Ervin Jr.'s mother, Velma, gave birth to him at a hospital in Tulsa, an hour north of Wildcat Junction, on August 18, 1964. As she had been with all of her children, Velma was a loving mother but even she was never able to protect her last-born child from his father. As a matter of fact, Ervin Jr. suspects his father was rough with his mother—"She got it a little bit too"—for what the elder Williams perceived was too much babying.

The old man wanted his boys to be tough.

It's why he put all three of them on full-sized bulls before they were even teenagers.

Ervin Sr. produced a series of jackpot rodeos, including an annual all-Black event that drew the top Black cowboys to Grayson every year, and used to trade bulls with the legendary Jim Shoulders, an all-around rough stock rider who had already started producing PRCA events.

The Shoulders and Williams families lived no more than five miles apart, and the rather impressionable Ervin Jr. used to spend a lot of time with Shoulders on his ranch.

Shoulders, who was known as the "Babe Ruth of Rodeo," was a tough, no-nonsense cowboy, and he expected the cowboys around him to be just as tough.

Quietly, Little Ervin, as he was known, would watch and learn.

Bull riders—local amateurs and nationally recognized pros alike—were always welcome. Jim and his wife, Sharon, would let them room in their bunkhouse in exchange for a hard day's work on the ranch. Afterward, they would head to the practice pen for a well-earned rodeo clinic led by Jim.

Though Ervin Jr. was far too young to ride bulls, those were his earliest and, perhaps, most influential lessons. Whether Shoulders knew it or not, he was a mentor.

Years later, Cody Lambert, another old-school cowboy known for his gruff exterior, became Williams's professional mentor. Lambert took a liking to Williams because he was a tough kid who was serious about making a career out of bull riding.

Shoulders and Lambert eventually became more like father figures to Williams, providing him with the one thing his own father failed to give him—their approval.

While Ervin Sr. wasn't the ideal father, he is responsible for steering his youngest son toward a rodeo career.

The elder Williams had his son roping calves at six and seven years old. Ervin Jr. kept falling off his horse, so his dad bought him a bucking barrel. Little Ervin never bothered to do any mutton busting (riding sheep) and, instead, started out riding calves. From there, he moved on to steers and quickly started riding full-size bulls. He was a couple years ahead of other kids his age.

It was surprising for some to see Little Ervin on the back of a bull, given his disinterest in horses, but he dominated junior rodeo, winning championships at the Oklahoma Junior Rodeo Association and the American Junior Rodeo Association before advancing to high school rodeo. In 1983, as a senior, Williams became the first African American to win a state high school rodeo title. That year, he won three Oklahoma High School Rodeo Association titles in bull riding, bareback riding, and the all-around.

That season, he battled Lane Frost for the bull-riding title. A decade later, Frost would be lionized following the release of the film *8 Seconds*.

Frost showed up at the state finals ranked the number one high school bull rider in Oklahoma, while Williams was number two in the state. The title came down to the final ride. The original bull that Frost was matched up with was injured in the bullpen area. His replacement bull was weaker and less athletic, allowing Williams to outscore Frost for the state title.

"I felt like I got lucky," said Williams, who recognized Frost was special and predicted in high school that he would one day win a PRCA world championship.

Frost did go on to win the 1987 world title in the PRCA, but unfortunately, in July 1989, he was killed when he was struck by the horn of Takin' Care of Business at Frontier Days Rodeo in Cheyenne, Wyoming.

As for Williams, his high school title earned him his first three trophy saddles and three championship buckles.

"I guess it felt good," he said, although he acknowledged that his father never congratulated him. As a result, he never thought those titles meant as much as they should have. "That's probably one of my downfalls. . . . Shoot, I just rode and got out of the arena."

Williams was far more talented and popular than he realized.

After graduating in May 1983, he started competing in the IPRA and headed to Labette (Kansas) Community College. He won the Central Region—arguably the toughest region in intercollegiate rodeo—and, in 1984, qualified for the College National Finals Rodeo. That year, he also qualified for the IFR, finished the season ranked tenth in bull riding and was named the IPRA Bull Riding Rookie of the Year.

Win at one level, move onto the next. Williams wanted his career to progress that way because he saw Tuff Hedeman, Jim Sharp, and Frost do it that way. But he also knew that he needed to get an education.

"I thought, shoot, I can't beat these guys," Williams recalled, "so I might as well get an education. That way, when I'm through riding, I could fall back on something. It's a shame all these world champions who don't have nothing. They're broke or beat up. I always wanted something to fall back on."

Back in his day, a lot of the top riders stayed up all night boozing and chasing women. Williams was almost never out all night. He wanted to make sure he got enough sleep and typically woke up early to train in the motel fitness room. Sacrificing the late nights with his friends and travel partners was better than the alternative of having to go home and face his abusive father.

Despite all of Ervin Jr.'s early success, the elder Williams never once told his son he was proud of him. "I was cool with it," said Ervin Jr., who compartmentalized the disappointment by telling himself that it was how a lot of men were in that era.

However, he admitted it would have been nice to hear.

"You gotta tell young kids that they can be a world champion," he said. "I didn't have that, so I didn't think I would be a world champion."

Ervin Jr. eventually made peace with his father.

Ervin Sr. died of pancreatic cancer in 1985 prior to his son's three best seasons in the PRCA. His father passed away while Ervin Jr. was recovering from a broken left leg suffered in Dodge City, Kansas. Everyone there knew it was a bad injury. The break was a compound fracture in which the broken tibia and fibula both penetrated through the skin.

Cody Lambert helped Williams to the locker room and told him he would be all right. In the dressing room, Williams got upset with the paramedics when they cut his left boot off before transporting him to a local hospital.

"I just bought them," whispered Williams, almost as if he was afraid a paramedic would hear him complaining more than thirty years later. Because of how his father treated him, Williams was hell-bent on not letting himself ever get angry, especially over something as trivial as having his brand-new boots cut and torn away from his broken leg. With an equally soft voice, he said, "I guess, I'm just determined to break that cycle."

The injury nearly ended his career when the recovery was complicated by an infection that forced doctors to reopen his leg.

"I was lucky," said Williams of the rough recovery that took all of 1986 and '87. "I could have got gangrene."

Today Williams considers his two-year absence from competition as a young bull rider part of paying his dues. He returned in 1988 and won Cheyenne Frontier Days.

A year later, he won the Fort Worth (Texas) Stock Show and Rodeo on the way to becoming only the fourth Black bull rider to qualify for the NFR—a feat he accomplished again in 1990 and '91. He finished the 1989 season ranked third in the PRCA world standings. He came in fifth in 1990.

Williams often traveled with his cousin Steve Washington and the two spent about a year traveling with Charlie "Pee Wee" Sampson, a native of Watts, California, who was the first African American to win a PRCA world title back in December 1982.

Williams and Sampson had two wildly different personalities. Williams was quiet and reserved, while Sampson was outgoing and charismatic. They used to call themselves Buffalo Soldiers in honor of the often underappreciated Black cavalry and infantry soldiers during the American Civil War. "Charlie always jibber-jabbered," joked Williams.

It was Sampson who encouraged Adriano Moraes, a Brazilian pioneer in his own right, to leave his home country and compete in the United States. Sampson arranged for Williams and Moraes to travel together.

Williams still remembers the long and quiet car rides.

Williams was not much of a conversationalist, and at the time, Moraes only spoke Portuguese. Williams was expected to do all of the driving from one rodeo to another—the closest Moraes ever came to sitting behind a steering wheel was in the bumper cars he enjoyed driving at state and county fairs.

"People don't know that I was with Adriano before he became what he became," said Williams of the season he spent traveling with the eventual three-time PBR world champion.

Williams's own professional career came to an unceremonious end following the 1994 season. With his aversion to horses, he didn't exactly ride off into the sunset. It was more like he flew off into the sunset by taking a job in Tulsa painting commercial aircraft for American Airlines.

To rodeo fans, Williams has become something of a recluse—not surprising for someone remembered as a reluctant champion.

Nevertheless, he still follows the PBR closely—he watches their weekly events on television, and when he's not at home he follows the event on his Ride Pass app—and enjoys tuning in to watch the NFR every December. Like so many others from his era, Williams is not active on social media, although he does quietly use his wife's Facebook profile.

Yes. He still has a love of the game.

Just don't ask him if he's a cowboy.

"I'm a bull rider," Williams emphatically said. "I don't know if I'm a cowboy or not. I think a cowboy is those guys who are on the range—wear cowboy hats or wear boots. My feet is so bad I don't even wear boots. I ain't put a pair of boots on in twenty years. When I was younger, shoot, I used to put my hat in a riggin' bag. Like J.W. [Hart] and them, you don't see those guys without a hat. I ain't wore a hat in a year or two. I was always a bull rider.

"I always loved riding bulls," Williams concluded. "Martin Luther King said, 'If you ain't doing something that you would die for, it ain't worth living for.' I loved it enough that I would die for it. Just like Lane did. He died for what he loved. How many people can say that?"

28

Charlie Reno and Steve Robinson

I don't mind being Black. I'm Black out loud. It's more than the people that they
are, it's the condition that they represent.
—MOS DEF

HARLEM AND BROOKLYN, NEW YORK

In death, the *New York Times* described former New York mayor Ed Koch
as "brash, shrewd, and colorful as the city he led." In life, he was a master
showman who—on multiple occasions—sat tall in the saddle on the back of a
horse as Steve Robinson led him around the edge of a makeshift rodeo arena
set up on one of four softball fields at Col. Young Park in Harlem.

A streetwise cheerleader and self-promoter, the famously feisty Koch
would smile and wave despite a rain of boos from the mostly Black crowd
that filled the temporary bleachers that, coincidentally, had been provided
free of charge by the City of New York.

The charismatic Koch was a three-term mayor who took office January 1,
1978. But New Yorkers had grown disenchanted with the longtime Democrat's
move to right of center, which many saw as "an act of betrayal," according
to another *Times* article.

Koch was unfazed by the crowd's response to his presence at the annual
springtime Black World Championship Rodeo. He kept waving.

Koch and his successors—David Dinkins in 1990 and Rudolph Giuliani in 1994—were always present for the celebratory parades and ceremonial grand entries in Harlem, Brooklyn, Queens, Bronx, and wherever else the rodeos were held on high school football fields, in city parks and empty lots among high-rise buildings.

There was no mistaking them for rodeo fans.

Future success in politics required Black votes, so the mayors came wearing honorary rodeo buckles and handed out proclamations like the one Giuliani brought in May 1997.

"The Black World Championship, founded in 1986 [Editor's note: It was founded in 1984] by Dr. George E. Blair, is an exciting, continually evolving rodeo and comprehensive educational program that identifies, documents, and presents information about American Black Cowboys, Black Cowgirls, Buffalo Soldiers, and Rodeos," read a release issued by the mayor's office.

But only Koch ever dared to ride horseback.

Robinson remembers him as the most personable of the three. Koch knew him by name, and would ask each year, "You have a horse for me?" Of course, Robinson did, and he always remembered to bring an experienced horse that knew how to take care of an inexperienced rider.

A politician's politician, Koch would make two laps around the arena in spite of knowing he would be showered with boos from the portable grandstands lined up on the sidewalk-long West 143rd Street and another set of stands on the first baseline of a city-owned softball diamond.

"That's taking a *big* chance," said Robinson, who was helping out before becoming the third cowboy—following Charlie Reno (aka Jesse C. R. Hall) and Dwight Judge—to serve as director of Black World Championship Rodeo. "Can you imagine if we had bucked off the mayor of New York?

"That would have been on the news."

George Blair was born in 1930 in Braddock, Pennsylvania.

He earned his PhD in education from St. John's University, after finding his way to Manhattan. He was an ordained minister, vice president at Long Island University, and assistant chancellor at the State University of New York. Fellow scholars knew him as an urban cowboy.

Various media accounts describe Blair as a fifth-generation Black cowboy, who grew up horseback riding on family farms in Virginia and Texas. In 1992 the *New York Daily News* led a July 31 story—"Black Rodeo Spurs Interest in the Old West"—by proclaiming, "George Blair's mama let her son grow up to be a cowboy—a Harlem cowboy."

Reno and Robinson question that story.

"I don't know how that story can be true," Reno said, while Robinson added, "He didn't even like being around the horses. He's not a cowboy."

From the early 1980s to the present day, Blair was profiled in dozens of newspaper articles. In addition to his own questionable story, he claims Black cowboys invented rodeo during the Old West while their white counterparts went to whites-only towns to drink whiskey and chase women.

Exaggerations like that deter from real trailblazers like Bill Pickett, who invented steer wrestling, or others like Bud Bramwell and Cleo Hearn, who were responsible for bringing an all-Black rodeo to Harlem in 1971. Yet in a 1986 article that was syndicated in the *Battle Creek (MI) Enquirer*, Blair claimed his Harlem events were the first of their kind.

"I looked at kids in Harlem and Bedford-Stuyvesant and said, 'What can I do to give them better role models?' The rodeo was the best answer I had," he told the *Enquirer*.

Three years later, in 1989, he told the *Boston Globe* his Black rodeo was the only one of its kind in the nation, which dismissed not only the 1971 event but also Hearn's new Cowboys of Color rodeos and the Bill Pickett Invitational Rodeo series, which Lu Vason started in 1984. There were others then and have been others since, but Hearn and Vason are regarded as originators by fellow Black cowboys throughout the United States.

For all his stories of grandeur, without Blair, dozens of all-Black rodeos held in New York, New Jersey, and Connecticut would never have been possible, and those events deserve to be recognized for the opportunities they provided *real* Black cowboys.

In 1984 Black World Championship Rodeo became a reality when Blair negotiated major corporate sponsorships with General Foods, Kool cigarettes, and a beer company. He worked with New York borough presidents and other local politicians like parks commissioner Henry Stern and wrote countless grant proposals that covered production costs of events that gave thousands of school-age children an opportunity to attend the rodeos.

Blair and a couple cowboys would visit local schools on Thursdays—despite the terrible optics of having tobacco and alcohol sponsors—and then host an exhibition rodeo for upward of a thousand or more young people on Friday afternoons.

"The place would be packed," Robinson said.

Blair's relationship with Stern gave him access to city parks and high school athletic facilities, while borough presidents provided Blair's rodeo directors—Reno, Judge, and later Robinson—with much-needed bleachers and security at no cost. The bleachers were fixed on the back of trucks and hydraulically folded out. The city provided everything from port-a-potties to garbage cans.

"Whatever borough it was," Robinson said, "you called the president and things happened. It was unbelievable. The whole thing was unbelievable."

For all his political savvy, Blair knew only one Black cowboy—Charlie Reno.

Blair may have ignored the existence of the American Black Cowboy Association, but he damn sure mimicked a formula started by the Urban Western Riding Program when he enlisted Reno to serve as his rodeo director.

Reno would drive out to Blair's house in Queens every Monday throughout the early months of 1984, and together, the two planned a series of rodeos.

"It was a lot of work and a lot of running around," Reno said. "I knew something good was going to come out of it."

Blair handled securing permits and sponsorships as well as applying for educational grants to offset the financial burden of producing rodeos, while Reno invited Black cowboys from near and far—Bud Bramwell, Willie Ed and Jimmy Lee Walker, Clarence LeBlanc, and Gary Richard, among them—as well as arranging for stock contractors and judges. Reno also handled everything related to assembling a temporary rodeo arena with bucking chutes and back pens for livestock.

Within months Blair scheduled six all-Black rodeos, including three in Harlem and one each in Brooklyn, Atlantic City, and Hartford, Connecticut. The first was held in September 1984 in a vacant lot in Harlem along Frederick Douglas Boulevard between 137th and 138th Streets.

"It was the curiosity factor that got those butts in the seats," Reno said. "They thought it was funny or this must be a joke or something."

Bobby Harrison, a Black cowboy from Port Arthur, Texas, agreed with Reno.

"The rodeo was completely over, and people were still in line paying to get in just to see the animals," wrote Harrison, in a Facebook thread about the rodeo on 138th Street, while Ronald Medley said, "A lot of kids had never seen a horse in person."

Medley, who befriended Reno at Pelham Bay Park in the Bronx, grew up in Harlem on West 143rd Street and entered his first rodeo five blocks away on 138th Street. Unbeknownst to his family and friends, Medley steer wrestled. It was a new experience for everyone. After touching a horse for the first time, one young boy told Medley that he "didn't expect it to feel like velvet."

Bill Perkins, a longtime Harlem councilman, saw the Black cowboys as thundering heroes on horseback more so than a circus, and he described the rodeo as very attractive to young inner-city New Yorkers.

Among those kids was a group of students who were part of the Upward Bound program at Columbia University. They were low-income high school students with at least one failing grade, which, according to former program director Kevin Matthews, "is the kiss of death to get into a good four-year school."

Upward Bound was started in the summer of 1965 as one of the first War on Poverty programs to come from the Lyndon B. Johnson administration.

Matthews, a graduate of Columbia, came to the program as an assistant director in 1985. He used the Black rodeos in Harlem, which were held within walking distance of the campus, as an honors trip for students with perfect attendance and all their assignments completed.

"If I'm sending them to a museum in Manhattan, I'm going to send a teacher with them," said Matthews, who is currently the chief of staff at the Schomburg Center for Research in Black Culture. "If I'm sending them to a rodeo in Harlem, *I'm* going with them.

"I had never seen Black cowboys. I had never seen a rodeo. I grew up in South Jamaica Queens and I was a New York City kid. I was low income and first-generation college. It was interesting for me, but for the kids, it was eye-opening."

They met and had an opportunity to talk with real cowboys, who shared real cowboy experiences. Matthews never intended, much less expected, that the rodeo experience would inspire any career choices among the fifteen to thirty students he took from 1985 to 1988, but it certainly taught his students "to realize there are opportunities beyond what they can see every day."

Those trips inspired curiosity. It taught them that anything is possible.

"Kids have an assumption that all Black people are the same," explained Matthews, who made it a point to impress upon those in the Upward Bound program that cultures are different, even among Black communities. "That's why the rodeo was so interesting. They actually talked to people with a different frame of reference."

In the late eighties, Kool Moe Dee returned to the Harlem neighborhood he grew up in and performed his hit single, "Wild, Wild West," during the intermission for one of the Black rodeos held at Col. Young Park.

Steve Jones—a Harlem street vendor for more than a quarter of a century—sells hats catty-corner from the Schomburg Center on the southeast corner of Malcolm X Boulevard and West 135th Street, but in the early part of the nineties, he was located down on 125th Street.

The cowboys always used to make it a point to frequent Jones's table.

The cowboys would buy hats and pose for photos. Jones was never sure why they stopped coming to Harlem, but always appreciated the history lesson provided by the mere presence of Black cowboys out on the streets.

"It was great to see them guys with their boots on, their cowboy hats, and the ruggedness about them," said Jones. "Everybody should know their history, and a lot of times . . . you can't understand where you come from. History is always important. I mean, every time I look at the TV, I never really see any Black cowboys, so how do we know they existed?"

Black World Championship Rodeo provided those opportunities throughout New York.

They once held a rodeo next to Yankee Stadium in the Bronx. They were in Queens and Coney Island and, of course, the Bedford-Stuyvesant neighborhood of Brooklyn, where Black World Championship Rodeo held events in mid-July for several years at Boys and Girls High School.

The neighborhood is located between Flushing Avenue to the north, Classon Avenue to the west, Broadway to the east, and Atlantic Avenue to the south. Chris Rock grew up there, along with rappers Mos Def and Ali Shaheed from A Tribe Called Quest. Norah Jones is from there, too. All of them were approaching their teen years when the Black World Championship Rodeos were held on the football field behind the high school.

The field was pinned between the backside of the school and the elevated train that ran parallel to Atlantic Avenue.

Just as they did in Harlem, the city supplied temporary bleachers in addition to the existing stands, so the seating stretched all the way around the makeshift rodeo arena. The natural grass, instead of dirt, was not the best footing for barrel-racing horses trying to make tight turns and proved to be unforgiving for rough stock riders. And then the steer wrestlers tore it up. Not on purpose—it is the nature of the sport.

"Most of the time, in the inner city, that's the only place you could put them on and it made it kind of tough because the grounds weren't really suitable," said Robinson, "but it was about going in there and showing kids there were Black cowboys."

In 1984, the first year Blair worked out a deal to use Boys and Girls High School, more than four thousand students were enrolled in the school—making it the seventeenth-largest high school in the country. They had a graduation rate of only 24.4 percent, and it took the late Frank Mickens more than twenty years of his no-nonsense approach to raise that rate to 47.7 percent.

"The Brooklyn kids were just cold-hearted," Reno recalled. "You had to find something that would resonate with them. When they saw Black cowboys over there, we got their attention. They sat there with their mouths open saying, 'Holy smokes.'"

"It meant a lot to the community," said Clive Harding, who was an African American officer with the New York Police Department in the 1980s and is now the head football coach at Boys and Girls High School. "I think Bed-Stuy was the perfect place for Black rodeo to come, based on the demographics of the community. Those were the days of the crack epidemic and a lot of crime in this area."

The front doors of the high school are just twelve blocks from where director Spike Lee filmed *Do the Right Thing*. Less than a decade removed from his critically acclaimed 1989 film, Black World Championship Rodeo returned to Bed-Stuy for one final event at the school.

Unfortunately, in July 1997, life imitated art on one of the hottest days of summer, leading to a racially provoked confrontation—only this one could have been avoided.

With the rodeo set to get started at 3:00 p.m. and temperatures topping ninety degrees, city officials notified Blair that he could not start on time. A citywide ordinance prevented any outdoor equine activity when the temperature is at or above ninety degrees.

Horse-mounted police officers in Midtown Manhattan had to stable their horses.

Horse-drawn carriages in Central Park had to halt their services.

And yes, city officials told Blair he would have to wait before leading the grand entry.

Robinson remembers Blair being visibly upset with anyone who tried to reason with him that it was okay to wait for the temperature to drop a degree or two. Instead, Blair caused a scene by getting on a microphone and making racial accusations.

Robinson vividly remembers Blair riling up the crowd of a few thousand onlookers.

"He made it sound like it was a Black or white thing," Robinson said. "It wasn't. Had we waited, it would have been good."

Instead, the rodeo was canceled.

Blair's outburst also cost him a lucrative sponsorship with General Foods, which made it all the more difficult to cover production costs related to producing future rodeos. Blair was never invited back to Brooklyn despite receiving a key to New York City from Giuliani.

Like Dwight Judge and Reno before him—Blair had been intimidated by Reno, who produced his own pro rodeos under the banner Hall and Sons and felt Blair was guilty of "shady dealings"—Robinson was now having his own tough time working with Blair.

"George was a difficult man to deal with," Robinson said. "He really wasn't a rodeo producer."

If the Brooklyn event was a defining moment regarding how bad things had gotten with Blair, the final straw came when the next rodeo was rained out. Blair did not want to pay top contestants the show-up check he promised or the stock contractors, even though they had trucked their livestock into the city.

Rodeo contestants and contractors were holed up at the Marriott Hotel next to LaGuardia Airport. Reno and now Robinson were strong-willed and saw to it that their Black rodeo colleagues were paid, especially friends who had flown in or driven from Texas and Oklahoma.

A short time later, Black World Championship Rodeo ceased operation.

Blair tried leveraging the rodeo brand, and despite claims to the contrary in recent interviews, he never produced another rodeo. Instead, he has overseen the New York City Riding Academy.

"It could still be going on today," concluded Robinson, who nearly twenty-five years later remains disappointed in how Black World Championship Rodeo came to such an unceremonious ending. "It just kind of fell apart and it didn't have to be that way."

"The history that the Black rodeo left is a great one," Clive Harding said. "We can pass it down to some of our kids who know nothing about Buffalo Soldiers or Black history . . . and have kids learn about something different other than video games."

29

Dwayne Hargo Sr.

One isn't necessarily born with courage; one is born with potential. Without courage, we cannot practice any virtue consistently.
—MAYA ANGELOU

SAN BERNARDINO, CALIFORNIA

For Dwayne Hargo Sr. it was the opportunity of a lifetime, and he was not about to let a little rain dampen his spirits.

He was unfazed.

As an alternate, all Hargo wanted was an opportunity to prove himself.

He got it on a rain-soaked afternoon in Wyoming, at the annual Cheyenne Frontier Days Rodeo—a career-defining matchup with an eight-year-old Mexican crossbred fighting bull named Crooked Nose. This bull had a distinct reddish-brown body with dark legs and one big horn on the left side. Legend has it that at two years old, Crooked Nose hit a barrel so hard in his first bullfight that he broke his right horn off.

As mean as fighting bulls are—Crooked Nose was meaner.

In July 1985 Hargo made one of the greatest freestyle bullfights of his legendary career against the animal, who would go on to be the first bull to be inducted into the Pro Rodeo Hall of Fame.

He was loose and cool as he circled Crooked Nose around to the right—staying within arm's reach, never tensing up under the pressure. He darted back and forth in front of the bull and challenged him—dared him, if you will—to hook him and try to run him over. As quick as Crooked Nose was, Hargo was quicker and all the more athletic. The first-time pro remained calm and maintained the composure of a seasoned veteran. In fact, no one would have known the kid from California was getting his first opportunity to compete on the now-defunct Wrangler Bullfighting Tour.

In a matter of forty unforgettable seconds he scored eighty-nine points. Hargo outscored a pair of legends—Jimmy Anderson and Skipper Voss—to win the round and the event.

More importantly, his professional debut defined his entire Hall of Fame–worthy career, and more than three decades later, it's apparent that fight did more than prove he belonged competing with the best freestyle bullfighters in the world—it foreshadowed the world title and gold buckle Hargo would claim five years later.

"I was proud for him," said fellow bullfighter Ryan Byrne, the first Canadian bullfighter to work the NFR, "and not just because he was Black. It was because he deserved it."

A decade earlier, the scene could very well have played out like the opening sequence to *The Andy Griffith Show*. A boy and his father walking side by side along a gravel road to their favorite fishing hole.

Except this was not the fictitious town of Mayberry.

It was real life.

More specifically, it was San Bernardino, California.

Set on the far east edge of the Greater Los Angeles area—fifty miles due east of downtown Los Angeles—the Inland Empire is a basin populated by four million people. The last bastion of urban society before continuing west on Interstate 10 into Death Valley. At one time, the Empire was a center for agriculture, but as the twentieth century unfolded, it became the urban setting it is today.

And Elmo Hargo was not an Andy Griffith–like father figure, taking his son, Dwayne, fishing on a midsummer morning. Nope. Elmo was in the process of divorcing his son's mother, Olivia, and every morning, the elder Hargo would drop the boy off at Glen Helen Regional Park.

He left him alone for the day with three things: a sack lunch, a fishing pole, and a promise that he would be back to pick him up before sundown. The car ride to and from the park was their only time together, and they did not spend it talking.

Elmo drove and Dwayne sat quietly.

His father never even asked about the lack of fish his son caught. Elmo had no idea that Dwayne wasn't much for fishing. If he was anything, Dwayne was curious.

One morning, he noticed horses going around the park.

The horses were following a trail that looped around the manmade lake where Dwayne was supposed to be fishing. They came from the far side of the park. After stashing his fishing pole under a bush, Dwayne followed the trail and found a stable across the street. Out front they had horses for rent. Dwayne, who was only eight, did not have any money, but that did not stop him from crossing over.

Just before dinnertime, he hustled back to where Elmo picked him up, and together they would quietly drive home. The elder Hargo never once asked his son how exactly he spent his day at the park. Either he did not care to know, or he just assumed Dwayne hadn't had any luck fishing. He would drop him off again the next morning. Like clockwork, Dwayne would stash his pole, run around the lake and cross the street.

After a few days, Dwayne met the stable owner.

Eventually, the ranch hands taught the young boy how to properly brush the horses and make sure they had water. Soon they let him lead the horses from the rent tent into the barn, tie them up, brush them down, and saddle them up for a trail ride around the park.

"Eventually, I got good enough where I could take guided rides out," Hargo said.

It was fun for an inner-city kid who was too small for football and too short for basketball—and one who had no desire to run the streets gangbanging with his friends and dealing drugs.

Hargo worked at the stables for five years before growing restless. His entire future changed on a trip to a local sale barn. He was thirteen when he met the Meisner brothers. David and Dale produced and promoted smalltime jackpot rodeos in their own backyard, while their other brother, Johnny, was a bullfighter.

Hargo started spending more and more time with the Meisners until he eventually spent all of his time with them.

He was feeding and watering horses. Saddling horses. Even tasked with sorting broncs and bulls. "If you're working for a rodeo company," Hargo explained, "you can do anything you want. You can try anything."

He tried roping and riding bucking horses, but never developed a passion for either. Surprisingly, he took a liking to bullfighting. Hargo had not grown up around animals—his parents did not even have a dog—but he was a natural. He started to shadow Johnny, who wanted to get away from bullfighting and work alongside his brothers.

"Let me try that," Hargo asked Johnny one day.

He loved it.

From that day forward, Dwayne Hargo was no longer a city kid from San Bernardino.

He was a rodeo cowboy—a *Black* rodeo cowboy.

Hargo had been feeding the Meisners' bulls and sorting them into various pens. He knew them. He knew their tendencies. He knew which ones were hot and which ones were less feisty, but they were all mean and being in an arena with them was, "a whole different atmosphere." Protecting bull riders is a dangerous role. Without hesitating, bullfighters need to be willing to step between a bull rider and a bull—even if that means getting injured.

It's not a matter of *if* you're going to get hurt. It's only a matter of when and how bad.

"The kind of bulls they had, they weren't just milk cows," Hargo joked. "They got some bulls that would hook you and run a horn up your butt. I was pretty athletic, so getting around bulls, I'm not going to say it was no problem, but I'm glad I have the athleticism. But when they want to get you, it's a whole different game."

Hargo was living at home with his mom and four sisters. Johnny Meisner was providing the paternal influence Hargo needed. At thirteen Hargo left home and moved in with Johnny's family. They looked after him, and more importantly, they thought of him as one of their own. Hargo's relationship with Johnny Meisner was similar to the one Bill Pickett had with Zack Miller decades earlier.

It was not a perfect situation, but it helped steer him away from the streets and gave Hargo, whom the Meisners nicknamed Chocolate, an opportunity to focus on a career in rodeo.

On Friday nights, Hargo would ride along with Johnny's older brother, David, to a livestock auction in nearby El Monte. That's where he met his future wife, Nanette. They would see each other from time to time throughout their teen years, but never dated until they were nineteen.

Eventually, he would move in with Nanette in Altadena, before they married.

Shortly thereafter, Hargo set his sights on making the IFR and spent the summer after his wedding working for Chicago-based rodeo producers Thyrl and Mike Latting.

Hargo also met a legendary rodeo coach from Cal Polytechnic State University, who encouraged him to get his permit with the PRCA, which would allow Hargo to work more prestigious rodeo events. To do so, Hargo would need three signatures on his permit—a PRCA bullfighter, a PRCA bull rider, and a PRCA stock contractor.

The signatures were hard to come by.

It was not the color of his skin that kept people from signing. They needed to see him consistently work at a high level. Living on the West Coast, that was not an easy task. It was his wife who encouraged her husband to enroll in a bullfighting school taught by legendary bullfighter Wick Peth. There were sixteen bullfighters enrolled at the start of a four-day clinic. Peth was an old-school, hardnosed bullfighter, who passed in December 2019. He did not go easy on anyone. Most of them did not last beyond the first day. On the final day, it was just Peth and Hargo working bulls. One after another. Tough and relentless.

Before leaving, Hargo asked Peth if he would sign his pro card.

"Yeah," he replied, "I'll sign it right now."

That was 1984. Charlie Sampson had won the world title two years earlier. He was born and raised in the Los Angeles neighborhood of Watts and was not happy with Hargo, who he thought was too mild-mannered and good-natured when it came to the Meisners calling him Chocolate. Hargo wasn't offended, but Sampson felt it was derogatory. At the time, he did not know about Peth calling Hargo Fudge Stick. Nanette described the difference in the personalities as the difference between growing up in Riverside County as opposed to LA's inner-city, where young men like Sampson learned as kids to stand up for themselves. Hargo kept his opinions to himself and simply said, "They didn't know any better, so let me befriend them."

Sampson was not happy with Hargo's passive nature. Still, he signed Hargo's permit and now he was one signature away from earning his PRCA card.

Hargo then started driving up to Gary Leffew's ranch in the Central Valley of California to work bulls in the practice pen. Leffew was a world champion bull rider who was now a stock contractor and was the third signature Hargo needed to fill his card.

In 1985 Dwayne began a twenty-year career providing cowboy protection at PRCA rodeos, and for a time, he was part of the Wrangler Bullfighting Tour. Dwayne and Nanette raised their boys—Dwayne Jr. and Aaron—on the rodeo circuit.

Four years into his PRCA career, in 1989, Hargo won the Wrangler Bullfighting Tour and became only the second Black world champion.

Afterward, the *Pro Rodeo Sports News* published a blurb recognizing Hargo's title but it did not include a photo of him. Nanette wrote a letter expressing her disappointment. She said they wrote her back saying, "We love getting feedback, whether it's negative or positive, but the fact is the Wrangler Bullfights are not a sanctioned PRCA event."

"Rodeo will never give him that recognition," said Nanette, who insists her husband was a pioneer who had made history.

Unlike his wife, Dwayne seems unfazed by it. He was hurt by the perceived lack of respect, but no longer cares about it today. Yes, he's mostly remembered for the Wrangler Bullfights, but what brought him the most joy were the rodeos he worked over the years and the entertainment he brought to the crowds, as well as the relationships he had with all the committees and the committee members who brought him back year after year.

Relationships, not buckles, are what he's proud of.

In 2005, when Hargo suffered an aneurysm, committee members from the Washington State Fair organized a special rodeo and raised more than $10,000 to help the Hargos with medical bills.

The aneurysm changed everything.

It was the first time Dwayne Jr. and Aaron were not going to be home for Thanksgiving. Dwayne Sr. woke up in the middle of the night and passed out on the floor. He eventually crawled back to bed and Nanette found him the next morning "in really bad shape." She took him to a local hospital, and they transferred him to a nearby location, where he was diagnosed. They transferred him again to University of San Francisco Hospital, where he spent nearly three weeks before going home.

His memory is not what it used to be. And sadly, the patriarch of the Hargo family lost his passion for rodeo. On occasion he will watch a local rodeo, but mostly to watch his sons—both of whom are bullfighters. And he almost never wears his world champion buckle, electing instead to wear a buckle from one of his longstanding rodeos.

Nowadays, in lieu of entertaining large crowds and protecting bull riders, the elder Hargo has retreated to a quiet life of doing yardwork in sweatpants.

It's his way and, therefore, to him, the cowboy way.

30

Fred Whitfield

I'm young, I'm handsome, I'm fast. I can't possibly be beat.
—MUHAMMAD ALI

CYPRESS, TEXAS

The Fred Whitfield story has never been foremost about the color of his skin.

Yes, he is a Black rodeo cowboy, and yes, he has faced his share of racism—in and out of the rodeo arena—but Whitfield's story is one of greatness that puts the eight-time PRCA world champion in a conversation among the greatest athletes of all time.

Michael Jordan and Larry Bird.

Tiger Woods.

Joe Montana and Tom Brady.

Michael Phelps.

Roger Federer.

Pelé.

Richard Petty and A. J. Foyt.

Babe Ruth and Willie Mays.

Wayne Gretzky.

Muhammad Ali.

Each one of those athletes knew the difference between merely competing at an elite level and knowing how to *win*, but every one of their competitors and legions of fans—then and especially now—were also aware of their greatness.

It was that undeniable lack of doubt—in themselves and from others—that separated them from everyone else, and it is what separates Fred Whitfield from other tie-down ropers.

The greats never blend in.

In fact, they often stand out at a young age.

"You can't instill a killer instinct in people," Whitfield said. "You either got it. Or you don't."

He added, "You know what I think it is? I was friends with a lot of people until I backed in the box, and I don't want to use the word 'hate,' because that would not be the right word, but we were not friends when it comes to competition. We were friends afterward, but as long as I was competing against you, you were my enemy. And that's just the way I approached it. There was no doubt that I could win anytime I wanted to. And I could beat anybody at any given moment, no matter who it was."

There are those who see Whitfield as arrogant or cocky, but decades earlier, many said the same about Ali and later Jordan. Truth is, like Ali and Jordan, the statistics and laundry list of accomplishments prove Whitfield to be as great as he said he was.

From 1990 until 2019, when he officially retired following his appearance at Rodeo Houston—that kind of longevity is unheard of in other sports—Whitfield was a dominating force in the sport of rodeo.

In being named Rookie of the Year, he was only the second first-year tie-down roper to qualify for the NFR. A year later, in 1991, he won his first PRCA tie-down title. He followed with six more in 1995, '96, '99, 2000, '02, and '05.

He added an all-around PRCA gold buckle in 1999.

He was the second Black cowboy to win a PRCA championship (third if you include Dwayne Hargo Sr.'s title in the Wrangler Bullfights), the first to do so in a timed event, and the first to win multiple gold buckles—eight of them in a sixteen-year period—in what TheUndefeated.com coined the "National Football League of rodeos."

Whitfield qualified for the NFR in seventeen consecutive years, proving not only his durability and resilience when it came to injuries—or lack thereof—but also a consistency that has galvanized him as the most successful and accomplished Black rodeo cowboy of all time.

If anyone else, regardless of their ethnicity, was going to win the PRCA tie-down title—be it Joe Beaver, Cody Ohl, Monty Lewis, Trevor Brazile, or Stan Smith—they were going to have to beat Whitfield in the midst of the golden age of calf roping, which later became known as tie-down roping.

"Fred Whitfield is a true American sports champion," said Cleo Hearn, who was the first African American to turn pro as a tie-down roper in the RCA.

As much as he loved winning, he hated losing even more.

Whitfield was known for competing with as much urgency at the first event in early January as he did at the finals in mid-December. He was never, ever relaxed until he damn sure knew he had qualified for Las Vegas.

"The season starts in January . . . and nine times out of ten, I could make my reservations for Las Vegas in June," Whitfield said. "There was never any question of *if* I was going to qualify."

He added, "I realized at about sixteen years old that I was pretty gifted and talented, but, I mean, I'd worked my tail off up until that point. It wasn't like I just woke up one day and was sixteen years old and was going to be a world champion."

Fred Whitfield was born August 5, 1967, in Hockley, Texas—halfway between Houston and Prairie View—and raised in nearby Cypress. He was one of five kids, but his parents, Willie and Marie Whitfield, could not afford to raise all five, so they gave two of them up for adoption.

In their earliest years, it was a violent homelife for Fred and his older brother and younger sister. Their father was a womanizer and alcoholic who regularly beat their mother. Twice she shot him. Twice he survived. "It was the Wild West around my house," said Fred, but in the mid-1970s, his father was sentenced to prison for murdering a man he suspected of sleeping with his girlfriend.

Now a single mother raising three children on her own, Marie went to work for Don and Joanne Moffitt. Fred remembers his mother having done everything from babysitting the Moffitts' children to working in the office of their family business to cleaning their home.

She did whatever was asked of her and was thankful the Moffitts helped look after her children. The Whitfields lived across the road and Fred, who was in grade school, befriended their son Roy. He was seven years Fred's senior, and although he was still in high school, Roy became something of a father figure. They developed a lifelong bond that is more like family than friendship.

Every day after school—without fail—Whitfield was with Roy.

He would help Roy with ranch chores, and together, they would work until after dark. This was years before Whitfield had a horse of his own. He would work cattle and push calves all day. It was hard work, but worth it, especially at night's end when Roy would say, "You can run one on this horse."

"It was the highlight of my day to get to rope [calves]," said Whitfield, who added, "I was around a lot of guys. I'd say Roy has helped me the most. He never roped that good, but he always had all the assets that I needed, and I stayed with it."

At thirteen, Whitfield "jumped ship." He left home and went to live with Roy "most of the time, because it was too unstable where I was. . . . I didn't let a whole lot of people in and around my circle.

"Fortunately, for me," Whitfield continued, "I always had the right people."

There was Rufus Green, Calvin Greely Jr., and Sedgwick Haynes. Eventually, as a PRCA rookie, Whitfield met Sylvester Mayfield. They were some of the great Black rodeo cowboys.

"I had all the guys around me," said Whitfield, who was careful never to let himself imitate any particular style of roping. "I took a lot of different things . . . that I liked, and I tried to incorporate it all into my skill."

Throughout high school, Whitfield would run 100 to 150, and sometimes as many as 200, calves a day and ride anywhere from ten to twenty of Roy's horses. On days he outworked the horses, he would do groundwork by running down the rope, flanking and tying the calf.

At sixteen, Whitfield was something of a phenom, and amateur rodeos did not provide him with much competition. Halfway through his senior year, Whitfield, who graduated in 1986, took a job training horses. He would get home from school between 10:30 and 11:00 a.m. every day, change his clothes and not get back until after midnight.

He came by his work ethic naturally, though he does credit his mother with instilling the idea of working hard for what you want out of life.

Shortly after coming of age, Whitfield, who was probably nineteen at the time, lost his way and briefly experimented with drugs. "[I] did all that bullshit, but it didn't take me long to figure out that that was a dead-end street."

One night, Whitfield and a so-called friend were, as he put it, "all jacked up," when the guy said, "Hey, if we ever get busted with this shit, you take the rap and I'll get you out of trouble." On a one-way road to nowhere, Whitfield realized, "I'm headed the wrong way with this dude."

He eliminated the distraction, tightened his circle of friends back up, and refocused on winning.

He honed his skills and stoked his drive and desire to win by competing at Bill Pickett Invitational Rodeo events. "Fred Whitfield brought out a lot of Black cowboys," said Larry Callies, founder of the Black Cowboy Museum, in an interview with FOX News in Houston. "I mean, they all want to be Fred Whitfield."

He used his brief time with the Pickett rodeo to prepare himself for transitioning to the PRCA.

As a PRCA rookie, in 1990, he started off the season by placing in San Antonio, doing well in Denver, and winning some more money in Houston. By springtime, he was ranked in the top five, and Whitfield laughed, "It was like, 'Oh shit, this Black son-of-a-buck right here is for real.'"

Midway through his first season, he said, "I knew then I was going to have a lot of success. Did I know I was going to be an eight-time world champion? Hell no."

In 1991 he had more success in the first couple months of the season, but then "hit a little bit of a stumbling block." He tallied up "a pretty good size credit card bill" before going on a run that lasted through spring and summer. That year, he said, winning his first gold buckle was "the best feeling ever" because "nobody thought I could do it."

He certainly proved them wrong and continued doing so.

At the finals in 1991, he placed in seven of ten rounds, including two round-winning times en route to winning his first world title. Less talked about was the first of his record-tying four average titles at the NFR, a feat he also accomplished in 1997, 1999, and 2002.

In 1993, after winning the Calgary Stampede, he used his payout of more than $100,000 as a down payment to buy a ranch in Hockley.

In 1997, in Vegas, Whitfield had the greatest week of tie-roping in his career.

He set an NFR record for an aggregate of 84 seconds in ten rounds of competition, and in round nine, he made history with the second of back-to-back-to-back, record-setting finals runs. His 6.9 seconds beat the 7.0-flat set one hour prior to his, but it lasted less than a minute when Jeff Chapman tied his calf in 6.8 seconds. That particular Saturday night, in 1997, remains one of the greatest nights of tie-down roping in history.

Coincidentally, a year earlier, Roy Moffitt was adamant Whitfield was letting a second buckle slip away every year, especially considering that year's all-around champ won fewer events, so Whitfield added team roping to his growing repertoire to give himself an opportunity to win an additional buckle.

Moffitt then told Whitfield, "You ought to start team roping."

Moffitt bought team-roping horses and steers, built a brand-new, private arena to practice in, and arranged for team ropers to come and work with Whitfield. He was working harder at team roping than he was tie-down roping and admitted, "When I very first started team roping, honestly, in my mind, it took away from my calf roping a little bit. It took me a couple of years to get it balanced."

He started team roping competitively in 1998.

In 1999 it paid off when he won the all-around title.

"A lot of people don't know this," said Whitfield, who was teamed up with a local kid from Cypress, "but I damn near made the finals heading steers in '99. I missed it by less than $10,000 and had only been roping steers—heading—for a couple of years."

Of course, he added, "We were kicking their ass. We were in the top ten in the world up until late July" and, unfortunately, fell out of the top fifteen by the end of October.

In 2002 Whitfield represented the United States in a three-day exhibition rodeo against Canada at the Winter Olympics in Salt Lake City, Utah; and then, a decade later, surpassed $3 million in career earnings.

It's safe to say, the color of Whitfield's skin never held him back in the rodeo area.

Jealousy, however, was a completely different story, especially when it came to his preference for dating and eventually marrying a white woman.

"It didn't ever affect me," said Whitfield of being a successful athlete in a sport where he believes less than 5 percent of the rodeo cowboys are Black. "There were guys who jacked with me a lot, man, and, I mean, that's been well documented. I wrote about it in my book. I had my eyes on the prize and I knew what they were trying to do.

"There was a guy that used to send stuff to my hotel room out there in Vegas and I knew what they were doing. They would say, 'Oh, I had fun with you this summer. Hope to see you during the finals and here's some roses to remind you of a time we had this summer.' That bullshit never happened. It was just guys trying to fuck with me and [start] turmoil in my camp."

He added, "Every once in a while, I'd have to slap one of them around if they got out of line, but I was never afraid of that either."

At the time of his 2004 Pro Rodeo Hall of Fame induction, Whitfield had the second most tie-down titles (seven) and the second most NFR qualifications (twenty).

In 2000, the same year he married his wife, Cassie, with whom he has two daughters, Fred was inducted into the Rodeo Cowboy Hall of Fame in Oklahoma City, followed by the Texas Cowboys Hall of Fame (2003), Cheyenne Frontier Days Hall of Fame (2005), Texas Rodeo Cowboys Hall of Fame (2005), National Multicultural Western Heritage Hall of Fame (2012) and the St. Paul (Oregon) Rodeo Hall of Fame (2012).

A year later, in 2013, he self-published *Gold Buckles Don't Lie: The Untold Tale of Fred Whitfield*, but unfortunately, according to courthousenews.com, he sued the co-writer of his as-told-to autobiography for breach of contract, conversion, and breach of fiduciary duties when she filed a fraudulent copyright. In 2014 a semiretired Whitfield entered and ultimately won the tie-down roping event at the Cowboys of Color Rodeo held on the Martin Luther King Jr. holiday at the Will Rogers Memorial Coliseum in Fort Worth, Texas.

Afterward, he told rodeo columnist Brett Hoffman, "There were a lot of pioneers who paved the way for me. . . . Let's honor the people who went before us because they paid a price."

While competing at the Calgary Stampede for the final time, in 2017, Whitfield was cast in the title role for some dramatic re-creations used in the documentary film *John Ware: Reclaimed*.

Before making the thirty-three-hour drive home from Calgary, trailering a pair of horses behind his truck, Whitfield auditioned for producers who were awestruck by his resemblance to Ware. Six feet two and muscular, he was a mirror image of Ware, who was known for driving cattle from South Texas to the railway in Kansas. In 1882 Canadians came to know him as the grandfather of the cattle industry when he drove a herd of more than three thousand north from Kansas into the southern region of Alberta.

That was the birth of the cattle and ranching industry in Canada.

Ware was tragically killed twenty-three years later, in 1905, when his horse stepped in a badger hole and flipped over while galloping across an Alberta pasture. Ware was crushed underneath his horse and broke his neck. He died a folk hero, and in February 2012, Canada Post honored his legacy with a commemorative stamp.

"I'd be lying to you if I said I ever heard anything about [John Ware] until they brought [the script] to me," said Whitfield, who used his downtime between scenes to explore.

"I had never been off the beaten path just riding around doing stuff until I started filming that movie. My goodness. Can you imagine what that country was like before man really showed up over there? Before we started building shit and some of them buildings that we filmed in, like barns and stuff, they told me were 100, 150, 200 years old with original wood. Unbelievable."

Two years later, following one final appearance at his hometown Rodeo Houston—"there's nothing else left for me to prove in the sport"—Whitfield retired from tie-down roping and rodeo.

Or did he?

"Well, the thing about rodeo, you never totally quit doing it," said Whitfield, who summarized his career with seven words: "Many were taught, but few were chosen."

31

Dihigi Gladney with John Davis and California Chrome

I look at where I'm at today and realize that most of my success is owed to the mentors that was in my life.
—KENDRICK LAMAR

WATTS, CALIFORNIA

The final bell of the day was followed by high-pitched shrieks from kids emerging from the front doors of Flournoy Elementary School. The random screaming quickly gave way to a chorus of grade-schoolers yelling, "They got horses. They got horses."

Nine-year-old Dihigi (pronounced Da-hash-ee) Gladney knew his fourth-grade classmates were yelling about his pony, Coco.

That wasn't a onetime memory.

Most afternoons, his cousins would ride horseback from the El Fig Stables at the corner of West El Segundo Boulevard and South Figueroa Street, leading Gladney's pony to the front of his school two miles from the stables.

He'd hop up on Coco's back—one of the few ponies from El Fig that was settled enough to ride on the urban streets of Los Angeles in the early to mid-1980s—and circle the school once or twice. His mother would not have been happy had she known he was riding in his school clothes, a definite no-no in his household. He and his cousins would ride down the block together so he could change into his Wranglers and cowboy shirt before continuing south on either Compton or South Central avenues, down to 120th Street and then west to Broadway.

Gladney loved riding his pony down Broadway to El Segundo. They did not always take the same route, but always wound up coming down Broadway because the little guy with a great big smile and oversized personality wanted everyone from the neighborhoods—both Watts and Compton—to see him riding *his* pony.

"That was my limo," Gladney said. "I'm getting picked up by my cousin in front of the school—on a *pony.*

"Those are memories that never leave, I mean, ever," continued Gladney, smiling and giggling as if he were back in grade school all over again. "When you look back at it, was it crazy? Absolutely. Was it fun? Totally. Did I love it? To the end of my life—"

Dihigi Gladney was born July 30, 1975, at Gardenia Memorial Hospital, but his mom might as well have given birth to him at El Fig Stables, where he spent nearly every day of the first eighteen years of his life, side by side with his granddad, John Davis.

He was only a couple days old when his granddad brought him to the stable for the first time. Within a few weeks, Davis would hold his grandson while sitting up in a saddle. For his second birthday, his granny wanted a picture of him sitting on a pony with his mom holding the reins as if she was going to lead them on a walk. One problem: His mom was terrified of horses, so when the pony sneezed, it startled her and she ran off yelling, "My baby. My baby."

"Good thing the pony just dropped its head and went to eating grass," laughed Gladney. "Can you imagine what could have happened to me?"

His mom ran a daycare, but her rambunctious son proved to be problematic when he bothered all the other kids during naptime. Who could sleep, Gladney recalled, when he knew he could be having fun with his granddad? She would call her dad and he would send over one of the stable hands to pick up his grandson.

By the time Gladney was six, he was riding a thirty-year-old thoroughbred, Major, that took care of the young, inexperienced rider.

"Everything I did was with adults," recalled Gladney, who said if he was too young to go along then his granddad simply wouldn't go. He'd send the others and stay with his grandson. "We did everything together."

Davis was originally from Macedonia, Oklahoma, and like so many of the other characters who found their way to El Fig, he got his start working for Tommy Cloud. Davis eventually started his own stable in the old tack house, in 1967 or '68, after he won his first horse, Little Big Man, in a game of dice against Gene Smith.

A Stringtown, Oklahoma, native, Smith traveled to California with his brother Johnny after they were encouraged by actor Ben Johnson, a rodeo cowboy who became a stunt double before becoming an actor, who would go on to win an Academy Award for Best Supporting Actor in *The Last Picture Show*. Johnson and his pal Clark McEntire—father of country music superstar Reba McEntire—assured Davis and later the Smith brothers that there was stunt work available for them and they would be treated more fairly at West Coast rodeos. Davis went first and then the Smiths joined him at El Fig.

Davis focused on stable work, while Cloud got plenty of movie work for Gene and Johnny.

Everyone worked, but it got pretty wild and Western on the weekends.

"They'd hook up on Friday night at the stables, shoot dice," recalled Robert "Tenderfoot" Brown, who grew up down the street from Davis near the corner of 111th Street and Compton Avenue in Watts and was one of the many kids Davis would round up and bring along in the summertime. Davis would oversee Barns 1 and 2 and lead the hayrides for Cloud, while the kids cleaned horse stalls and helped with the rent horses and pony rides.

By the time Gladney was old enough to help, those kids working for Davis— Tenderfoot and Kevin Ford, among them—were knowledgeable enough to mentor him. In lieu of being on the streets with gangs, drugs, and other crime, little Gladney was surrounded by a motley crew of Black cowboys. There were celebrities, too—Woody Strode, Iron Eyes Cody, Larry Holmes, the cast of *The Dukes of Hazzard*, and Academy Award nominee James Caan, who started coming around the stables at the same time he starred as Sonny Corleone in *The Godfather*.

But if anyone made an impression, it was Charlie "Pee Wee" Sampson.

Gladney was eight when Sampson made history at the NFR in December 1982.

Like Gladney, Sampson was from Watts, and he was a bull rider like Gladney wanted to be. Sampson was a hometown hero before winning the gold buckle and whenever he happened to visit El Fig, Gladney followed him like a shadow. Even though he knew him, personally, Gladney would wait in the autograph line when Sampson was competing or appearing in Los Angeles.

Gladney grew up riding steers, and by high school, he moved on to riding bulls. He attended Centennial High in Compton, because it was only two miles west of the El Fig Stables.

He recalled a school project he did for Black History Month in which he had to write an essay about who he most wanted to be like. Everyone else wrote about baseball and football players, actors, and musicians. He wrote about Sampson and bull riding.

"A lot of the parents knew who he was," Gladney said. "Oh my God, they thought that was the best thing in the world because I brought something different on who I idolized. I wanted to be this Black bull rider coming up out of the 'hood."

To his own surprise, Gladney rode his last bull when he was only nineteen and instead became a jockey.

"I did not want to be a jockey. I knew nothing about being a jockey," he said.

It all started when he took a job helping his cousin exercise quarter horses at Los Alamitos Race Course—a twenty-minute drive from Watts. He learned the basics of working with racehorses and would ride them up and down the dried riverbeds every morning. That was the summer of 1993, and by the start of the 1995 season, Gladney was riding as a jockey. He rode in forty-eight races that year and made it to the winner's circle twice.

Each year, he rode more and more.

His granddad lived long enough to see his early success as a jockey. When local horseracing scribes asked Davis what he thought of his grandson's success, he replied, "Well, goddamn, he loved to go fast and whoop one, and now he gets paid for it."

They laughed.

Gladney laughs, too.

Davis died in 1997, a day after his birthday. "He was my best friend," said Gladney.

The laughter continued as he shared the memory of the first time he told his granddad he wanted to be a cowboy. Davis just shook his head and said, "Oh, yeah, that sounds good, but you wouldn't make a patch on a cowboy's ass."

Still, he knows the old man was proud of him.

In 2001 Gladney mounted four hundred times and claimed thirty-one victories. He was becoming something of a local legend at the racetracks when it all damn near ended on January 5, 1993.

His mom and his granny had always worried when he rode bulls, but it was as a jockey that the injuries mounted—he broke both ankles and his nose, fractured his ribs, and had a rock tear through his pantleg and embed in his kneecap. But all of that was nothing compared to the day he nearly lost his life. He broke four vertebrae in his back and all the ribs on his left side.

"One minute, you're battling to win a race, the next minute you're battling for your life," he later told LosAlamitos.com.

When he was finally discharged from the hospital, he wore a custom metal brace for eight months. He could not walk without assistance for the first year, much less bend over to tie his shoelaces. He began to experience muscle atrophy to his upper and lower body. Water therapy was so painful, he had to stop. When he finally started walking, what normally would have taken a few minutes took as long as an hour.

As the weeks turned to months and then years, the kid who always was known for his positive disposition grew more and more depressed.

He suffered terrible nightmares.

He was sidelined for five years and it was his family—especially his three kids—who inspired his comeback. Like his granddad, he started offering pony rides and then was able to sit on a horse and gallop for the first time in 2007. Soon after, he rode everything from quarter horses to thoroughbreds and even an old mule.

And then came racing.

His first postinjury win was at the Fresno Fair and eventually he was back at Los Alamitos until his career of injuries proved to be too much and he fell into what TheNational.ae described as "the journeyman rut." He last raced in 2012 and officially retired as a jockey in 2013. According to track records,

Gladney rode in 2,610 races, finished in the money 766 times, and recorded nearly 300 career wins.

In October 2015 Gladney got a call from Art Sherman. Gladney had been exercising a trio of Derby contenders—I Want Revenge, Mr. Commons, and Tale of a Champion—for Sherman and another trainer when Sherman reached out to him ahead of bringing California Chrome, the 2014 Kentucky Derby and Preakness winner, back to his home stable inside of Barn 2 at Hollywood Park.

Sherman had let Chrome's longtime exercise trainer go earlier in the year when he overslept prior to the Dubai World Cup and missed the final session. Chrome finished an embarrassing third place, a full two-and-three-quarter lengths behind the winner. At the time, Chrome was a five-year-old, headstrong stallion that was a handful for anyone on his back.

On race day, Chrome—the richest Kentucky Derby winner in history—was a legend. Any other day of the week, he had a prickly attitude and was something of a sonofabitch for his exercise rider to handle on the racetrack. But damned if he didn't like cookies. He also liked Gladney. Or perhaps the kid who up grew up in Watts and had his hands full breaking unruly ponies before they could be put out for rent simply wasn't intimidated.

"He's probably one of the biggest thoroughbreds I've ever seen in person," said Gladney of the ornery chestnut stallion with four white stockings.

Gladney developed a strict routine that began every day at 5:30 a.m. Training sessions were followed by a bath, hot walks, a little time to eat, and an hour-long nap. He would jog him on Mondays and Saturdays and gallop on the days in between. Chrome developed a reputation for rearing up on his hind legs, and for other riders, once around the track could be the fight of a lifetime. In three months' time, Gladney and Sherman had Chrome ready. He won his first race and then left for a trip to Dubai. It was tough for Gladney leaving three kids behind for three months, but the sacrifice paid off when Chrome won the Dubai World Cup. In the thirteen months they worked together, Chrome raced nine times, including seven first-place wins along with a second- and third-place finish. In their time together, Gladney spent more time on Chrome's back than anyone else, including Victor Espinoza, the jockey who rode him to nearly every penny of the more than $13 million he won.

"Everything I have now, everything I've ever done, I directly owe it all to El Segundo and Figueroa stables," Gladney said, "without a doubt. I'm that stable's own child."

Now he is back to what he loves: ponies.

Oftentimes, prior to the COVID-19 pandemic, Gladney would be set up with Fancy, Cali, Maverick, and Chocolate at Santa Anita Park during the week and Del Mar Racing at the fairgrounds on the weekends. Like his granddad and Tommy Cloud did for so many kids, Gladney has used his pony business—Got Ponies?—to provide opportunities to help other young Black cowboys like Chris Byrd. Just as Gladney looked up to Sampson, Byrd looks up to Gladney and followed him like a shadow before moving to Northern California to work at the famous Flying U Ranch.

Now Gladney's two teenage boys help with pony rides, and his daughter, London, hopes to one day become the first Black barrel racer to qualify for the NFR. She won two of the first four races she entered and, in 2019, qualified for the Junior World Finals Rodeo and won the second round of competition. A year later, in 2020, London was a junior barrel qualifier for the Vegas Tuffest and was the California Junior Rodeo Association junior barrel-racing champion.

When it comes to horses, her daddy always puts her on the fastest and strongest horse her skill level will allow. She turned fourteen in May 2020 and already runs barrels against adult women at the BPIR as well as jackpots and open rodeos against pros and amateurs. "That's one of my main goals is to watch her try to become something successful," said Gladney. "It's like watching me with ponytails all over again."

32

Gus Trent (aka Harlan Tyrone Ware) with Sedgwick Haynes

It ain't where you start in life, it's where you end up, and what you did along the way.
—COLIN POWELL

PITTSBURGH, PENNSYLVANIA, AND HOUSTON, TEXAS

Sedgwick Haynes was an undersized calf roper with an oversized personality.

He was a husband, father, friend, mentor, teacher, manager, and, more importantly, a cowboy at his core. He let his opinions be known, and yes, Sed—as he was known to those closest to him—could be stubborn. But he was never one to brag. He did not demand respect—he earned it.

In a letter that Haynes wrote just prior to his death and later was published in a rodeo-style program distributed at his funeral, he let it be known he had no regrets. He lived his life doing what he wanted, how he wanted, and when he wanted.

And he wanted those who were mourning his passing—he died February 23, 2018, at age sixty-three—to "know that I am at peace" and to "always remember life is too short."

Haynes learned that lesson the first time he met the late Lu Vason, founder of the Bill Pickett Invitational Rodeo.

Haynes was in Gary, Indiana, competing in a calf-roping event at a rodeo produced by legendary Black cowboy Thyrl Latting. Haynes appreciated

Vason's passion and dream of one day producing an all-Black rodeo series in cities like Denver, Los Angeles, Atlanta, Washington, and Haynes's hometown of Houston.

He wished Vason well that day and never really thought much more about their conversation.

Then, in 1984, Vason produced the first-ever Bill Pickett rodeo in Denver. When it came time to plan the second event, scheduled to take place in Houston, he called on Haynes to help.

For the next thirty-four years, the little guy with a heart and work ethic as big as the Lone Star state worked just about every job associated with producing the popular all-Black rodeo series, including his longtime role as co-general manager.

During that time, Haynes and Vason shared their passion for educating and promoting Black rodeos and openly talking about the history of Black cowboys who came from America's inner cities.

Haynes had a profound impact on the lives of many, including eight-time PRCA world champion Fred Whitfield and Hollywood actor Reginald T. Dorsey.

He not only came to appreciate the dreams of others, but also did his best to help make those dreams a reality. That's why, in 2011, when Vason introduced Haynes to Gus Trent, he told the newcomer to stay close and pay attention. They were in Kansas City that weekend, and Trent was in awe of the five-foot-six-inch Haynes.

"That was a great introduction to the fact that in rodeo, it's about respect," Trent explained. "And you knew it in that moment, man. This guy has *it*."

Gus Trent was born May 4, 1965, in Pittsburgh.

The legal name on his birth certificate reads Harlan Tyrone Ware.

He did not grow up poor—far from it—but throughout the 1960s and '70s, he lived in Pittsburgh's inner city. His father, Seymour Ware, owned a commercial printing company, and his mother, Lois, was a credit manager.

His parents provided a great example for Harlan and his siblings, but his biggest influence came from playing football. He joined his first team in fourth grade and continued to play through college, where he started as a linebacker and evolved into a down lineman at Edinboro University of Pennsylvania.

Harlan was not the greatest athlete. He was not as big as others at his position, but he was generally faster, which complemented the defensive scheme for the Fighting Scots.

More importantly, football gave him self-confidence and discipline.

When Harlan was not studying or practicing, he was lifting weights. He graduated in four years as an ROTC student with a degree in speech communication, but readily admits football filled 75 percent of his time. When he graduated from Edinboro, he was commissioned a second lieutenant in the Air Force Reserve Command.

He spent nine months overseas as a result of the first Persian Gulf War.

His time over there is nothing to be glamorized nor was it, by his own admission, a horrible experience leading a petroleum transportation unit. He made a career of serving active duty and took on a laundry list of special assignments ranging from assisting a two-star general to traveling to Korea and Germany and teaching military science at Ohio's Youngstown State University for two years before being called back overseas. He served a two-year stint in Iraq and Afghanistan beginning in 2005 with just one trip home on a fourteen-day leave.

He considers himself fortunate, but his fortunes were tough on his family.

Being gone affected his wife and daughter. Harlan was twenty-three when he married his first wife in 1988. Their daughter was born ten years later. The couple divorced in 2013.

"Things just didn't work out," Harlan said, "and it was time to move on and you learn from your mistakes and try to be the best person you know that you possibly can be."

For someone who struggled as a kid—had it not been for football, he would not have had the incentive to attend college—the military taught him how to be a leader. Truthfully, becoming a rodeo cowboy was the last thing anyone ever expected from a onetime football player who became a military officer.

Harlan never owned a horse, much less rode horses at any of the nearby stables. Yet as a youngster, he would tell anyone who would listen that one day he planned to own horses and live on a ranch in the countryside.

He was eight years old at a neighbor's birthday party the first time he rode a pony. Harlan was mesmerized. From that day on, he never stopped thinking about them. His dream went unfulfilled until he bought his first horse in June 2010. He was forty-five years old.

Dealing with the horrors of war—he was still serving active duty—changed how Harlan saw life, and the divorce represented an ugly period for him.

Buying his first horse marked a new beginning.

"I rebuilt my life," Harlan said. "I lost a lot and had to start over. . . . Horses and that kind of thing just filled me and put me in a better place."

As with so many veterans who deal with posttraumatic stress disorder, horses provided Harlan with a sense of calm and a foundation for healing that had been a decade in the making. A few months after buying his first horse—in the ensuing years, he's bought and sold several of them—Harlan reached out to Vason, who Harlan knew only as a fan of the BPIR.

When the two talked on the phone, Harlan introduced himself as Gus Trent.

He was creating a whole new image for himself. He took the name Gus after Capt. Augustus McCrae from the classic Larry McMurtry novel *Lonesome Dove*. There is no special origin or meaning to the name Trent. He just liked how it sounded when he introduced himself.

In Plant City, Florida, with a home and a new life he's made for himself following a protracted divorce, and at rodeos and, more often, mounted shooting events, he's Gus.

When he's back home in Pittsburgh, he's still Harlan.

"I got a rule that nobody from Pittsburgh is allowed to call me Gus because they don't know me as Gus [Trent]," he said. "They know me as Harlan [Tyrone Ware]."

As Trent, he grew closer to Sedgwick Haynes, who encouraged him to remain positive through his difficult divorce. It was a powerful message from a man who had tragically lost his son in an automobile accident.

Trent was an outsider of sorts, but with the support of Haynes and others, he gained the acceptance of the entire community.

Harlan had been a career-minded military officer. Gus was a cowboy with a small ranch and his own stable of horses.

One goal remained elusive. Trent wanted to bring the BPIR to Tampa, but Vason never took him seriously. They were in Memphis the last time Trent asked about it over breakfast. Vason wiped his mouth with a napkin, looked up at Trent and asked, "How many rodeos have you actually done?"

The answer was none.

That was April 2012.

In 2013, and every August since, Trent has produced his own annual rodeo in Tampa. And there have been others, too, including Pinellas Park just across the bay from Tampa. All are open to pro and amateur contestants alike and none of them are sanctioned by an organization.

His growing list of events provided Trent with another new opportunity he never would have considered taking on in his earlier years.

Oklahoma native Marcous Friday, a rodeo announcer who was and remains behind the mic for the BPIR in Washington, had worked Trent's first event, but a scheduling conflict a year later kept him from returning a second time. Trent valued Friday's talent and even considered changing the date of his rodeo to accommodate the longtime announcer's schedule. As flattered as he was by the idea, Friday convinced Trent to announce his own event.

"You have the right personality," Friday insisted. "You don't need me or anybody else. You ought to do it yourself."

A self-described people person, announcing came naturally to Trent, but he was initially apprehensive.

His style defies tradition. While most in-arena announcers call the event from a booth or in the arena on horseback, Trent never restricts himself to any one location. He moves with relative ease from behind the chutes or on the dirt to going into the stands to interact with rodeo fans. He especially likes getting young, impressionable kids involved.

Given his own charisma and ability to relate to people of all types—he spent twenty-eight years in the military and served in eleven different countries—he has a welcoming persona that appeals to both first-time rodeo fans from urban settings and long-established rodeo enthusiasts. In 2019 newly elected Tampa mayor Jane Castor served as the grand marshal and, according to Trent, "was totally blown away by how diverse my rodeo was."

In all, producing has been a sharp learning curve for the Pittsburgh native.

Trent has shared his second act with his father and daughter, Madison. But in 1999, his mother died, taking her last breath in the arms of her son. He remembers his mother as an incredible lioness who fought cancer with everything she had.

"She was a great mother, raised three kids, married to the same guy," said Trent, who for a moment was once again Harlan Tyrone Ware as he continued to reminisce. "I really had a great set of parents."

She would be thrilled to see the realization of her son's dream of owning a horse ranch, producing rodeos, and competing in horse-mounted shooting events. She always told him he could accomplish anything, and today, when Gus Trent is introducing young kids to Western culture, he models that same kind of positive reinforcement.

He finds joy in helping others—a characteristic Sedgwick Haynes reinforced in the wake of Trent's mother's passing—and, more importantly, shares his passion for horses and horsemanship.

Haynes, who was born September 7, 1954, was raised in the inner city of Houston and once said half the kids from his hard-scrabble neighborhood were either on drugs or wound up in jail.

But he was never easily influenced, even then.

Not one to be typecast, he grew up playing golf. In fact, he was a top player for Booker T. Washington High School, and as a senior, he was offered a full scholarship to continue playing at Texas Southern University.

After much self-introspection and despite disappointing his parents— Robert and Dorothy Haynes—he politely declined the offer and elected to pursue the uncertainty of a rodeo career.

Prior to Sedgwick, no one in the Haynes family had shown the least bit of interest in rodeo or Western culture, much less any sort of inclination of one day becoming a rodeo cowboy.

When Sedgwick was not in school or on a golf course, he would walk more than a mile to a local stable, where he learned how to ride horses. His childhood neighbor, calf roper Alvin Penrice, took Sedgwick to his first rodeo, and throughout his teen years, another neighbor, Eugene Tucker, allowed Sedgwick to use his horses to practice roping.

After choosing to forgo college, Sedgwick sought the instruction and tutelage of some of the all-time greats—regardless of color or ethnicity—including the likes of Calvin Greely Jr., Rufus Green Sr., and Nelson Jackson Jr., along with Walter and Bonnie Beaver, all of whom encouraged the youthful, yet determined newcomer.

Later, despite being a single father of his two oldest sons, Sedgwick traveled from coast to coast to compete as a calf roper and steer wrestler.

A decade into in his career, he met Lu Vason. The friendship changed the course of his professional career and, perhaps, more importantly, affected his personal life in a profound way. Haynes met his wife of twenty-six years, Stephanie, who is best known in rodeo circles by her nickname, Cookie.

Together they won titles and set records—Cookie has won more Bill Pickett titles than any other competitor in its more than thirty-five-year history—and Sed became the father of three more children and eventually a grandfather of seven.

Unfortunately, in early 2014, he was diagnosed with multiple myeloma, a type of cancer that forms in bone marrow.

In the program passed out at his funeral, Haynes wrote a letter to his loved ones telling them cancer "did not determine my destination." He had no time for self-pity. Instead, Haynes continued working with the BPIR throughout much of his courageous four-and-a-half-year battle. He made some adjustments and learned to live with the disease. As anyone who knew would have expected, he worked hard and held himself accountable for his role with the rodeo.

"If you're going to do it, do it right," Haynes often said.

In the same spirit, he continued his willingness to be a mentor—offering advice to Gus Trent and countless others right up until his passing.

33

Dennis Davis with Alvo Tucker and Donald Goodman

You must never be fearful about what you are doing when it is right.
—ROSA PARKS

RUNGE, ROSENBERG, AND WINNIE, TEXAS

There is not a lot known about Alvo Tucker prior to his coming to America.

He was born in Germany and lived there until he was six years old. His eldest grandson, Dennis Davis, is not sure of the details or circumstances involved in the decision made by his grandfather's family to immigrate to the United States prior to World War II.

Of all the places to call home, the Tuckers settled in Runge, Texas. Not much has changed in this rural ranching community—located seventy miles southeast of San Antonio—which has maintained a population of just over one thousand people and is barely one square mile in size.

Tucker, who already spoke German and Polish, learned to speak fluent English and Spanish. He had an eighth-grade education and yet he went to college.

He was in his early twenties when he met and married Lilly Viesta, and together they raised five children, including grandson Davis's mother, Gloria Jean.

The elder Tucker became the town mechanic but earned a reputation as a sharp businessman. In addition to owning his own shop, he acquired land in and outside of town and kept a relatively small herd—by Texas standards—of cows.

Years later, Tucker became a big influence on his firstborn grandson.

Davis was born March 22, 1968. His grandfather owned about three blocks' worth of property in town and the entire family lived within a few houses of each another.

"It was me and him," said Davis, who was up before dawn every single day before school and would go out to the ranch and ride through the pasture with his grandfather to check on the cows.

When Davis heard his grandfather rev his truck engine, that was the signal for him to run out the door and hop in the front seat. The old man would never squeal the tires, but once the two of them were out on the highway, he would give it little extra gas just to watch his grandson's reaction.

They talked about life. They talked about opportunities. If they came upon a sick cow, together they would nurse it back to health. Whenever fall gave way to winter, they would haul hay out into the pasture. When wintertime turned to spring and then summer, they fed the cattle grain.

Tucker introduced his grandson to all aspects of how to work with livestock, and more importantly, he taught Davis how to be responsible and how to be a man.

Davis's father, Leonard, was in the restaurant business and worked nights. He almost never made it home before Dennis and his sister, Denise, went to bed. Their parents split when the two kids were young, but they didn't officially divorce until Dennis was a senior in high school.

After school Davis played sports and hung out with his friends, but he always found his way back to the ranch. Together, he and his grandfather would wind up in the pasture.

"I was interested in what he had going," recalled Davis.

While he loved his father—"That's where I got my work ethic," Davis said—if he's being honest, he spent more time with Grandpa Tucker.

In Runge, it was commonplace for everyone to have horses, whether it was a few in the backyard, on a small ranch, or a large working ranch.

His paternal grandfather managed a ranch. While his dad was overseeing a restaurant, his dad's brother, Robert, "would ride crazy horses" and calf rope locally at what Dennis described as "backyard rodeos."

At seventy, Robert—or Uncle Bob, as Dennis refers to him—is still in good shape, and when he's not training horses, he still competes in breakaway roping.

"Everyone was sort of a cowboy," Davis recalled.

And cowboys were cowboys—whether they were white or Black. Davis said no one ever paid much attention or made a big deal out of him being the only Black kid in his class. They were all just young cowboys, who would one day grow up to be South Texas ranchers—including Davis.

"It's not prominent in history books," Davis said, referring to the lack of stories featuring Black cowboys and Hollywood's own history of casting Black cowboys out of Westerns for fear of putting a Black man on the back of horse and calling him a hero.

"I still just assumed there were always Black cowboys," he said. "Why not?"

It wasn't until the family moved two hours east, from Runge to Rosenberg, Texas, which is just outside of Houston's metropolitan area, that Davis "started to really notice there's a big difference in treatment. I started to experience more of a difference" based on how some people would treat him because of the color of his skin—something he never faced in Runge.

Davis's aunts and uncles from both sides of his family would compete locally in timed rodeo events like barrel racing and calf roping, while he briefly tried his hand at bull riding. It's not that Rosenberg or Houston was any different than Runge and San Antonio, so much as Davis was older, more mature, and would sometimes think, "Oh, that wasn't fair" on those occasions when his scores were lower than usual.

Davis used the skills his grandfather taught him to compete in local rodeos, and that's where he met all-around cowboy Donald Goodman, who would become his rodeo mentor.

Goodman took Davis under his wing and gave him the confidence to believe he was a professional rodeo cowboy, that his talent and skill transcended the local jackpot rodeos his family frequented on the weekends.

The two hit the road together and Goodman taught Davis how to rodeo in the big leagues.

Donald Ray Goodman was born November 18, 1964. He was one of seven siblings—two girls and five boys—born to Joseph and Jonnie Mae. After graduating from South Park High School in Beaumont, Texas, in 1983, he followed three of his brothers—Donelle, Lloyd, and Ben—and began to rodeo professionally.

The Goodman boys were steer wrestlers—none better than Donald and his horse Linda Lou.

In a 2008 article in the *Brownsville (TX) Herald,* Donald Goodman said that it is important for rodeo cowboys to "keep a little fear or bad stuff would happen." He spoke from experience. After recovering from a broken neck he suffered in 1992, Goodman won a series of championships from 1994 to as recently as 2016.

He was the all-around average champion at the BPIR in 1994, 1997, and again in 1998, when he also won the bareback-riding title. In 1995 he was the all-around cowboy at the Cowboys of Color Rodeo during the State Fair of Texas.

The day before Barack Obama was inaugurated as the forty-fourth president of the United States, on January 20, 2009, Goodman was competing at the annual African American Heritage Rodeo of Champions—held every year on Martin Luther King Jr. Day—at the Denver Coliseum during the National Western Stock Show.

Goodman and his brother-in-law had planned to travel to Washington for the history-making inauguration, but Goodman thought better of the idea and told his local Beaumont newspaper, "Right now, I'm focused on this. The reins Obama's being given tomorrow, I'm not even sure I'd want those. I'll stick with rodeo."

He earned a trio of steer-wrestling titles—Ike Carden Rodeo Association (2004), Louisiana Christian Production (2011), and Oklahoma Texas Connection (2016)—before retiring from competition.

He and his wife, Angela, had made a home in nearby Winnie. He found work as a truck driver, while also managing his own ranch and promoting rodeos.

Unfortunately, Goodman, who is remembered for mentoring up-and-coming cowboys like Davis, was found dead February 2, 2019, at age fifty-four. His death remains a mystery.

Goodman was on his way to work the morning of January 23 when he called his wife at 7:45 a.m. to let her know that his truck had broken down on the Taylor's Bayou Bridge along Highway 73. Less than three hours later, at 10:30 a.m., authorities called Angela to inform her that Donald was not with his truck.

Although local police did not wait the customary twenty-four hours to begin a missing persons search, the investigation into Goodman's disappearance has been widely criticized by locals for what they thought was a lack of urgency on the part of authorities. Ten days later, his body was found floating in the water one hundred yards from the bridge where his truck had been.

An obituary that chronicled his career and love of rodeo concluded with an alternate version of Clem McSpadden's cowboy prayer: "Welcome to heaven, cowboy. Your entry fees are paid."

"I'll forever talk about him," said Davis, reminiscing about his mentor and best friend.

The two men—Goodman was three years Davis's senior—spent the better part of a decade on the road together. They met just before Davis graduated from Texas Southern University.

Davis spent two months living in Beaumont finishing an internship. There he met fellow Black cowboy Nathan Wilson and they would compete together in small backyard rodeos. One of those events was in nearby Cheek, Texas, where Goodman was working as a judge.

Davis did not even make a qualified ride that night, but Goodman approached him later that evening because he saw the potential Davis had and liked how he handled himself in the face of defeat. He did not offer to let Davis travel with him, so much as he said, "I'm going to take you under my wing and I'm going to take you to some real rodeos."

Davis was twenty-three years old and, until then, had never thought of himself as a professional-caliber bull rider.

"I couldn't see past just being where I was," he recalled, "but Donald opened my eyes and said, 'Why not?' Well, I guess, you know, why not me?"

Goodman had the vision and was a powerful influence on Davis at a time when he needed someone to believe in him and lead the way. The support and words of encouragement and the lessons—both professionally and personally—gave Davis all the confidence in the world.

"I didn't know it was possible," Davis said. "Never even crossed my mind."

His grandfather raised Davis to be a cowboy, and his dad instilled in him his work ethic. Goodman would combine those early lessons to develop Davis into the consummate professional he is today.

Rodeo is an individual sport, but as travel partners, they learned about each other and gained a new perspective on rodeo. They once "went three weeks without turning the ignition switch off on a truck." They left Beaumont, went to the Midwest, and then headed west before finally making their way back to Beaumont.

Goodman's most important lesson may have come at an event sanctioned by the IPRA—the second-largest professional rodeo organization in the world—in Oklahoma, when a bareback horse came out of the bucking chute backward and flipped over on top of Goodman.

He saw Davis on the back of the chutes and hollered for him to jump down into the arena and sit on the horse's head. Horses use their necks when standing up, so having Davis sit on him afforded Goodman the valuable time he needed to crawl out from underneath without having the horse jump to its feet and potentially stomp on him.

"He was just calm," said Davis of Goodman's demeanor in the face of danger, "as if we were sitting next to each other eating a hamburger."

With Goodman, Davis experienced firsthand the possibilities and opportunities that he and his grandfather had talked about all those years earlier. After a decade of traveling from coast to coast and competing at rodeos damn near every weekend, Davis returned home to Texas and pursued a passion be shared with his grandfather—raising cattle. More specifically, bucking bulls.

After years of working for other stock contractors and other jobs in the industry, Davis struck out on his own and started Dennis Davis Bucking Bulls. He trains, handles, and hauls bucking bulls on behalf of his investors. He favors working with younger bulls—two-year-old futurity bulls along with three- and four-year-old classic bulls—over mature bulls ridden by bull riders at the professional level of competition. In fact, his most famous investor is UFC president Dana White. The two had success with a bull is named F-Bomb and have since partnered on several other ABBI bulls.

Davis might be the only Black stock contractor competing professionally at ABBI, PBR, PRCA, and IPRA events.

Much like Dr. Martin Luther King Jr. once said—"*I look forward to the day when people will not be judged by the color of their skin, but by the content of their character*"—Davis sees the importance of character.

"The only way we can change the way we're being viewed is up to us, as Blacks, to handle ourselves, to handle our business. . . . We have to focus on the content of our character because that's what we will be judged on. And if our character is out of whack, that's how you're going to be judged, but that goes across the board for all races," he concluded.

34

Steve Reagor with Sidney Reagor

One important key to success is self-confidence. An important key to self-confidence is preparation.

—ARTHUR ASHE

TULSA, OKLAHOMA

Steve Reagor was making the drive, some 960 miles, from Casper, Wyoming, back to Tulsa, Oklahoma, when his cell phone rang. He had just won the 2003 National Championship in calf roping at the College National Finals Rodeo, so his phone was ringing quite a bit on the drive.

Friends and family and fellow ropers were calling to congratulate him.

This call was different. This time it was a rodeo reporter and he wanted to know how Reagor felt about becoming the first African American to win a collegiate rodeo title.

"No," said Reagor, who thought there had to have been others, "but I didn't know the history. I really didn't."

In 2003 he could not google it on his phone. Social media was not what it is now, so no one was making a big deal about his accomplishment.

Even after he got home, Reagor thought the reporter probably had his facts wrong.

So many other Black rodeo cowboys had gone to college, he thought, "Somebody had to have."

The College National Finals Rodeo (CNFR)—known as the Rose Bowl of Rodeo—dates back to 1949 and the formation of the National Intercollegiate Rodeo Association. Bud Bramwell and Cleo Hearn, who attended Oklahoma State University in the 1950s, are believed to be the first African Americans to have earned a rodeo scholarship. Neither qualified for the CNFR.

The first Black cowboy to qualify was Mike Latting, a junior from Southern Colorado State College in Pueblo, in 1973.

In the thirty years between Latting and Reagor's historic win, no other Black cowboys—Ervin Williams and Mike Moore, among them—won a national championship. And no other African American has won a national title in the nearly twenty years since Reagor.

It's great to know that he's *the* guy, but Reagor is disappointed to still be the *only* guy.

"That's very, very surprising," Reagor said, "but it's coming. There's going to be another one. There's no doubt in my mind."

The only thing Reagor ever questioned was why in the world Buddy Lassiter, a college rodeo coach, would have ever offered him a scholarship to attend Bacone College in nearby Muskogee, Oklahoma.

He never won a dime in high school rodeo events and there was no indication he would win in college. But in 2003, as a sophomore at Bacone, he won the Central Region and then earned an opening-round win at the CNFR. He placed in the next two rounds and was second in the average to earn a spot in the championship round.

When Reagor looked at the draw, he was slotted between Cade Swor and Sterling Smith.

Smith, who went on to become the PRCA Rookie of the Year in 2007, did not have a great finals, while Swor, who has since qualified for the NFR several times and won well over $1 million as a tie-down roper in the PRCA, was the cowboy to beat.

Reagor was confident on the back of a horse raised by his father. It was not a career-best time, but it was a career-defining moment, to say the least.

"I've never been a stat guy," said Reagor, who does not remember his combined winning time of 34.9 seconds on four calves until he's reminded of it. "I just know that I went and done my job."

There was never a doubt in his or anyone else's mind that Reagor was going to grow up to be a professional calf roper. His daddy was a roper. All three of his daddy's brothers were ropers. His older cousin was a roper. And Steve was going to be a calf roper, too.

"It's just something I grew up wanting to do," he said.

Steve was born in 1983 and raised in Tulsa, Oklahoma.

His father, Sidney, was an aircraft painter for McDonnell Douglas and his mother, Shirley, worked there until she went back to college and became a schoolteacher.

Sidney was forty-four when Steve was born, and his own amateur rodeo career was pretty much over by that point. Steve remembers seeing his father compete four, maybe five, times when he was a child, but mostly he grew up hearing stories about what a great horseman his old man was.

He still hears those stories today.

Sidney had a roping horse named Pino. Oklahoma legends like Nelson Jackson, Bud Bramwell, and Cleo Hearn would compete on him. In 1979 Sidney won riding Pino in a rodeo in Topeka, Kansas, but he mostly stayed within three or four hours of home.

"Daddy, he didn't like to travel," Steve said, "so he didn't go to the New York rodeos and all of that."

When the elder Reagor finally gave up competing, he spent the better part of a decade judging rodeos. Steve grew up going to Cowboys of Color events and other rodeos his father was judging in Oklahoma and Texas. By that point, Sidney still roped a little bit around the house or at least enough to keep his son's horses tuned up.

And while he helped with Steve's horses and offered advice, Sidney never forced or pushed his son into roping calves. "That's one credit I can give him," Steve said of his father, "he never once said, 'You have to do this.'" But if Steve was ever going to have an opportunity to compete, he knew his father would expect to see him out in the roping pen on his own every night after school.

Steve was eight when he started roping calves at home. When he caught his first calf, it felt like what he imagined winning a world title would feel like. It was exciting. There was a joy and a rush, and he was ready for the next one.

He even thought he was ready to compete at junior rodeos.

His friends were already competing, and so were his cousins. They would tell him about how much fun they were having. Steve and his father would go to the events, but they sat in the bleachers and watched. Sidney held his son back and made him wait.

"I would be like, 'Man, I know I can get out here and do this,'" said Steve, but Sidney would nod and tell him maybe next time. "He just kept leading me on."

The elder Reagor wanted to make sure his son could catch calves consistently. And he didn't mean roping two or three in a row and then missing one. Sidney's version of consistent was hitting the practice pen hard and not missing a single calf. He also wanted to make sure his son had a passion for the sport and a desire to win, so Steve roped for an entire year before his father agreed to let him enter a junior rodeo.

Together, they made the short drive to Skiatook, Oklahoma.

Steve was so excited to be competing that his adrenaline got the best of him and he missed his first calf.

"I cried like a baby and my dad used to tease me about it all the time," Steve said. "I was hurt. I spent a year catching calves at home, went to the rodeo, and missed."

He was in shock.

In the six months before entering Skiatook, he might have missed six calves, but there was nothing he could do about the timing of having missed his seventh. He had learned how to rope. Now he needed to learn how to harness the energy and the adrenaline of competing and make it work in his favor. He had to learn how to win.

Sidney explained to his son that he did not believe it bothered his friends when they missed. For them, roping was a pastime. Sidney was actually proud that missing a calf bothered his son to the point of tears.

That conversation with his father stayed with Steve.

"I think my dad was making me hungry," Steve said. "I think it helped now that I look back on it. As a kid, you don't understand, but he was just fueling that fire in me. When you pay your entry fees, you better plan on winning. The ultimate goal is to win, and I never lost that drive."

He went again two weeks later and caught his first calf in competition.

As a reward, Steve was back in the roping pen the next evening.

His relentlessness paid off. At fifteen, a year before he could legally drive a truck, he won his first horse trailer at the Ernie Taylor Classic, a U.S. calf-roping event in Durant, Oklahoma. It was a three-round event held Thanksgiving weekend, and he was in a draw with men—some of whom had already turned pro.

He won a round and, as Steve put it, hustled hard enough in the other two rounds to score more points on three calves than everyone else.

In the rush and excitement of winning, he did not realize he had won a horse trailer. His parents waited until Monday to tell him. It was strange for Sidney, who had since retired, not to be home to greet his son when he came in from school. It was even more strange when the sun went down and dinner had not been served, so Steve asked his mother where he was. She said she didn't know. It was the best surprise of his life when Sidney finally pulled in towing the trailer with all the running lights lit up.

"When I backed in [the box] on that last calf," Steve recalled, "I never thought, well, I have a chance to win a trailer. Had I known, I might have puked it up."

Father and son stood next to the trailer and Sidney told Steve he had roped pretty good.

"Thank you, Daddy," he replied.

"But you could have did this and won two rounds instead of one," Steve recalled his father telling him as they walked toward the house. "That's how he was. He kept me hungry."

Then came high school.

"You can put this down," Steve emphasized, "I was no good [at rodeo] in high school."

Steve attended Booker T. Washington High on the far north side of his hometown. He did not enter many high school rodeos and never placed.

He did, however, make a name for himself as a standout baseball player. Truth be told, his father hoped Steve would go on to play ball in college.

His mother still has a stack of scholarship offers—all but one for baseball. Missouri Valley College wanted Steve to play third base, so did Hill College and Missouri Southern State University. And had it not been for Bacone College and its offer for him to rodeo, he would have chosen from among the other three.

Instead, Coach Lassiter gave him a full ride to rodeo.

"I wouldn't have gave me a scholarship," Steve said, only half-jokingly. "I guess the word got around that I could win at open rodeos."

Despite his troubles at high school rodeos, he had been competing alongside men—amateurs and pros—and consistently winning $500 to $1,000 at open events since he was fifteen.

Education was important to his parents, so there was no doubt Steve was going to college. When he received Lassiter's letter in the mail, he decided to enroll at Bacone.

"I don't know what clicked," Steve said, "but I won my first college rodeo."

He qualified for the College National Finals Rodeo as a freshman, sophomore, and junior. His senior year, Steve needed to place first or second in the opening round of the last regular-season event. He was third. He won the short round and the average but missed out on qualifying for a fourth consecutive trip to Casper, Wyoming, for the CNFR by five points.

Steve turned pro in 2005, but it was not until 2009 that he headed out to California for his first major pro events outside of Oklahoma, Texas, and Kansas.

He didn't win any money at his first two rodeos out West and started to feel like he did when he missed his first calf as a nine-year-old. So he called his father. Sidney was tough, but he also had a calming presence. He had never been to California, much less competed there, but he told his son to stick to the basics.

Steve's third event was in Red Bluff. He can still remember it like it was yesterday. He split the opening round win and when the event was over, Red Bluff served as Steve's first big professional win outside of Oklahoma. He then placed in Clovis, California, before heading home.

Though he dabbled with the PRCA, Steve elected to compete full time at the more regionally focused American Cowboy Rodeo Association (ACRA). He eventually partnered with longtime family friend Marcous Friday to produce and promote their own series of rodeos, stand-alone roping events, and timed-event rodeos.

Steve had already started producing an event for his father and was looking for an opportunity to approach Friday, who had known Steve since "he was knee high to an adult." Friday had befriended Sidney years earlier and knew the Reagor family was raised right. They were a family of faith, with good morals.

It was 2016 and Friday said, "I was at the point where I was tired of doing everything by myself. You would have a few guys who said they wanted to help you, but they never would. . . . I kind of mentioned it to Steve and he was gung-ho about it, so we went for it."

One of their first ventures was the annual Juneteenth Rodeo at the Owasso Round-Up Club Arena in Tulsa.

Friday had started the rodeo in a tiny building at the fairgrounds before moving to Turley Rodeo Arena and later Owasso after the event began attracting competitors from Texas and as far away as California, Illinois, and Michigan. In the early 2000s, the Juneteenth Rodeo laid over the top of the same dates as the CNFR and it made Steve "sicker than a dog" to think he could not compete.

"It's what, like five miles from my house?" Steve rhetorically asked. "That's like a hometown rodeo."

For the first ten years, the Juneteenth Rodeo was billed as an all-Black rodeo, but Friday said he had a hard time selling sponsorships.

"It was a fast-growing rodeo," he recalled, "but they had a foot on our neck and eventually we had to open it up." More white cowboys entered and so did Native Americans. "It was an open rodeo with world champions," said Friday, who is proud to have drawn, "the baddest of the bad."

The first year, Steve not only worked with Friday to produce the entire event, including all the preproduction, but he also was entered in the calf roping. Steve made sure his run was scheduled for the slack that followed the rodeo performance.

He and Friday were in the production trailer taking care of post-event settlements when Friday said, "Now go out there and take care of *your* business."

Friday missed Steve's run.

Later, he laughed when he learned Steve won the event.

A year later, in 2017, Steve tore his groin. It was a career-ending type of injury. He tore the adductor muscle from the bone. But the competitor in him still has a passion for winning. The last time he roped a calf prior to the injury was the final round of the ACRA Finals. He finished second. After two years of undergoing therapy twice a week, there was hope of one day returning to competition.

His desire to rope again is the competitive cowboy in him.

But he hesitates to refer to himself as a cowboy.

"I got a cowboy upbringing," said Steve, regarding the way of life his father Sidney introduced him to, "but they were real cowboys. What we're doing now isn't half of what they used to do. It's totally different. The cattle were 150 pounds bigger than they are now. You had to really want it if you wanted to rope calves or ride bulls, steer wrestle. Now the calves weigh 170, 180 pounds. My dad said he'd run some calves he couldn't hardly [reach] over to their flanks. They were 300 plus. They were fresh, never been roped before. These calves we rope now, they're pushovers. Trust me. I roped some pretty good-sized calves, but—"

After pausing to contemplate whether or not he thought of himself as a cowboy, Steve continued, "Nah, *they* were cowboys."

35

Glenn Jackson

Life is not a spectator sport. If you're going to spend your whole life in the grand-stand just watching what goes on, in my opinion, you're wasting your life.
—JACKIE ROBINSON

HOUSTON, TEXAS, AND PAWNEE, OKLAHOMA

Alice Jackson knew her son was disappointed in himself, and that it was going to be a long and somber five-hour drive home to Houston from Ardmore, Oklahoma. But when they pulled out of the parking lot of the Hardy Murphy Coliseum and Fairgrounds, she never imagined having to pull over on the side of I-35 for a heart-to-heart moment with her son, Glenn Jackson, before they even crossed the Texas state line.

Glenn, who was fifteen at the time, summed up his appearance at Barry Burk's Eleventh Annual Championship Jr. Calf Roping Roundup with five words: "It was a complete bust."

He felt embarrassed by his performance.

The Hardy Murphy is a legendary facility, and every world champion tie-down roper since it opened in the 1930s has competed at one event or another in that same building. And every top junior roper has been going to that Memorial Day weekend event since Burk held the first one in 1986.

For a teenager with aspirations of becoming a professional roper, this was not the weekend to come away with "nothing."

Alice understood her son's desire to win, but when Glenn told her he was thinking about filling out some job applications and taking on a summer job instead of competing full time at junior rodeos, she had something to say and wanted to make sure she was looking him in the eyes when she said it.

She pulled off on the gravel shoulder of a major interstate connecting Oklahoma City to the Dallas/Fort Worth metroplex.

"I don't care if you win or lose," she told him. "If you put forth the effort, I'm going to be extremely proud of you."

At that moment, something clicked.

And for Glenn, everything changed.

"I realized it was okay to lose," recalled Glenn, as long as he was giving everything he had to win, "and I did not have to be afraid to lose, and that enhanced my winning.

"That's the moment I became a winner."

Glenn Jackson was born March 19, 1981, in Houston, and his earliest memories are of the family business: rodeo. For the Jacksons, rodeo was never a hobby or a sport. It is and always has been a family business, going all the way back to the 1940s.

Glenn's father, Tommy, was raised by Robert "Money" Jackson. Tommy's father—Robert's brother—died when Tommy was a boy and Robert raised him as if he were his own son. In turn, the elder Jackson treated Glenn as if he were a grandson.

Unlike Robert's sons and his other grandsons, Glenn did not play any other sport.

His focus was rodeo. More specifically, tie-down roping. Period.

He started roping when he was seven or eight years old, and at ten, Glenn sat down at the table and wrote himself a letter. In it, he clearly stated that he wanted to be a cowboy, and that meant following in his grandfather's bootsteps.

"That was my goal in life," Glenn said.

Robert had competed and later hauled livestock and ran a rodeo company. He not only made his living being a cowboy, but also supported his family.

Every decision he made was a business decision, and that's how Glenn saw his future—"making a living doing it."

Robert taught his sons what it meant to work hard.

And they taught their sons the importance of having a work ethic.

"We spent more time trying to accomplish more than we spent talking about what we accomplished," Glenn said. "It's the guy who works the hardest who is going to achieve the most."

Life consisted of three things as Glenn and his brothers were growing up: schoolwork, chores, and roping.

Glenn wasn't just a cowboy on the weekends. He was a cowboy Monday through Friday, and his classmates learned to accept him for who he was.

"My attire was starched jeans, buttoned-up shirt, and a pair of boots," said Glenn, who never dressed any differently for school than he did if he was headed to a rodeo. "Periodically, I wore sneakers."

At sixteen, only a year after he and his mother talked on the side of the highway, Glenn took off and started to compete in amateur rodeos on his own. He made his way around Texas, and on Easter Sunday, he placed at Hearn and then again in Liberty that evening, but he still had a lot to learn. Sometimes he traveled with his best friend, Justin Richard. But had it not been for the conversation with his mother, there is a good possibility that he would have been just another very talented Black tie-down roper from South Texas.

Instead, his career took off. "I didn't think there would ever be another broke day," he said.

At eighteen he befriended Sedgwick Haynes and the two traveled together to Atlanta for a Bill Pickett Invitational Rodeo.

Glenn may have known how to rope, but he quickly discovered he didn't know anything about rodeoing. Haynes taught him everything from how to manage his money to how to look after and care for his horse when they were away from the familiarity of home. Hell, he didn't know it beforehand, but Haynes had to teach him the importance of keeping good tires on his truck and horse trailer, especially if he was planning on driving seventy-five thousand to one hundred thousand miles a year.

In 1999 Glenn rode along, watched, and learned. By 2000 he was competing, and in 2002 he had first tie-down title won before he even arrived at the finals. He still had goals he wanted to accomplish, including setting an arena record and winning all four rounds to emphasize he was, in fact, the best. That year, he won three of four rounds at the Bill Pickett Finals, the finals average, and the year-end title, but he "did not spend much time celebrating" before he was focused on the 2003 season.

He won six Bill Pickett tie-down championships, but the most satisfying came in 2007.

Glenn arrived in Las Vegas in a tight race and was going to need a repeat of his 2002 finals in order to win the title. His family was there to encourage him.

"I always felt that if I can beat you mentally then if I worked hard enough I can beat you physically," said Glenn, who delivered on expectations, "It was a great feeling . . . knowing I could step up to the plate and knock it out of the park when I needed to—when it mattered the most."

Glenn never actually preplanned his transition from the Bill Pickett series to the IPRA. It just sort of happened.

He was seeing a woman in Oklahoma and, in 2007, went to stay with her and wound up establishing a life for himself in the Sooner State. He moved to Pawnee, where he still lives today when he's not traveling. Like he did his first year with Bill Pickett, he laid back, watched, and asked questions. In January 2008 he got his IPRA permit and qualified for the IFR in his first season. That year, he became the first Black cowboy to win the finals average in the tie-down roping and ended up as the reserve champion.

He was second in the IFR two more times and was competing semiregularly at both American Cowboys Rodeo Association (ACRA) and Cowboys Regional Rodeo Association (CRRA) events. In subsequent years, he's worked hard to develop a balance between rodeo—meaning, he is no longer going to every event—and stunt work.

He was only sixteen when he first appeared in a documentary film for the Houston Livestock Show and Rodeo—commonly referred to as RodeoHouston—and various local and regional television commercials, but his career started in earnest in 2018 on the set of *Yellowstone*.

"I was busy working on *Yellowstone* quite a bit," said Glenn, who worked as a stunt double on every episode of the first three seasons of the Paramount series starring Academy Award–winning actor Kevin Costner. "Fortunately, the job requirements are something that is natural to me—that's being a cowboy."

He and the other stuntmen are featured in all the scenes taking place on horseback, especially when cattle are present.

It's become a hugely popular show. The season three finale drew more than five million viewers, which was a series high and made it the most watched cable program of 2020. Glenn is oftentimes identified by rodeo announcers for his work on the show. Despite his growing popularity among rodeo fans, Glenn passed on working on the fourth season and, instead, took a job on the feature film *The Harder They Fall*, a Black Western being produced by Jay-Z for Netflix.

"I feel like I've reached my peak in *Yellowstone*," he admitted.

Production for *The Harder They Fall* was shut down in March 2020 after the film's lead actor, Idris Elba, tested positive for COVID-19. A few months later, in late August, Glenn was asked to return to Santa Fe, New Mexico, where he and the entire crew were quarantined for fourteen days before filming resumed.

Glenn was one of forty-two stunt doubles on set—"It's a pretty big production"—but only three of them were skilled cowboys. Elba has his own action double, while Glenn, Ora Brown, and Tim Cook "swapped off his horse action" stunts, but there was plenty of other cowboy work to be done in front of the cameras throughout the entire four-month shoot.

The Harder They Fall co-stars Academy Award winner Regina King and relative newcomer Jonathan Majors, who is tentatively hoping to portray Myrtis Dightman in a possible biopic of "the Jackie Robinson of Rodeo."

Though his film and television work dictate his schedule—he is a member of the Screen Actors Guild and the American Federation of Television and Radio Artists—Glenn managed to win both the ACRA and CRRA roping titles in 2019 and qualified for the PRCA Prairie Circuit Finals and IFR. He also was the first Black cowboy to receive the award for having the IPRA Horse of the Year.

And he would like to add one more Bill Pickett title to his list. Because there are only six events spread out over ten months—Denver, Memphis, Oakland, Los Angeles, Atlanta, and Washington DC—Glenn concluded, "Forty doesn't seem very old to me. I'm active and my body is in good shape. I'm going to go on with this for as long as I can."

36

Dwayne Jr. and Aaron Hargo

I think people who have faults are a lot more interesting than people who are perfect.

—SPIKE LEE

SOMERSET, CALIFORNIA

The arrest photo tells you everything you need to know about Dwayne Hargo Jr.

His eyes, bloodshot from crying, were glazed over as he seemingly stared into his unknown future—the guilt and shame of his past weighing heavily on his shoulders. He had just turned himself in on two charges of armed robbery.

The agony he felt had nothing to do with being a thirty-year-old Black man who had jeopardized a promising career in rodeo and as an up-and-coming Hollywood stuntman. Instead, it was because he had brought shame and embarrassment to his family.

For Dwayne Jr.—the firstborn of Nannette and his namesake, Dwayne Hargo Sr.—the worst of his pain was the idea that friends and neighbors in Somerset, California, and others throughout the rodeo world could mistakenly think that it was his father who had robbed a liquor store and later held up a gas station with an air-powered BB gun.

Dwayne Sr. was a pillar in the community and a legend in rodeo.

The elder Hargo was a six-time NFR qualifier and the 1989 Wrangler World Champion Freestyle Bullfighter—the first African American to win the title.

And the idea of damaging his father's reputation was worse than any sentence he might face.

It was February 5, 2013.

Dwayne Jr. spent almost a year in jail awaiting sentencing before being sent to a receiving center for three months and then prison for another three. He spent the last year at fire camp fighting wildfires in California.

The first time his fiancée came to visit, Dwayne Jr. asked her not to give up on him. Initially, they were separated by a glass wall when she visited. The first time they were allowed to meet face-to-face, she broke off the engagement.

He hit rock bottom emotionally and wondered how he could have made such a big mistake.

"When I was locked up," Dwayne Jr. recalled, "my mom sent me an article about [PBR bullfighter] Frank Newsom—of his hard times and the drugs and all that stuff he'd went through."

He read the 4,800-word article and then read it again.

Like Dwayne Jr., Newsom was a promising bullfighter. Not only had he worked events for both the PRCA and PBR, but Newsom also was widely regarded as having the potential to become one of the greatest of all time. He overloaded his schedule and to keep up the pace, a couple of *friends* introduced Newsom to methamphetamines.

He doesn't know why, but Newsom told the Matt West Now Podcast, "Sin comes easy to me."

Newsom avoided prison but spent two years putting his life back together before reclaiming his career. In November 2012, he shared his personal story of redemption in a longform feature, "Running on Faith," published online at www.pbr.com.

Three months later, Nannette Hargo printed Newsom's story and mailed it to her son. Call it a mother's intuition, but Nannette knew her son needed to see he could still have a future—if he would only believe in himself.

"When he went off to prison," Nannette said, "I didn't want to give up on him and I was hoping he could come out of it. . . . I just hoped he wouldn't give up. To hopefully make him see there was life ahead.

"I sent it to give him hope."

It worked.

"I was like, 'Man, I still got a chance,'" said Dwayne Jr., thinking about the impact Newsom's story had on him. "I'm still young. I got some years in me."

Dwayne Jr. was born January 1, 1983. His younger brother, Aaron, was born June 19, 1986, and less than a year later, the Hargo family moved to Somerset, California, where all four have lived since.

Somerset is thirty minutes south of nearby Placerville, which was originally settled as Hangtown in 1849, a year after the discovery of gold at Sutter's Mill triggered the California Gold Rush. One hundred years later, in 1950, Somerset was founded and named after the hometown—Somerset, Ohio—of its own present-day settlers.

The Hargos were the first Black family to live there.

From an early age, the brothers were different.

Dwayne Jr. learned to walk at nine months and soon was running away from his mother. Aaron did not start walking until he was almost a year old, and as his mother likes to say, he's been a "rule follower" ever since. Dwayne Jr., on the other hand, thought it was funny when his mother would ground him.

"They were such different personalities," Nannette said.

As kids, Dwayne Jr. and Aaron spent their summers traveling from one rodeo to another. The family would be gone all summer. Dwayne was a month shy of turning seven the year his father won the world title in freestyle bullfighting. Aaron was three.

"We grew up going to rodeos," Aaron said.

Dwayne Jr. added, "That was our life. That's all we knew at the time. I don't think I really thought much of it until I got a little older."

In school, the brothers were the only two Black students in their classrooms.

"I definitely had some problems with the redneck-type people," said Dwayne Jr., who recalled some derogatory racial remarks being written on his car with a permanent marker.

"If you asked my mom, she would tell you that I used to get pulled over every week. I had a convertible—a cheap [Chrysler] LeBaron. It was my first car, and one time I got pulled over for having my music too loud."

There was one problem: There was no music playing. His car stereo was not hooked up.

"Just crazy stuff like that," Dwayne Jr. said, "but, honestly, now we're pretty well-known around here and I don't have any problems."

The boys were good students and even better athletes. Dwayne Jr. was a three-sport athlete—karate, baseball, and basketball.

Both boys excelled on the basketball court. Dwayne Jr. was a flashy point guard who led the team in scoring, while Aaron was an old-school, traditional point guard who looked to involve his teammates in the offense. He led the team in assists and never led the team in scoring.

His first two years in high school, Dwayne Jr. was the only cowboy, much less Black cowboy, at his high school. Yet, he did not get involved in rodeo until his junior year. He was fifteen years old the summer between his sophomore and junior years when he made a trip with his father to a pair of rodeos in Omak and Caldwell, Washington. When they got home, Dwayne Jr. informed his mother that he not only wanted to rodeo, but also ride bulls.

"She was pissed," Dwayne Jr. said, "but there was nothing she could say."

Or so he thought. Her oldest son might have been a ball hog on the basketball court, but she reminded him of his commitment to his team. She told him he could rodeo, but not during basketball season. He agreed.

"That's a good compromise," Dwayne Jr. said, "but it didn't work."

When his high school season was over, he joined a local recreational basketball league while also competing at rodeos on the weekend. He was bucked off and got his arm stepped on. It was sore and swollen, but not broken. His mother made him play his rec game.

"She's like, 'You're playing,'" recalled Dwayne, who went directly from having his arm examined to the gymnasium. "I played in my jeans and a tank top. That's just kind of how it was. She was like, 'You're playing. This is our deal.'"

A year later, in 1999, he won his first buckle riding bulls at a local rodeo in King City, California. His father was working as a bullfighter. After graduating, the younger Dwayne still shied away from bullfighting and rode full time. He made the circuit finals four times—2002, '03, '04, and '06—and also went to the Dodge Circuit Finals in 2006.

Although his mother would hold up a pair of cleats and tell him he was better on his feet, Dwayne Jr. thought he was establishing his own legacy instead of becoming a mirror image of his legendary bullfighting father.

He loved his father and looked up to him, but said, "Nah, I'm good. I want to be a bull rider, and then some things went *down*."

He dabbled here and there with drugs—his father had found evidence of cocaine use—but it was nothing compared to the addiction that followed his moving out on his own after taking on work as a ranch hand. He was running their bucking bull program and went from dabbling to addict in a year's time.

"When I went to this ranch," Dwayne Jr. said, "everybody did it around there, so that's all we did every day. It fucked up my life for a while."

After being fired by the same ranch hands who introduced him to meth in the first place, he begged, borrowed, and stole money to fund his addiction.

And then came the day he robbed a liquor store and gas station. As soon as photos from the surveillance video were released, everyone in El Dorado County recognized him. Dwayne Jr. turned himself in and used his one call to phone his mother.

They cried.

Technically, he was classified as a violent offender, but thankfully, the system did not treat him as one. He sat in a county jail awaiting his sentencing. They gave him three years instead of six.

Emotionally, he had to deal with the guilt and shame on his own. Physically, the worst of his time behind bars was the time he spent at a receiving center, where he transitioned to life as an inmate. He was evaluated by a counselor and determined to be a Level I offender, but for an hour a day, he was among Level IV offenders serving life sentences. The other twenty-three hours were spent in a cell "that I could reach both arms across and touch both walls, with another dude, the toilet, and the sink."

He stayed quiet and kept to himself.

Soon enough, he was granted honor status and when fire season started, they sent him off to join California's inmate firefighter program. He was still dressed like an inmate, but there were no walls and he fought on the frontlines alongside commissioned firemen. Having grown up in a logging community and being naturally comfortable working in heavily wooded areas, Dwayne Jr. was soon positioned at head saw and that's where he was until his release on August 31, 2015.

His supervisor offered to work some backchannels to get Dwayne Jr. hired on as a fulltime fireman. He declined. "A lot of people don't get second chances and I got one," said Dwayne Jr., who wanted to prove himself personally and professionally. He added, "I just couldn't wait to get out to prove everybody wrong."

When he got release, his mother was as scared as she was the day he turned himself in. As a hospital administrator, she knows all too well that addiction is a "horrible illness, disease," and admits she might always worry.

Dwayne Jr. almost immediately faced a tough test when he broke his leg and had to miss ten months of the rodeo season. His first event back, he broke his other leg and missed another ten months.

Instead of feeling sorry for himself and turning to drugs, he picked up one of his four guitars and began playing local wineries, open-mic nights, and parties. Songwriting filled his time until a friend called with an opportunity to do some stunt work.

Like his father, Dwayne Jr. had dabbled in stunt work a decade earlier. He took jobs on *Flicka* and a Coors Light commercial in 2006, and *Jackass 2* and *Wild Hogs* a year later.

In 2018 Dwayne Jr. got the opportunity to work on the set of *The Mustang*, doubling for Jason Mitchell, who had just played Eazy-E in the blockbuster film *Straight Outta Compton*.

He followed with work on *Harriet*, NCIS, season two of the Paramount series *Yellowstone*, with Kevin Costner, and Ethan Hawke's Showtime miniseries *The Good Lord Bird*, about a white abolitionist who sparked the Civil War.

"I actually had more of an acting part in this," Dwayne Jr. said. "Ethan [Hawke] is cool and he's a rodeo fan, too. Very passionate guy and, yeah, deep thinker. I don't know what the hell he's saying sometimes, but it sounds good."

He did enough stunt work in 2017, '18, and '19 as a member of the Screen Actors Guild to qualify for a pension and, more importantly, health insurance for his daughter, Nakiahh.

And 2019 also saw him working rodeos with his brother, who didn't pick up bullfighting until after he finished two years of college. Together, they are two of the eleven bullfighters working PBR events at the Velocity and Touring Pro level of competition. They also worked several PRCA events until the COVID-19 pandemic brought the entire bull-riding and rodeo community to a grinding halt.

"Honestly, when I come out of prison, my mind was riding bulls the whole time I was in there," Dwayne Jr. said, "and then I was like, 'Man, I'm over this gambling stuff. I like to get paid a for-sure check.'"

He stepped in at the PRCA rodeo in Red Bluff, California, when a bullfighter got injured by the first bull. Like all bullfighters, he kept his gear in the trunk of his car, whether he was planning to fight bulls or not. His first PBR event was in Lexington, Kentucky

"That was the coolest event I've ever been to in my life," he recalled. "There was seventeen thousand people stacked up the walls to the ceiling."

The Hargo brothers worked several PBR events together, in 2019—Oakland, California, and Reno, Nevada, near home, and also Utah, Ohio, and Massachusetts—and 2020 would have seen Fresno, California, which was postponed and then canceled because of the pandemic, added to the list of events the brothers would have worked together.

"If they want to follow in their father's footsteps or whatever, you kind of show them and put them in the right position to do that," said Dwayne Sr.

Noting that everything is a test, Dwayne Jr. described life and career as "survival of the fittest." Like Newsom before him, Dwayne Jr. is now keen to share his story of redemption and hopes others learn from it.

"I have a good support system around me," concluded Dwayne Jr., who better understands the importance of prioritizing his family nowadays. "I had it back then, too, but I wasn't listening."

37

LaMontre "Tre" Hosley, Chris Byrd, and Stanley "Ray Ray" Taylor

I'm about seeing long-term, seeing a vision, understanding nothing really worthwhile happens overnight, and just sticking to your script long enough to make something real happen.

—NIPSEY HUSSLE

COMPTON AND MARYSVILLE, CALIFORNIA

America's first introduction to the inner cities of Los Angeles came in August 1965, during national news coverage of the Watts Riots.

Twenty years later, in 1986, Dr. Dre, Ice Cube, Eazy-E, MC Ren, and DJ Yella formed N.W.A. and pioneered the popularization of West Coast gangster rap with their groundbreaking 1988 debut, *Straight Outta Compton*. It was an autobiographical account of gang violence, drug use, and police brutality, a way of life that was further dramatized in John Singleton's 1991 critically acclaimed film *Boyz n the Hood*.

Another two decades later, in 2015, Dr. Dre opened his most recent solo project, *Compton*, which served as the companion piece to N.W.A.'s Academy Award–nominated biopic, with a one-minute sample from a television news documentary, *Compton, Black City*, which was originally broadcast back in 1971.

Compton was the American dream. Sunny California with a palm tree in the front yard. The camper. The boat. Temptingly close to the Los Angeles ghetto in the Fifties and Sixties, it became the black American dream.

Open housing paved the way as middle-class blacks flooded into the city. Whites don't buy houses in Compton anymore. Now, at 74 percent of the population, black power is the fact of life from banks to bowling alleys, but the dream that many blacks thought they were buying has turned sour.

Though the Mayor and four other of five city council members are black, they have been unable to solve the problems of crime and growing welfare, which is slowly turning suburban Compton into an extension of the black inner city.

Crime is now as high as the ghetto. 47 homicides last year, gave Compton one of the highest per-capita rates in the country. Juvenile gang activity, muggings, and small robberies want to make some blacks want to leave, want to leave, want to leave.

Lost in that narrative is a history of Black cowboys in south and west Los Angeles neighborhoods dating as far back as the 1950s and carried on today by a trio of Black rodeo cowboys—LaMontre "Tre" Hosley, Stanley "Ray" Taylor, and Chris Byrd, who were born and raised in Compton.

"You're not a gangster."

If Hosley heard his mother lecture him once about his future, then he "heard it seventeen million times," and for good reason. Even though being a gangster "felt like the easiest thing to do," his parents and grandparents had other ideas.

His grandmother has a photo of him sitting on a horse at twenty-one days old. By the time he was eight or nine, Hosley was riding solo in a saddle.

In the summertime, he would leave the house by 9:00 a.m. His uncles, who were headlong into the gangster life, would tell him which streets to avoid that day and he'd walk to Richland Farms. He would be gone all day. His elders knew he was safe.

Hosley may have been from Compton—he was and is proud of where he's from—but his mother was not about to let him go to high school there, so she enrolled him at Jordan High School on the opposite side of the 710 freeway in Long Beach.

"My mom had a better outlook on my group of friends than I did," Hosley said. "She pretty much told me, 'Your cousins are stirring up shit and if you go there, I feel like you're going to be right in that shit.'"

His father was never into gang banging, but according to Tre, his father had eight brothers and every one of them earned a reputation on the streets. By the time the younger Hosley boys—Tre and his first cousin—reached their teen years, there was an expectation that they were being groomed to one day run the streets like their uncles had done in the 1980s and '90s.

That said, Compton gets a bad rap (pun intended).

"There's actually nice parts of Compton," Hosley explained, "but you never see that on TV or in the media because of N.W.A., that's what sold Compton, that's what put us on the map.

"But it's about how you present yourself, your whole demeanor," continued Hosley, whose upbringing was nothing like what had been portrayed in movies and on television.

Those images showed one element, and as with any other American city, Compton was more textured than it's given credit for.

Some incredibly successful people have come from Compton: Dennis and Marques Johnson played in the NBA in the eighties, while Tyson Chandler and Brandon Jennings made the league in recent years; Pro Bowlers Larry Allen, James Lofton, and Richard Sherman all played in the NFL; Serena and Venus Williams have established themselves as two of the greatest women's tennis players of all time; rapper The Game and thirteen-time Grammy winner Kendrick Lamar followed N.W.A.; while Paul Rodriguez, Anthony Anderson, Niecy Nash, and Ava DuVernay have experienced success twenty miles away in Hollywood.

Still, Hosley's cousin chose the streets.

"It's about the choices you make," said Hosley, who recognized that just being in his own front yard could be dangerous, but he was old enough and wise enough to know there were other opportunities. "At school, I played football and then I rode horses. That was something I was proud of and—I didn't know it at the time—it was keeping me out of trouble."

By the time Hosley aged out of the Compton Jr. Posse—founded by May-isha Akbar in 1988 with a mission of "keeping kids on horses and off the streets"—he still thought there was a chance of playing college football, but the idea of rodeo seemed more and more plausible, especially pursing rodeo along with Chris Byrd and Stanley "Ray" Taylor.

Hosley was "scared as hell of bulls," so he learned how to rope. But much like a lot of other would-be tie-down and team ropers—regardless of ethnicity—Hosley did not have the financial resources to buy a good $20,000 roping horse, much less a reliable truck and trailer to pull his horse up and down the highway from one rodeo to the next. Before long, he discovered a YouTube video of Clint Cannon riding barcback horses.

"I was totally wired through the whole thing," Hosley recalled. "I'm there, like, no shit, I've got to do this."

Cannon is a five-time NFR qualifier who has earned more than $1 million riding bareback horses in the PRCA. He was the 2003 PRCA Resistol Bareback Riding Rookie of the Year, and in 2009 he set a PRCA record for the most regular-season money won in any event with $233,504. He split first in two of ten rounds at the NFR that year and finished the season as the reserve world champion.

Hosley friended Cannon on Facebook and then sent him a direct message.

Cannon invited Hosley to his annual Southeast Texas Bareback Riding School.

It was a pivotal moment for Hosley, who rode a Greyhound Bus to Houston.

"I was familiar with cowboys being from Compton and from the inner city here in Houston," Cannon said, "so when he said he was from Compton, I knew he would come give it a shot. . . . Bareback riding is the most brutal sport there is. Bull riding don't even compare to it."

Cannon sized up Hosley after his first attempt, "I remember how scared he was and he got on and this horse turned back and he rode it about three jumps before it bucked him off, and he let out this yell, like, 'Ahh.' He was like, 'Man, I freaking love it,' and he was ready to go. He probably got on eight horses and, yeah, that's a lot. He was just rolling with it."

Hosley got on twice as many horses as the other students.

By the end of the first day, Cannon told him to take it easy and that it was more important to make it through the whole clinic. On the second day,

Hosley was in a bad position so Cannon blew the eight-second whistle early, but Hosley did not bail out.

"I got rocked over on my hand and it was pretty extreme," he recalled. "Clint blew the whistle, but it was like three seconds into my ride."

Hosley recovered and got squared up on the backside of the horse and really rode him for eight. Afterward, Cannon asked, "Did you hear the whistle?"

"I did," replied Hosley, who wanted to make the most of a trip he really could not afford. "I still had more to do. I'm trying to get everything I can out of this school."

Cannon was amazed, "That's impressive."

He was not the only one who was struck by Hosley's effort and determination.

Sean Amestoy has been the rodeo coach at nearby Wharton County Junior College for more than twenty years, and he was impressed enough to tell Hosley, "If this is what you want to do, I'll give you the opportunity to come to my school right now."

Hosley nodded his head yes and Amestoy offered him a rodeo scholarship to attend Wharton County Junior College in Texas. He was about to get a free education in a county that almost fifty years earlier would not let Tex Williams—a three-time high school state rodeo champion—even compete in the same event as his white classmates. In school and around town, people were surprised to learn the kid with "a good head on his shoulders" was from Compton. Hosley said he often heard one of two responses: "Oh my God" or "No shit?"

It was a great experience, but after two years, Hosley was ready to go home to California. He just never expected to end up in Northern California.

While Hosley was in Texas, Byrd and, later, Taylor—who were both born in the early 1990s—moved six hours north to Marysville, California, to live and work for legendary rodeo producer Cotton Rosser.

Rosser and his son Reno operate the Flying U Rodeo Company and, at one point, produced as many as fifty rodeos a year. They still regularly produce events up and down the California coast, including the LA area, where Byrd and Taylor were regulars.

"They would just show up and enter our open bull riding," Reno recalled. "Now they live with me. They basically . . . to be honest with you, I couldn't get rid of them. They would do anything, and I felt horrible, because I really didn't have a lot of housing, but they didn't want to get caught in the trap again."

They worked as ranch hands and then helped at the rodeos and also competed.

Byrd and Taylor, and later Hosley, not only had a great work ethic, but they were eager to learn whatever they needed to know in order to help out on the ranch—from feeding cattle to mending fences and hauling livestock to and from the Flying U rodeos. Byrd and Taylor have been in Marysville for almost ten years now.

"They're all pretty good kids, but you gotta handle, well, not handle them differently, but you always have to remember they had a pretty tough upbring-ing," Reno explained. "They're really good guys. Ray is one of the nicest guys you'll ever meet, and Chris, too. We love having them around and they are more or less part of our family. They live at our ranch and we celebrate holidays with them."

As a kid, Byrd was hanging in the streets and playing sports at the park.

His mom was barely making enough money to get by, so Byrd, who was eleven at the time, and his cousin would go door-to-door in the neighborhood asking if there was any yardwork or chores around the house they could help with. Unlike Hosley, Byrd was never introduced to horses or rodeo as a young kid, so it was a random coincidence when he knocked on the house of a married couple—Louie and Stephanie Alloutufuli—who offered Byrd an opportunity to clean their horse stalls at a nearby stable.

"It was just an accidental deal," Byrd said, "right there in Compton."

He did not earn any money to help his mom, but he learned how to ride a horse and eventually started making a little money on the side by helping run the popular pony rides. Byrd, his mom, older sister, and little brother had spent two years living together in a motel room when the Alloutufulis moved all four of them into their "nice big house."

"They let us stay and let my mom get on her feet and build her money up," Byrd said, "And me, I was just riding horses and staying out of the way and stuff—staying busy. I was just kind of going with the flow."

He may have grown up in poverty, but he was never out on the streets selling drugs or running with a gang. It just wasn't his style. Instead, he was interested in rodeos. That's when he met the Rosser family and discovered the Bill Pickett Invitational Rodeo, where he met Dihigi Gladney, who was riding bulls and riding horses in the relay races at the time. Later, Hosley became the exercise trainer for California Chrome, winner of the Kentucky Derby.

Byrd was fifteen when Gladney put him to work helping with the pony rides. He looked up to Gladney and wanted to ride bulls. He started out at the Calf Riders Only down in Orange County, and at sixteen and seventeen years old, he started entering open-rodeo events promoted by the Rossers.

"I started kind of helping them out little by little," said Byrd.

His mom eventually moved to Las Vegas, so he just hopped in the truck with Reno Rosser and went home with him. "It's lovely. They treat me pretty good here. Just living the life.

"You stay busy here. We're into everything—whatever needs to get done."

Taylor's journey from Compton to the Flying U Ranch was a passion torn between football and horseback riding. From seventh grade until his sophomore year in college, Taylor played football. He loved contact, playing fullback on offense and linebacker on defense. But prior to those eight years and every day since, his focus has been on rodeo—first as a bull rider and eventually transitioning to bullfighter.

He grew up on the backside of ponies and horses.

Before he ever laced up a pair of cleats, Taylor said, "You couldn't get me away from a horse when I was younger."

Taylor was a regular at El Fig Stables in its final years, long after the last of the legendary Black cowboys had left and before The Hill side of the property was mysteriously burned to the ground. He'd also ride in nearby Long Beach and Gardenia or make a little further trip to Thompson. His uncle had a horse and his dad had a couple of Shetland ponies for the kids to ride, so they knew where all the stables were.

"I got friends that lived in Compton their whole life and I'd be like, 'Man, you want to go to the stables with me,' and they don't even know where the stables are at," Taylor said. "I'll take them over there and they're like, 'Man, I never knew there were horses over here.'"

Not a day went by without riding horses—until football consumed his life.

Taylor attended Manuel Dominguez High School in East Compton. He was a freshman the year after Richard Sherman graduated. Sherman went to Stanford University before becoming a five-time Pro Bowl cornerback in the NFL and a Super Bowl Champion with the Seattle Seahawks.

Taylor hoped to run in Sherman's footsteps, but ended up wearing a pair of cowboy boots instead.

He briefly played football at Bacone College in Muskogee, Oklahoma—the same school Steve Reagor had attended on a rodeo scholarship a decade earlier—for two years and then transferred to College of the Canyons, an hour north of Compton in Santa Clarita. By then the dream of professional football had faded, so he was down at the Orange County Fairgrounds helping Byrd and the others tear down the bull pens and rodeo arena and load fencing on the Flying U semitrailer.

"I just stuck around and helped them," said Taylor. "From there, I was coming to their shows every weekend—just drive up to where the show is and then go back home."

After two years of driving back and forth, Taylor moved to Marysville full time. Truth is, he has no desire to go home.

"I'd rather stay up here and just work," Taylor said.

One of his last memories of being home is the death of his older half-brother, Jerrod Taylor. Ray had been out East and gotten back to California around 6:00 p.m. He was tired from the trip and told Jerrod he would see him the next day. Instead, Ray went to watch the first half of a high school football game and then went home early to lie down. About 1:00 a.m. he was awakened by a phone call from Jerrod's mother.

"She's telling me he's been shot and shit like that," Ray recalled.

Jerrod and a couple of friends had been hanging out on a porch drinking beer when one of the others brandished a handgun. Jerrod told him it wasn't cool and to put it away. A struggle ensued that ended with Jerrod being accidentally shot and killed. His friend became so despondent over what happened that before police arrived, he turned the gun on himself and took his own life.

"I lost two people over the same deal," said Ray. "It was real tough."

The loss of his brother made it easier for him to join Byrd in Marysville.

"I remember it like yesterday," Reno recalled. "Chris and Ray Ray were like, we don't want to go home."

There was a problem. It was November, and anyone who has ever produced rodeos or raised bucking stock understands Reno's predicament, "We're millionaires in June and July and then we're borrowing money in December." They were financially strapped, but Reno and his father, Cotton, felt horrible turning them down. Neither of them wanted to send those boys back to Compton, so Reno "decided we'll put them in the bunkhouses . . . and they kind of became part of the family."

They had Thanksgiving and Christmas together, and in January it was time to get back to work.

Still Reno was worried about Taylor's well-being, "I think the whole brother thing with Ray Ray, that haunts him every day." Though it has not been openly talked about, Reno worries that Taylor has post-traumatic stress, and for that matter, he added, "Chris has damn sure seen some stuff that none of us wants to see."

After returning home, Hosley would meet up with them on weekends. A short time later, Taylor was leaving for a week and suggested Hosley fill in for him. He found more than a new opportunity; he found a family—a rodeo family. "It was contagious," said Hosley of the passion and drive for all things rodeo that consumed his every waking moment. "It got to me."

He had already met Cotton, but on his second day he got to *know* the man. Hosley was mistakenly left behind at the house and wound up at the kitchen table with Cotton. They talked and then drove together out to the property where everyone was working. "I didn't know who Cotton was, honestly, until I was at his house sitting at his table," Hosley said. "I'm just like, damn, everybody respects this guy."

Together, all three boys became cowboys.

They worked cattle and Byrd rode bulls, while Taylor developed his skills as a bullfighter—both cowboy protection and freestyle—and Hosley continued riding bareback horses. Taylor is still at the ranch. Byrd works there, too, but in July 2020 he bought a small place of his own not far from the Flying U. He plans to add to it, but for now, it is a great start to a dream of one day having a working ranch, raising cattle, and producing his own rodeos.

Hosley found his way back to Compton, where he has since been featured in a mural painted on a wall at Gonzales Park.

He started to rodeo more—Hosley won the 2020 California Circuit title in bareback riding—but went back with the intention of being a mentor and introducing other young Black kids to the cowboy culture. He loves Compton and finds purpose working with inner-city youth—he sees himself in them. Hosley offers riding lessons and speaks at schools and community organizations.

"I always tell [kids] now that if you want to find trouble, I can point you right to it," said Hosley, who was profoundly impacted by the death of two-time Grammy winner Nipsey Hussle, who was thirty-three years old when he was gunned down in the parking lot of his clothing store not far from where Hosley was giving riding lessons, "but if you want to get around it, I can show you how to do that, too."

It can certainly be a tough place to call home, but Hosley does not hesitate to make it known, "I'm proud of where I'm from."

38

Bill Pickett and the U.S. Postal Service

Most of my heroes don't appear on no stamps.
—CHUCK D

WASHINGTON DC

It began as just another Sunday morning for Mark Hess. He poured himself a cup of coffee, sank into a comfortable chair in his living room, and switched the channel on his television to ABC so he could watch the rest of *This Week with David Brinkley.*

Hess had already missed the one-minute "lighter" essay, a weekly favorite the oftentimes dry and humorless Brinkley was known for reading. When the camera turned to Brinkley coming out of the final commercial break, the venerable news veteran took delight in saying, "Well, the United States Postal Service has done it again. They hired an artist who put the wrong person on a postage stamp. Can you believe it?"

Or at least, all these years later, that's how Hess still hears it in his memory. It was Sunday, January 23, 1994.

The new year was cold, and it only felt colder when Hess saw the picture of a Black cowboy, Bill Pickett, flash across his television screen—if only for a second or two—but that is all it took for him to feel an overwhelming sense of confusion that quickly turned to anxiety.

Brinkley was not concerned with Pickett being the first and, to this day, only Black cowboy to ever appear on a U.S. postage stamp or, least of all, Pickett's historical significance as the inventor of bulldogging. No. He merely saw the mistake as another opportunity to belittle the Postal Service, whom he had taken great pleasure in lobbing insults at over the years. Brinkley never even mentioned Mark Hess by name.

Instead, his sarcasm was directed at what he perceived as the unreliability of the Postal Service. Though, Hess recalled, Brinkley did twice mention "the artist made a mistake."

"Mistake?" thought Hess, who was the *artist* in question.

He had been commissioned to paint a series of twenty stamps for the upcoming Legends of the West collection. Hess fancied himself as an amateur historian and offered to provide research in uncovering archived photos used to create the unique, one-of-a-kind portraits and had found an often-used photo that was hand labeled "B. Pickett" on the backside of the original print sometime around the turn of the century.

But Hess wondered, how could Brinkley have known of such a mistake before him? A short while later, Hess received a phone call from Terrance "Terry" McCaffrey, who was head of stamp development for the U.S. Postal Service and has since retired.

"Have you heard?" McCaffrey asked.

"I'm just now watching this," Hess replied.

"Yeah, ah, we're in trouble," said McCaffrey, who then informed Hess, "I got to see all the research you did on Bill Pickett because this isn't the right guy."

Mark Hess grew up in a modest Southfield, Michigan, home typical of 1950s Detroit. His parents were nineteen when they married and bought the house. By the time Mark was three, they divorced, and he was raised by his mother in a single-parent household.

His father, Richard, was the son of a milkman and later became a well-known graphic designer and illustrator. In high school, the elder Hess famously entered an annual competition through the Detroit Art Directors Club. When it was discovered that Richard entered three different pieces under three different names—he won first and third prize—they "almost took away both prizes."

Thankfully, he was allowed to keep his first prize, which was an opportunity to work for Palmer Show Card Paint Company, which created the original paint-by-number kits. In a 1991 obituary that was published in the *New York Times*, Richard was credited with inventing the craft of paint-by-numbers.

"He wasn't the inventor," said his son, Mark. "He just popularized it."

In the eighteen months Richard worked for Palmer Show Card, he not only created more than one hundred paint-by-number kits, his marketing skills helped turn it into something of a pop culture phenomenon. He left the Detroit-based company after separating from his wife; another eighteen months later, he moved to Philadelphia and then to New York City. He designed political advertisements and helped redesign the *Washington Post* before, later, becoming the art director for *New York Magazine*.

Mark would spend his summers in New York with his father and an eclectic collection of illustrators and designers Richard knew as friends—namely Chuck Haden, who owned some woodsy suburban land outside Philly.

Haden turned Richard on to horses and the two traveled to Oklahoma to buy Richard a quarter horse. Haden saw himself as something of a cowboy and started a rodeo camp. In the summertime, during his visits, Haden would put Mark on a horse way too advanced for the young lad.

Mark was nine when, on a Saturday night, Haden took him to a rodeo in Cowtown, New Jersey.

"Coming from Detroit," Mark said, "I thought we were in Oklahoma. I mean, everyone there was bow-legged and wore cowboy hats."

The younger Hess eventually moved to Boulder, where he enrolled in an art program at the University of Colorado. "I thought that would be a good place to go ski," said Mark, as he chuckled at the memory. "That's how serious I was about college."

He was putting himself through school, and once his money started running out, Mark was growing increasingly antsy with the idea of getting his own career started in earnest, especially having already met his future wife. So he curried a favor from his father, who "was jet-setting around the world," and asked if he could return to New York fulltime "and sort of like hang around him and learn to illustrate."

They were father and son, but they did not have a typical loving, nurturing father-and-son relationship. The elder Hess was forthright and would often describe his son's work as nothing more than *interesting*. Then he would take out a brush, some paints, and paint right over the top of Mark's work.

It was tough love, but make no mistake, Mark remembers his father as an "incredibly charismatic guy," and more importantly, the lessons were exactly what he needed.

Instead of all the existential conversations artists and instructors often have with one another, Richard was able to simplify the process and show his son "what I wanted to learn." Six months later Mark signed with an agent, and by the next year, he was designing covers for *Time* magazine.

The first time Hess was ever commissioned by the U.S. Postal Service, he was asked to paint a four-stamp transportation series featuring the first car, first ship, first paddle wheel, and first biplane.

In the mid-1990s, the Postal Service developed roughly 250 commemorative stamps a year—inventors, politicians, philanthropists, history-makers—each of which had to be painted by an artist on a four-by-six-inch card. Artists were paid a onetime fee of $5,000 per stamp. Hess, who painted several stamps over the course of a few years, developed a friendship with Richard Sheaff and was in Washington DC, meeting with the now retired art director. The two were having lunch when Mark, whose stories can be as captivating as his father's, began to amuse Sheaff with childhood stories of urban rodeos and wild horse rides.

Sheaff was delighted with the stories and said nothing of a planned series they intended to call Legends of the West.

Instead, he waited six months before calling Mark with details of a collection that would include twenty stamps. The list started with eight names—Buffalo Bill, Kit Carson, Geronimo, Charles Goodnight, and, of course, a famous Black cowboy, Bill Pickett, among them—before expanding to sixteen and then settling on twenty personalities because, as Hess recalled, "We realized, oh my God, there are so many people to honor."

Terry McCaffrey spent thirty years as the stamp director with the Postal Service. He and Sheaff worked with Hess, who offered to research the subjects in exchange for painting all twenty stamps in the collection, to finalize the list. During the process, Hess sketched several ideas, including Billy the Kid and Butch Cassidy, before the trio decided that including outlaws was not consistent with *honoring* the Legends of the West as opposed to the Wild West.

Hess had a thriving business doing album and magazine covers for *Esquire*, *Newsweek*, *Forbes*, and *Fortune*, but in order to devote his attention to a single project that would include twenty stamps, Hess and his agent cleared his schedule for the next four months.

He was now singularly focused on a project that would pay him a career-high $100,000.

Hess quickly realized the one cowboy he was not familiar with was Pickett.

He had never read about Pickett or any other Black cowboys, and to the best of his recollection, old Hollywood Westerns were "movies about bad Indians and good cowboys." By *good* cowboys, Hess was referring to *white* cowboys like John Wayne.

Certainly not *Black* cowboys like Bill Pickett.

The decision was made to print twenty million sheets totaling four hundred million stamps with a special run of one hundred thousand limited-edition sheets they were planning to sell for $30 each. The others would be the standard $8.

However, in order to appeal to collectors, each sheet from the limited-edition series had to be individually numbered by hand and then signed by Hess. They flew him to Minneapolis, Minnesota, where Hess said the Postal Service has seven printing presses. In 1993 he made three separate trips to Minneapolis, where they locked him in a vault for eight hours a day, Monday through Friday, for two weeks at a time.

Hess signed his name over and over and over again—one hundred thousand times in all.

The signings always took place in a secured vault area with two, sometimes three, people helping to shuffle through the sheets faster and keep them in numerical order. Every couple of hours one of the assistants would recommend Hess take a break because his signature was becoming increasingly illegible. The otherwise empty room had only a table, stacks of printed sheets (otherwise known as panes) that needed to be signed, and a small portable television.

Only in hindsight was it discovered that William Pickett—otherwise known as Bill—and his brother Benjamin had posed for professional photographs in the late 1890s. This was well before Bill ever moved to Ponca City, Oklahoma, and famously toured the world with the 101 Ranch and Wild West Show; and at a time when Ben was still president of the Pickett Brothers Bronco Busters and Rough Riders Association.

The photographer labeled the back of Bill's photo W. Pickett and labeled Ben's photo B. Pickett.

No one knows whatever happened to Bill's photo—it was likely used or sold or borrowed, stolen, or mistakenly destroyed—once he became a world-famous cowboy, but after the photographer passed away, a photo collector happened to come across a glass negative labeled B. Pickett and assumed it was a rare never-before-seen photo of a young Bill Pickett and relabeled the frontside to read: "Bill Pickett, famous Negro cowboy. First man bulldogger. Also used his teeth bull dogging instead of hands on horns method used by cowboys today."

The photo was mistakenly published in several books, magazines, and newspapers, including the August 1989 edition of *Smithsonian* magazine, and was even on display at the Pro Rodeo Hall of Fame, in Colorado Springs, Colorado. Hess, who referred to the mislabeled image as "a defining photograph," also found a catalog listing of an exhibition at the Library of Congress from March 26 to October 2, 1983, which included the same photograph identified as Bill Pickett.

Unlike the other photos of Pickett, which captured him in the later years of his life, this was the only photo of a much younger Bill Pickett that was made available, so Hess decided on using the younger version for the stamp collection.

Ultimately, Hess, Sheaff, and McCaffrey skipped one vital step in the research process. For lesser-known figures like Pickett, the Postal Service generally required photo identification by two family members. However, their research had indicated Pickett had no known family, so relied on the accuracy of the previously published photo.

Not only was the photo misidentified, but their own research regarding his family was also wrong.

There were 215 living descendants, including Pickett's great-grandson, Frank Phillips Jr. His grandmother, whom Frank lived with as boy was Pickett's daughter, Bessie Pickett Phillips.

Frank, who has since passed away, was living in Silver Spring, Maryland, less than ten miles north of the Postal Service headquarters in Washington DC; he began writing letters in 1982 urging the postal agency to consider Bill Pickett for a commemorative stamp.

His requests had gone unanswered.

A decade later and independent of Frank's request, the Legends of the West collection was set to be unveiled December 7, 1993. But on November 22, Ruth and Jerry Murphey of Corpus Christi, Texas, collectors of Old West memorabilia and owners of more than 4,500 historical artifacts from the 101 Ranch, received a fax of the Bill Pickett chapter of a commemorative book that would accompany the release of the Legends collection. It included a photo of the stamp.

With one glance, Ruth immediately noticed the error.

According to a detailed account in the *U.S. Stamp Yearbook of 1994*, published by Linn's Stamp News, Ruth contacted PhotoAssist—publishers of the book and the same agency typically tasked with researching photos used for potential postage stamps.

She was told it was too late and that the stamp was already printed.

Seven weeks later, Jim Etter, a columnist who had retired from the *Daily Oklahoman* in December 1993 and was now working as a freelance writer, called Ruth on the eve of January 6, 1994, and Ruth confirmed she had contacted the Postal Service about the mistake. Later that day, Ruth is said to have called Etter and pleaded with him not to publish the story.

"They're liable to not even issue the stamp at all. Just let it go," she said, according to a comment she's attributed as having told Linn's.

Ruth and her husband were afraid the Postal Service would never be willing to endure the trouble or the cost associated with reprinting the stamps of a relatively unknown Black cowboy, who was arguably the least famous subject featured in the collection.

But the next morning, Etter broke the news on January 7, 1994, in a front-page story under the headline "Cowboy's Fans Fear Stamp Inaccurate," and in that moment the U.S. Postal Service had a multimillion-dollar problem on their hand. They had printed 5,201,000 sheets with more than 104,020,000 stamps, all of which had been distributed to 137 stamp distribution centers and 330 post offices, according to Linn's reporting.

It was not until eleven days later, on January 18, that the Postal Service announced a recall of the Legends series.

In a written statement, Postmaster General Marvin T. Runyon wrote, "Subjects selected for American stamps represent America's culture and heritage. To release a stamp that's less than our best would be a disservice."

Runyon went on to explain the intent was to honor Pickett's memory and his "significant contributions to American society and American culture," and then took exception with the process or lack thereof. "We found that the design, research, and validation process was not followed thoroughly," Runyon continued. "We are now in the process of historically validating each of the subjects of the Legends series to ensure accuracy."

McCaffrey had been summoned back to Washington from a business trip to Hawaii and given five days to validate every image. It took two weeks and when he was done, historians and family members provided him with a laundry list of issues Linn's termed subjective, ambivalent, and "some no more than quibbles."

There was no evidence that Jim Bridger wore a bear-claw necklace. Bill Tilghman would more likely have been in a business suit and not the cowboy outfit he was pictured in. Geronimo was a desert Indian and not the mountain Indian he was identified as. Kit Carson should have been pictured without a mustache, and Wyatt Earp's hat was wrong.

Hess sent McCaffrey a list of all the publications that Pickett had appeared in.

"It wasn't even a mistake," said Sheaff. "All of the archives had it that way, virtually all of them. It was labeled that way and, again, I wasn't the official researcher who did all the leg work, but every credible source had it listed that way and everybody thought that was correct until some relative—some cousin or second cousin or something—came to light and said, 'Hey, that wasn't Bill.'"

Sheaff explained there had been a change in the administration and the new executives leading the Postal Service "didn't know a heck of a lot about what they were doing" and "got in a tizzy about it." Sheaff further explained that the previous administrations he worked under would have said, "'Well, geeze, look at that, the archives had it labeled wrong. It's the wrong picture. Sorry about that.' That would have been the end of it. They would have issued the stamp. It would have been noted down that it was a mistake and the world would have moved on and then there would've been almost nothing to it."

Today Sheaff still doesn't see the mistake as a big deal and that "Hess did the best he could" considering "everybody thought it was the right" photo.

Instead, Runyon determined that only the Pickett stamp would be changed.

With approval from the Phillips family, Hess repainted only Pickett's face using an image from the movie poster for *The Bull-Dogger* as a reference. They also changed a reference to the year he was born, from 1871 to 1870.

Rather than fly Hess to Washington DC, the Postal Service mailed him the original artwork themselves, which remains on a file in a vault at the U.S. Postal Museum along with the artwork from every single commemorative stamp.

Once he received the package, Hess said he could not help but to call a collector and inquire about its value.

"Am I really going to paint over the top of it or should I just throw it in a closet and paint another one?" he asked himself. "I didn't. I painted over the top of it."

Instead, he and his wife sat together as Hess took a brown acrylic paint and painted a square over the original head and repainted an older looking Bill Pickett based on the movie poster for *The Bull-Dogger*.

After sending the painting back to DC, they digitally changed the entire color pallet for the photo, making it look almost nothing like Hess's original.

Asked, all these years later, whether he pulled a fast one and, in fact, still has the original, he laughed, "I'm too squeaky clean. It's like, why would I cheat the Post Office? I love those people and they were so great to me."

Hess doesn't feel the same way about David Brinkley.

He reached out to the veteran newscaster and asked for an on-air apology in a letter that read in part "with all due respect, you really put the blame at my feet." Hess wrote that Brinkley's report was "grossly unfair" and included copies of all his research. Brinkley wrote him back. He evoked a quote from Abraham Lincoln—*Truth is the daughter of time*—saying "The television audience will little note or long remember my few words about this," and went on to explain "Your name was not mentioned nor was the Hess Design Works and so I see no reason for you to be seriously annoyed."

Brinkley signed the letter: "My best wishes to you."

The *U.S. Stamp Yearbook 1994* said Hess followed up with a phone call to Richard Wald of ABC News, who in turn convinced Brinkley to apologize.

However, missing from that account is the fact that Hess's brother-in-law worked as an associate producer for ABC's primetime news magazine program *20/20*. He provided Hess with a guidebook from the news department detailing ethics for the company, which clearly stated: "If a mistake is ever made on any subject matter for any reason, a correction has to be made in the same way that mistake was made."

Brinkley thought the entire situation was "silly."

ABC's lawyers wrote back, and according to Hess, their message was to "basically go away." He didn't. Instead, he pressed on with the help of his brother-in-law, who risked his own job by going to his bosses from *20/20*. Together with Wald, the entire group pressured Brinkley and "three months later, he went on and apologized and corrected the record and said that it was not the artist's fault."

It was the first of only two on-air apologies Brinkley ever made in his nearly fifty years on television.

In the aftermath, the U.S. Postal Service informed Frank Phillips of their intention to destroy the entire first printing, correct the image, reprint the entire Legends of the West series and issue the corrected collection at a later date.

They sent out a release asking for all Legends panes—twenty million sheets in all—to be sent back to the distribution center in Kansas City, Missouri.

It was the start of a $1.1 million correction.

Or, as the *New York Times* noted, it was a $1.1 million mistake.

But the Postal Service incurred yet another problem when 184 panes turned out to be missing, including four that were sold from a Bend, Oregon, location in December 1993—more than three months prior to its scheduled March 29, 1994, release.

"A lot of people made a lot of money off of it for a while because the price went way up," said James E. Lee, former president of the American Stamp

Dealers Association. "It started out at about $100 and went up to about $300 [per sheet] and it collapsed."

Ultimately, the Postal Service specially packaged the collection and sold 149,816 copies, thereby flooding the stamp market with 150,000 less-than-rare copies and rendering their 184 *missing* panes—all of which had been mistakenly or purposely sold ahead of time to collectors—worth far less than they otherwise would have been.

Lee said the decision was a gimmick on the part of the Postal Service to make lemonade out of lemons.

"You had to order them through the Postal Fulfillment Service in Kansas City," recalled Lee, "and if your number came up, you got to buy a sheet.... It was a great boom for stamp collecting for about three or four months because it got a lot of publicity, and that's exactly what they wanted to do—get publicity to sell more stamps. Keep in mind, all the stamps that they sell to collectors, those are never getting used for postage, so that's bottom-line profit to them. They don't have to provide a service for that stamp."

Contrary to Ruth Murphey's concern that the Postal Service would never go to any lengths, let alone great lengths, to correct a stamp involving a Black cowboy, Bill Pickett went from being the first (and to this day only) Black cowboy on a U.S. postage stamp to, arguably, becoming the most famous cowboy ever to appear on a stamp.

"Once they realized the mistake," Lee continued, "they saw a way to profit from it and they saw a way to use it as a vehicle to promote stamp collecting, so from that perspective they may have been successful, but it was contrived."

Acknowledgments

Danny Glover, Esailama Artry-Diouf, and Carrie Productions: I was overcome with emotion when I received your text message—"Let's do this!"—but even that pales in comparison to the tears I shed reading your foreword. Your heartfelt contribution means the world to me. Thank you for your unrelenting passion when it comes to the truth and setting the record straight. I will be forever grateful for your willingness to work with me on this project and love you both.

Rob Taylor, Courtney Ochsner, Nathan Putens, Claire Schwinck, Leif Milliken, Bridget Barry, Sara Springsteen, Karen H. Brown, Tish Fobben, Rosemary Sekora, Mark Heineke, and everyone at the University of Nebraska Press for caring enough to give these stories, which have been orphaned for so many decades, a warm and welcoming home.

Julie Dwyer for being the first to read the entire manuscript, for always understanding my voice, and, more importantly, seeing to it I delivered clean copy. LB Cantrell and Sabrina Tyson for helping me sort through many of the interviews when I could not keep up with them on my own.

Ruta Sepetys (and Michael Smith) for talking through several book ideas with me, in April 2017, and assuring me I had the experience and the mental strength to write an entire book. And then saying three magic words, "yes, yes, yes," when I said I wanted to write about Black cowboys.

Books do not write themselves, especially when you spend more than three years working on it. These profiles of courage and heroism are based on more than five hundred conversations for a total of nearly eight hundred hours with the following people, many of whom were sharing the most extensive conversation of their lives or, in some cases, speaking for the first time on the record: Denise Abbott, Lee Akin, Mary Akin, Melissa Akin, John Ashby, Jim Austin, Obba Babatundé, Bailey's Prairie Kid, Randy Bernard, Bud Bramwell, Sharon Braxton, Minniejean Brown, Robert Brown, Tony and Sharon Brubaker, Dr. Lonnie Bunch III, Art Burton, Dean Butler, Ferrell Butler, Chris Byrd, Ryan Byrne, Larry Callies, Harold Cash, Sue Cermak, Sherral Clayton, Fannie Criswell, Heather Atlas Crow, Darlene Crowley, Jadie David, Dennis Davis, Jesse Davis, Gregory Dightman, Myrtis Dightman Sr., Myrtis Dightman Jr., Dr. Thomas Dorhety, Reginald T. Dorsey, Charles Eckel, Kevin Ford, Fletcher Forte, Elisabeth Frank, Ingrid Frank, Preston Frank, Marcous Friday, Walt Garrison, Don Gay, Neal Gay, Andrew Giangola, Jim Gibbons, Dihigi Gladney, Freddie Gordon, Bubba Goudeau, Dr. Aram Goudsouzian, Rachel Lindsay Greenbush, Jesse C. R. Hall, Clive Harding, Aaron Hargo, Dwayne Hargo Sr., Dwayne Hargo Jr., Nanette Hargo, Doug Harmon, John Harp Jr., Willie Harris, Cleo Hearn, Mark Hess, Dr. Karlos Hill, Cody Hollingsworth, Neil Holmes, LaMontre Hosley, James Isabell, Bobby Jackson, Glenn Jackson, Nelson Jackson, Ramone Jackson, Ryan Jones, Shavon Jones, Steve Jones, Jeff Kanew, Johnny Kimbrough, Manda Kowalczyk, Mike Latting, Doug Lawrence, Rev. James Lawson, Clarence LeBlanc, Kenneth LeBlanc, James E. Lee, Margie Lee, Dr. Debbie Liles, Dr. Patty Limerick, Kody Lostroh, Larry Mahan, John "Reverend" Marshall, Kevin C. Matthews, Sylvester Mayfield, Chauncey McClain Jr., Ronald Medley, Pam and Billy Minick, Bob Minor, Calvin Mitchell, Ezekiel Mitchell, Barry Moore, Abe Morris, Jacob Morris, Jimmie Munroe, Ty Murray, Carl Nafzgar, Corey Navarro, Ted Nuce, Charlie Parnell, Councilman Bill Perkins, Josh Peter, James Pickens Jr., B. Byron Price, Nathanial "Rex" Purefoy, Bill Putnam, Steve Reagor, Gary Richard, George Richardson, Beverly Robertson, Steve Robinson, Barry Rosen, Cindy Rosser, Cotton Rosser, Reno Rosser, Charlie Sampson, Richard Sheaff, Marvin Paul Shoulders, Sharon Shoulders, Arlene Smith, Jimmy Smith, Larry Solomon, Bobby Steiner, Donald and Ronald Stephens, Dr. Quintard Taylor, Stanley Taylor, Rufus Thomas, Willie Thomas, Charlie Throckmorton, Gus Trent, Glynn Turman, Jay Ventress, Carol Walker, Jimmy Lee Walker, Cindy Donovan Wallis, Steve Washington, Fred Whitfield, Ervin Williams Jr., Russell Williams, Tex Williams, and Dr. Yohuru Williams. And of course, for other important and ongoing contributions to this project: Erin Alvardo, Tanya Barbour, Art T. Burton, Jonathan Eig, Elisabeth Frank, Nelson George, Andrew

Giangola, Lindsey Kimrey with LitKey Events, Alan Light, Julanna Read Mahan, Justin and Jill McBride, Dr. Louis Moore, Gretchen Jackson Odin, Shirley Reagor, Steve Reiss and *The Undefeated* / ESPN, Deborah Schriber-Miller, Blair Underwood and Maria Rivera Savoy.

Archives and museums: 1867 Settlement Historical District (Texas City), African American Museum at Oakland, African American Museum of Dallas, American Heritage Center at the University of Wyoming, Arlington National Cemetery, Black American West Museum and Heritage Center (Denver), Black Cowboy Museum (Rosenberg, Texas), Brazos Valley African American Museum (Bryan, Texas), Buffalo Soldiers National Museum (Houston), Bull Riders Hall of Fame (Fort Worth, Texas), California African American Museum, Center of the American West at the University of Colorado, Donald C. and Elizabeth M. Dickinson Research Center (Oklahoma City), Frontier Times Museum (Bandera, Texas), Harlem Historical Society, Houston Museum of African American Culture, Hutchins Center for African American Research (Cambridge, Massachusetts), Idaho Black History Museum, James E. Walker Library at Middle Tennessee State University, John F. Kennedy Presidential Library and Museum (Boston, Massachusetts), Library of Congress, Martin Luther King Jr. Center for Nonviolent Social Change (Atlanta), Multicultural Cowboy Hall of Fame and Museum (Fort Worth), National Civil Rights Museum at the Lorraine Motel (Memphis), National Cowboy Hall of Fame and Western Heritage Museum (Oklahoma City), National Cowgirl Museum and Hall of Fame (Fort Worth), National Museum of African American History and Culture (DC), National Postal Museum (DC), Oklahoma History Center, Oshkosh (Wisconsin) Public Library, Pro Rodeo Hall of Fame and Museum (Colorado Springs), Schomburg Center for African American Research (Harlem), Texas Civil War Museum (Fort Worth), Texas Trail of Fame (Fort Worth), Western History Collection at the University of Oklahoma Libraries, Widener Library at Harvard University, and Williamson County Historical Society (Georgetown, Texas).

Associations and organizations: 101 Ranch Oldtimers Association (Ponca City, Oklahoma), American Black Cowboy Association (Newark), American Bucking Bull Incorporated (Pueblo, Colorado), American Cowboy Rodeo Association (Tahlequah, Oklahoma), American Junior Rodeo Association (Bronte, Texas), American Pro Rodeo Association (Cochranville,

Pennsylvania), Atlanta Black Cowboy Association, Bill Pickett Invitational Rodeo (Centennial, Colorado), Black Professional Cowboys and Cowgirls Association (Crosby, Texas), Black World Championship Rodeo (New York), Compton Jr. Posse (California), Cowboys of Color Rodeo (Dallas), Federation of Black Cowboys (Brooklyn), International Pro Rodeo Association (Oklahoma City), Louisiana Christian Rodeo Productions (Sulphur, Louisiana), National High School Rodeo Finals, National Intercollegiate Rodeo Association (Walla Walla, Washington), National Little Britches Rodeo Association (Colorado Springs), Negro League Baseball Museum (Kansas City), Oakland Black Cowboy Association, Oklahoma High School Rodeo Association, Oklahoma Historical Society, Oklahoma State University Rodeo Team (Stillwater, Oklahoma), Pelham Bay Horseback Riding Trails (Bronx), Professional Bull Riders, Inc. (Pueblo, Colorado), Professional Rodeo Cowboys Association (Colorado Springs), Texas High School Rodeo Association (Center), Texas State Historical Society (Austin), Urban Western Riding Program (Bronx), Williamson County Historical Commission (Taylor, Texas), and WME / IMG (New York and Los Angeles).

I wrote a majority of the manuscript at Starbucks #53847, and I want to thank Molly and her entire staff. Much love and may each of you accomplish your dreams and ambitions.

To those who have impacted my life personally and professionally: Clint Adkins, Leon Alligood, Brandon Bates, Alexandra Boulay, Sara Broun, Johnny Coffin, Niki Coffman, Mitch Covington and Monster Energy, Jay Daugherty, James and Adrianne Evans, Bill Farley, Scott Feinberg, Justin Felisko, Rich Florio, Alex Gautzsch, Tim Ghianni, Sean Gleason and the entire past and present staff at the PBR, Harvard University and the Department of Continuing Education, Jim and Kathy Haworth, Kendall Hinote, Alex Hubbard, Craig and Jennifer Hummer, Richard Jones, Dana Joseph and *Cowboys & Indians*, Lori Kampa and Carey Ott, Cody and Leanne Lambert, Beth Lee, Steve and MaryBeth Leib, librarians and booksellers, Marc Lieberman and CBS News, Andrew Maraniss, Sarah and Hank Mathewson, Jeff and Jenny Mathwig, Richard McVey, Jon Meacham, Jennie (Treadway) Miller, MTSU and the College of Media and Entertainment, Mark Nielsen, Tom Norwood, Thom Oliphant, Rob O'Neil and Los Angeles Pierce College, Rae Ann Parker, Parnassus Books, Ann Patchett and Karen Hayes, Dr. Greg Pitts, Jeffrey Pollock, Gwen Poth,

Stevie Rachelle and TUFF, Flint Rasmussen, John Paul Rollert and George Wendt, Rutherford County Board of Education—teachers, administrators, central office and board members, Kathleen Samsing, Eric and Elizabeth Schallhorn, Alec Shane and Writers House, Mike Sherry, Southeastern Young Adult Book Festival—Liz Hicks and Barb Collie, Michael and Josie Sutcliffe and the Simpson Family, Rob Taylor and Kimberly Whelan and the staff at Wiles + Taylor & Co. PC, Joe, Julie, and Anna Vanden Acker, Deborah and David Wages, Karen Weintraub, Shawn Weise and Brad Bensinger and XD Sports, Matt West, Dave Wilson, Ann Yakes, and George Zakk.

My mom, grandparents, family, and friends.

Much love to all who have shook my hand or wrapped me with hugs.

Selected Bibliography

In addition to the following sources, numerous online resources and other historical and biographical reference materials were consulted, as well as nearly five hundred separate interviews with more than 150 primary sources, including firsthand accounts from the cowboys whose lives are chronicled.

Abdul-Jabbar, Kareem, and Alan Steinberg. *Black Profiles in Courage: A Legacy of African-American Achievement*. William Morrow, 1996.

Amick, George, and Donna O'Keefe Houseman. *U.S. Stamp Yearbook 1994*. Linn's Stamp News, January 1, 1995.

Bell, Bill. "Black Rodeo Spurs Interest in the Old West." *New York Daily News*, July 31, 1992.

Berkow, Ira. "The Rocky Trail of a Rodeo Cowboy." *New York Times*, September 25, 1981.

Beyette, Beverly. "People: Ride 'em Cowboys." *Los Angeles Times*, August 24, 1992.

"Black Rodeo Show to Ride at Boys & Girls High." *New York Daily News*, July 24, 1987.

Bleiberg, Larry. "Oklahoma's Black Legacy Hangs On." *Orlando Sentinel*, February 7, 1999.

Bogle, Donald. *Hollywood Black: The Stars, the Films, the Filmmakers*. Running Press, 2019.

Boyer, Edward J. "Stabilizing Influence: Horsemanship Offers El Fig Riders a Respite from Inner-City Living." *Los Angeles Times*, January 3, 1994.

Boyer, Paul S. *The Oxford Companion to United States History*. Oxford University Press, 2001.

Bracks, Lean'tin. *African American Almanac: 400 Years of Triumph Courage and Excellence*. Visible Ink Press, 2012.

Brown, Jennifer L. "Cowboys of Color: Rodeo with a New Look." *Albany (OR) Democrat-Herald*, August 1, 2002.

Byfield, Natalie P. "Way Out West in Harlem." *New York Daily News*, April 17, 1989.

Carter, Joseph H. *Never Met a Man I Didn't Like: The Life and Writings of Will Rogers*. Avon Books, 1991.

Cartwright, Keith Ryan. "When Black Cowboys Paraded through Harlem with Muhammad Ali: A Path-Breaking All-Black Rodeo in New York Helped Introduce America to a Little-Known Piece of Western History." *The Undefeated*, February 3, 2020.

Collings, Ellsworth, and Alma Miller England. *The 101 Ranch*. University of Oklahoma Press, 1971. First published 1937.

Coplon, Jeff. "Riding Ugly." *New York Times Magazine*, April 12, 1992.

Donovan, Sandy. *Will Rogers: Cowboy, Comedian, and Commentator*. Compass Point Books, 2007.

Duncan, Dayton, and Ken Burns. *The Dust Bowl: An Illustrated History*. Chronicle Books, 2012.

Durham, Philip, and Everett L. Jones. *The Negro Cowboys*. University of Nebraska Press, 1983. First published 1965.

Eig, Jonathan. *Ali: A Life*. Houghton Mifflin Harcourt, 2017.

———. *Opening Day: The Story of Jackie Robinson's First Season*. Simon and Schuster Paperback, 2007.

Fraser, C. Gerald. "Association of Black Cowboys Brings a Rodeo to Jersey City." *New York Times*, April 25, 1971.

Giest, William E. "About New York; Bedford-Stuyvesant: New home on the Range." *New York Times*, July 27, 1985.

Gipson, Fred. *Fabulous Empire: Colonel Zack Miller's Story*. Riverside Press, 1946.

Glasrud, Bruce A., and Michael N. Searless. *Black Cowboys in the American West: On the Range, On the Stage, Behind the Badge*. University of Oklahoma Press, 2016.

Grossfeld, Stan. "Rodeo Rides in Brooklyn." *Boston Globe*, August 9, 1989.

"Harlem Rodeo Show Set For Central Harlem." *New York Voice*, September 8, 1984.

Hernandez, Efrain, Jr. "City Pupils Are Thrown for a Loop by Tales of Black Cowboys." *Hartford Courant*, June 6, 1985.

Hibdon, Glenn. "LeBlanc: Steer Wrestling's Running Man." *Tulsa World*, April 18, 1991.

Hintz, Martin. "Inner-City Kids, All Comers Find Fun, Inspiration in Thyrl-ly Good Rodeo." *American Cowboy*, May/June 1996.

Johnson, Cecil. *Guts: Legendary Black Rodeo Cowboy Bill Pickett*. Summit Group, 1994.

Jones, Meghan. "Debt, Feud Destroyed Jackson Estate." *Brazos Monthly Contributor*, February 21, 2017.

Ketchum Richard M. *Will Rogers: The Man and His Times*. Touchstone and Simon and Schuster, 1973.

King, Martin Luther, Jr., and Clayborne Carson. *The Autobiography of Martin Luther King, Jr.* Grand Central Publishing, 1998.

Krueger, Ray. "Black Rodeo Ropes the Past." *New York Daily News*, June 3, 1990.

Kyle, Jim. "Judge Stages Black Rodeo: Thousands of New Yorkers Enjoy Show." *Baytown Sun*, September 20, 1984.

Lacy, John. "The Kid from Connecticut Who Became a Cowboy." *Hartford Courant*, October 17, 1971.

Light, Nanette. "Lancaster Resident Cleo Hearn Paves Way for Black Rodeo Cowboys." *Dallas Morning News*, March 2014.

Lipsey, Rick. "On a Bull's Back He Had Few Peers: Myrtis Dightman Refused to Be Bucked Off the Pro Circuit by Racism." *Sports Illustrated*, January 11, 1999.

Love, Paula McSpadden. *The Will Rogers Book*. Bobs-Merrill, 1960.

McCallister, Jared. "Black Rodeo Invites You to Go along for the Ride." *New York Daily News*, July 3, 1986.

McLellan, Dennis. "Herb Jeffries Dies at 100; Hollywood's First Black Singing Cowboy." *Los Angeles Times*, May 25, 2014.

Meyers, Roward. "Reno Hates Loving a Rodeo." *News Tribune* (Woodbridge NJ), June 25, 1971.

Miller, Jeff. "Former Jockey Dihigi Gladney Enjoys Ride of His Life with California Chrome." *Orange County Register*, September 7, 2016.

Miller, Michelle M. "El Fig Stables: A Home Off the Range." *Los Angeles Times*, July 31, 1989.

Milloy, Courtland. "Yo-Ho Baby!" *Washington Post*, May 23, 1981.

Montville, Leigh. *Sting Like a Bee: Muhammad Ali vs. The United States of America, 1966–1971*. Doubleday, 2017.

Morris, Abe. *My Cowboy Hat Still Fits: My Life as a Rodeo Star*. Prong Horn Press, 2005.

"Myrtis Dightman Sr. the Man behind the Crockett, Texas, Rodeo and Trailride." *Texas Informer*, September/October 2007.

Nichols, Bill. "Hearn Was a Black Cowboy before Being a Black Cowboy Was Cool." *Dallas Times Herald* and *Del Rio News Herald*, July 18, 1986.

Nir, Sarah Maslin. "The Last of New York's Black Cowboys." *New York Times*, January 10, 2020.

Noel, Pam. "The Fancy Roping Man." *Ebony*, May 1984.

Odum, Charles. "Rodeo Reinforces the Role of Blacks in History of the West." *Los Angeles Times*, June 2005.

"On Harlem Streets: Black Rodeo." Associated Press, September 1971.

Paulick Report Staff. "From Compton to Chrome: Dihigi Gladney's Life Has Been an Incredible Ride." PaulickReport.com, November 1, 2016.

Peter, Josh. "California Chrome's Exercise Rider Used to Ride Bucking Bulls." *USA Today*, November 4, 2016.

——. *Fried Twinkies, Buckle Bunnies & Bull Riders: A Year Inside the Professional Bull Riders Tour*. Holtzbrinck Publishers, 2005.

Potter, Joan. *African American Firsts: Famous, Little-Known, and Unsung Triumphs of Blacks in America*. Kensington, 2014.

Pouncy, Joe. "Juneteenth Rodeo Expecting 17,000." *Dallas Morning News*, June 19, 1975.

Rivera, Madeleine. "Famous Black Texas Cowboy Inspires African-Americans to Join the Sport." FoxNews.com, March 1, 2019.

"Rodeo School: Enterprising Cowboy Brings Tradition of Old Wild West to Suburb of Chicago." *Ebony*, June 1964.

Rogers, Will. *The Papers of Will Rogers: The Early Years, November 1879–April 1904*. University of Oklahoma Press, 1996.

Roper, Chris O'Shea, and Tom Linton. *Legacy of the Early Gulf Coast Cowboys*. Self-published, 2019.

Russo, Dorianne. "Blacks Regain Their Place in the Realm of the Rodeo: The Big Apple Gets a Sampling of Old-Fashioned Western Fun." Gannett News Services, September 5, 1986.

Sanders, Caroline. "How Bull Rider Zeke Mitchell Is Bucking Convention." *Garden & Gun*, August/September 2020.

Schlesinger, Arthur M., Jr. *The Almanac of American History*. G. P. Putnam's Sons, 1983.

Shepard, Louisa. "Blacks Saying, 'Ride 'Em, Cowboy!'" *Hartford Courant*, June 26, 1988.

Shultz, Alex. "The Lonely Journey of the Nation's Best Black Bull-Rider." GQ, February 27, 2020.

Shyer, Marlene Fanta. "The Story Behind Stamp Gaffs." AARP *Bulletin*, June 2, 2011.

Smith, Jessie Carney. *Black Firsts: 4,000 Ground-Breaking and Pioneering Historical Events*. Visible Ink Press, 2013.

Smith, Red. "Red Smith's Views of Sport." *New York Times*, June 22, 1967.

Stratton, W. K. *Chasing the Rodeo: On Wild Rides and Big Dreams, Broken Hearts and Broken Bones, and One Man's Search for the West*. Harcourt Books, 2005.

Taylor, Quintard. *In Search of the Racial Frontier: African Americans in the American West 1528–1990*. Norton, 1998.

Thomas, Pete. "Cowboy from Watts Rides Trail in Saddle: Charles Sampson Has Overcome Injuries and Diminutive Size to Reach the Top." *Los Angeles Times*, June 21, 1986.

Villarosa, Clara. *The Words of African-American Heroes*. Newmarket Press, 2011.

Wachter, Paul. "Fred Whitfield and the Black Cowboys of Rodeo: The Champion Calf-Roper Is a Legend and an Outlier." *The Undefeated*, October 31, 2016.

Wagner, Tricia Martineau. *Black Cowboys of the Old West: True, Sensational, and Little-Known Stories from History*. National Book Network, 2011.

Wallace, Christian. "The Jackie Robinson of Rodeo." *Texas Monthly*, July 2018.

Ward, Geffory C. *The West: An Illustrated History*. Little, Brown, 1996.

Whitfield, Fred, and Terri Powers. *Gold Buckles Don't Lie: The Untold Tales of Fred Whitfield*. Self-published, 2014.

Wright, Mike. *What They Didn't Teach You About the Wild West*. Presidio, 2000.

Zinn, Howard. *A People's History of the United States*. Harper Perennial Modern Classics, 1980.